THE FIFTH GENERAL ORDER

JONATHAN A. PHILLIPS

Copyrighted Material
The Fifth General Order
Copyright © 2024 Jonathan A. Phillips

All Rights Reserved.
No part of this publication may be reproduced, stored in a retrieval system or transmitted, in any form or by any means—electronic, mechanical, photocopying, recording, or otherwise—without prior written permission from the publisher, except for the inclusion of brief quotations in a review.

For information about this title or to order other books and/or electronic media, contact the publisher:

The Fifth General Order LLC
Website: https://bit.ly/tfgo-signup
Facebook: https://www.facebook.com/TheFifthGeneralOrder

ISBN:
979-8-218-49748-4 (Hardcover)
979-8-218-49749-1 (Paperback)
979-8-218-52473-9 (Ebook)

Printed in the United States of America

All the stories in this work are true.

Cover Design: Jessie Eck: JessieEck.com
Interior Design: van-garde.com

Two non-negotiable covenants comprise being a United States Marine and the hallowed ethos of "Semper Fi," meaning *Always Faithful*. The first is the Fifth General Order. The second is "No Marine left behind." Period. No Exceptions. No political abdications. No abandoning core values no matter the current war or level of controversy. Wars are meant to conform to those traditions and constant values, not the other way around.

The Fifth General Order is the bedrock of military wartime service. It is drilled into warriors from day one. It states unequivocally: I shall not abandon my post until properly relieved. To do so would constitute treason.

He who dwells in The Secret Place of The Highest shall
abide under The Shadow of The Almighty.
I will say of The Lord, He is my refuge and my fortress;
My God, in Him I will trust.
Surely, He shall deliver you from the snare of the fowler
And from the perilous pestilence.
He shall cover you with His feathers
And under His wings you shall seek refuge;
His truth shall be your shield and buckler.
You will not fear the terror of the night,
Nor the arrow that flies by day,
Nor the pestilence that stalks in the darkness,
Nor of the destruction that lays waste at noonday.
A thousand may fall at your side,
And ten thousand at your right hand,
For He shall give His angels charge over you,
To keep you in all your ways,
In their hands they shall bear you up,
Lest you dash your foot upon a stone.
You shall tread upon the lion and the cobra,
The young lion and the serpent you shall trample underfoot.
But it shall not come near you.
Only with your eyes shall you look,
And see the reward of the wicked.
Because you have made The Lord, who is my refuge,
Even The Highest, your dwelling place,
No evil shall befall you.

Psalm 91

Contents

Chapter 1: Rebellion 1

Chapter 2: Kill! Charlie Company School of Infantry 11

Chapter 3: Umbrella Corporation: Golf Company 17

Chapter 4: Sink or Swim 25

Chapter 5: Tale of Two Cities: FOB Riviera 35

Chapter 6: Baptism of Terror 55

Chapter 7: Burn The Boats: Sharpen the Wood 71

Chapter 8: Freshman JSOC 91

Chapter 9: Testudo 111

Chapter 10: The Mad King 123

Chapter 11: Mutiny: 20 Days Prior to Deployment's End . . . 129

Chapter 12: Kill Zone 145

Chapter 13: Interrogation 179

Chapter 14: New Battlefield 199

Chapter 15: Best Laid Plans 223

Chapter 16: Article 134 237

Chapter 17: Public Enemy #1 241

Chapter 18: Muzzled 277

Chapter 19: Emancipation 293

            Epilogue 301

            In Closing 307

            My Fellow Veterans 311

Dedication

This book is dedicated to the fallen men of 2/8 Golf Company '06-'07 Al Anbar Province Deployment and the subsequent war stateside fighting for medical care valiantly earned. Your voice and spirits march on with reverberating echoes through the minds of all who served under the grace of your presence.

> "He wanted to get back to the platoon. It's my personal belief that he was doing anything he could to get back in the fight and support his boys. He expressed to me, 'I've got to stay with this platoon. This is my family. I don't want to go anywhere. This is what I came here for. I've got to do my job, my duty.' I certainly believe that, frankly and sincerely. That's as real as it gets."
>
> Marine LT Cameron Browne to Prosecutor

> "Phillips was a great young Marine. He followed all orders and commands. He was always there to help anyone. He was a Marine of Marines."
>
> SSGT Alfred Rivers – United States Marine Corps

One isn't born with courage. We're a product of our environment, as the poet Hawthorne once wrote. We're all highly subsidized by mentorship, whether we realize it or not. Both consciously and subconsciously. Influenced by exceptional and subpar leadership. To adequately convey my story in a manner befitting justice and to deliver literary value, I must begin embryonically, as life itself does. I find the most efficient way to do so involves interweaving tribunal testimony throughout the narrative, as the factual Q&A format chronicles what did and didn't happen.

Seven more days. If only I could survive this madness for seven more days. Then I can wake up from this bad dream and be back home mowing and watering my lawn in peace. But seven days is an eternity in this foreign realm. How had it come to this? Barely eleven months prior, I graduated from high school in Massachusetts.

It was all hands on deck. I was standing in the open courtyard, gazing up at the Iraqi night sky and counting the days until we left the front line. I had just grabbed a caffeinated beverage as we were about to depart the compound and be relieved by the next rotating squad. Enemy gunfire broke the silence. I geared up rapidly and was the first one to make it to the rooftop. Insurgents quickly ambushed the Iraqi Police Station from multiple directions. As I made it to the top of the stairwell, a hail of enemy gunfire came within inches, so close I felt my intestines being dragged past along with the bullets. Someone was firing from an elevated position. There was no other position to see over the short rooftop walls at that angle, making the direction and muzzle flashes easier to get a bead on. My mind automatically visualized the feeling of whether one of those projectiles should impact my flesh and bone and create a highway throughout my body. Anticipation was my default mechanism for courage. If I could anticipate how bad it was, it wouldn't hurt as much, and I could transcend any counter-intuitive momentary paralysis. It makes you question everything about yourself and life in an instant.

I immediately dropped to my knee, went online with my light machine gun, and stood back up. I began gliding forward, engaging the exact direction while moving forward to the North-West portion of the rooftop wall about twenty yards away, suppressing.

Once against the short wall, I quickly set up shop, deploying bipods for precision suppression. I leaned in and began engaging targets with complete violence of action, establishing fire superiority via machine-gun mounted night-vision scope.

CHAPTER 1:
REBELLION

Arlington, Massachusetts

I wasn't raised in a geographical locale lacking inspiration. It was marked by fierce rebellion against overwhelming odds of tyranny. I was raised in Arlington, Massachusetts, right down the road from the location of The Battle of Monotony. I grew up playing and biking down the same neighborhood streets that Paul Revere traveled on horseback during his famous Midnight Ride to warn of the arriving British forces having made their initial incursion. The next town over was Lexington and Concord, where the infamous battle commenced during those opening days of revolt, and the shot marking The American Revolution was fired, echoing the defiant sound projecting freedom, democracy, and independence and sending a message to the tyrants around the world. The American Armed Forces would go on to become the fiercest in the history of our species.

First Grade

I was born double-tongue-tied and learned to fight and not back down an inch from kindergarten onward. There was some attempted bullying, but I immediately put any doubt to rest that it would be tolerated through aggressive and disproportional responses. There's no virtue in proportional responses because it perpetuates the fighting. Words didn't flow even after multiple tongue surgeries and endless speech therapy. I had so much to say, but the words wouldn't come through. I learned to accept more responsibility than your average first grader, whereas everyone else had been focused on academics, recess, socialization, and athletic endeavors. I learned to supplement the added dimension of augmenting speech therapy and practicing reciting words in the mirror for hours at night. It required doing more with less. I couldn't speak, so I learned to listen and observe more, which heightened my other senses. The adverse setback also taught me to fight and defend others in similar walks of life. If someone thought I or they were a soft target type to be intimidated, they learned quickly about the fallacy of that miscalculation. The speech issues also made me self-aware, and I realized eventually that many people would stand passively by as others were bullied and not so much as resist, let alone raise a hand defiantly. That didn't work for me.

My grandfather was a Paratrooper and Recon Platoon Commander in the infamous 82nd Airborne Division in World War Two. It was a completely voluntary subset of the American Military assembled to drop large amounts of troops and gear behind enemy lines with the main objective of fighting through enemy defenses, punching holes in their perimeters, and linking allied ground units for a solidified push onward. If a Paratrooper refused to jump from the plane even once, they were dropped from the unit on the spot. You needed to be a little crazy to be a Paratrooper because it was a counter-intuitive novel form of warfare. You couldn't be controlled by fear.

My grandfather was subsequently assigned to military intelligence tasked with hunting Nazi war criminals attempting to flee Europe and abandon their legacy of evil. He was instrumental in the capture

Chapter 1: Rebellion

and execution of Nazi Germany's top bioweapons expert and sadistic medical doctor, Dr. Claus Karl Schilling. Below sits my grandfather behind captured Dr. Schilling, who testified at the Dachau Trials shortly prior to sentence and execution by hanging outside. He would later go on to serve in Naval Intelligence.

LT Charles Houghton
Recon Platoon
Commander

LT Charles Houghton sits behind captured Nazi Bioweapons Expert Dr. Claus Schilling at The Dachau Trials shortly prior to execution outside.

Obituaries

Charles Houghton, 75; helped capture Nazi war criminals

By Tara Yaekel
GLOBE CORRESPONDENT

Charles H. Houghton, a lawyer and former Army colonel credited with capturing Nazi war criminals after World War II, died Monday in his Somerville home after a lengthy illness. He was 75.

Born in Medford and raised in Somerville, Mr. Houghton was educated in Somerville public schools and enlisted in the Army in 1943, serving as a paratrooper.

After the war, he remained in Europe with the Occupation Forces, and was assigned to a military intelligence unit in Vienna. His work included identifying and locating suspected Nazi war criminals, and he helped capture a number of Nazis attempting to flee Europe.

He was later transferred to the American section of the Landsberg Prison in Augsburg, Germany, the execution site for Dachau war criminals and the prison in which Adolph Hitler had written his book "Mein Kampf." Mr. Houghton's job was debriefing and recording the works of Dachau Commandant Martin Weiss, among others.

When Mr. Houghton returned home, he studied at the University of Utah and graduated from Boston College Law School in 1950. He opened a private law practice and reentered federal service as a special agent with the Naval Intelligence Agency.

He later served as civil defense director for the city of Somerville, and was appointed director of the US Naval District One Office of Military Intelligence.

He remained in this position until the mid-1970s, when he was appointed administrative judge for the Equal Employment Opportunity Commission. He retired from federal service in 1985.

Mr. Houghton served as president of the Somerville Bar Association and St. Catherine's Holy Name Society, and was a member of the American Legion, the 82d Airborne Division Association, and the St. Vincent DePaul Society. He was also a former member of the Walnut Street Center board of directors.

He leaves his wife, Agnes (Fitzgerald); a son, Charles Jr. of Somerville; seven daughters, Maureen Foster, Sheila Tracy, and Rita, Kathleen, Brenda, and Mary, all of Somerville, and Eileen Phillips of Arlington; and 12 grandchildren.

A funeral Mass will be said at 10 a.m. tomorrow in St. Catherine of Genoa Church in Somerville. Burial will be in Oak Grove Cemetery in Medford.

The Boston Globe
WEDNESDAY, JANUARY 19, 2000

Obituary of Charles H. Houghton

From the time I remember, my grandfather drilled into me the quality of never abandoning your duties. He taught me in fourth grade the sacred nature of the Fifth General Order. My Aunt Mary

Chapter 1: Rebellion

was born with severe cerebral palsy and has been confined to her bed and nonverbal since birth. My grandfather taught me that the more precarious the situation, the more imperative it is to honor your obligations and never abandon your responsibilities and family. An attack on one is an attack on all. He would have me, and others stand on a line for extended periods of time, at attention, to instill a paradigm of holding the line in the face of temptation to run. He would hold contests to push our limits. He designed a reward system for excellence and performance. I never heard him so much as raise his voice, yet his soft-spoken demeanor commanded all around him. He read quotes from Ulysses S. Grant: "In war, anything is better than indecision" and "If I am wrong, we shall soon find out, and can do the other thing, but not to decide wastes both time and money and may ruin everything."

My Aunt Sheila told me this story of when she was young and my grandfather was with Naval Intelligence. He came home one day with burns up and down his arm. She asked him what happened. He told her that they were testing an experimental biological agent, and he didn't want any of his subordinates to have to be subjected unnecessarily, so he took their place and assumed the liability and uncertainty. That's what leaders do. They don't abdicate their responsibilities and let others suffer needlessly for their pride and ego. They don't pawn off responsibility under the guise of delegation. He bore the burden of command to spare his subordinates from unnecessary cruelty.

Little did I know the value of the lessons in which he was instilling or the extent of his clandestine and professional service in the cause of freedom. It was all youthful games to me at the time, yet there was always this underlying and innately palpable sense of something deeper being imparted. Profound lessons of fierce masculinity bestowed by a seasoned veteran of the Greatest Generation, having vanquished evil under no rules of engagement other than victory at all costs. For only in doing so are the valiant sacrifices of the fallen made reverent in effect.

In middle school, while studying in the library, I was captivated by the plaque commemorating the members of Arlington who were involved in the famous Doolittle Raid on Tokyo punching back following the deceitful ambush at Pearl Harbor. It showed how ordinary men rose up in the face of extraordinary circumstances and put their lives on hold for a higher calling.

I spent all of high school mowing my neighbor Miss Daily's lawn through the spring and summer months. The endeavor was quantitatively more than I could handle at first, but it pushed me mentally. She was an old-school Catholic like my grandparents had instilled in me, and as such, her expansive yard held some of the most serene statues, among them the Virgin Mary. Before I realized it, mowing that yard every few weeks, which took about five hours each time, I was looking forward to just being up that hill on that plateau around that statue with complete serenity. She was one of the sweetest women I'd ever met, along with my mom and her mother, my grandmother. Miss Daily's late husband had been a Marine. Something special happened to me, spending all that time in that yard with her. Things throughout my life have always had a way of being guided by some innate force beyond me.

When I wasn't mowing lawns, I was training assiduously for wrestling. Wrestling is different from most other athletic endeavors. Tournaments and meets run all weekend long. Multiple matches per week. Weight-class criteria and operating at max capacity while ravaged by dehydration and hunger. I learned to work harder in school

Chapter 1: Rebellion

with less downtime due to wrestling applications, work at the local gym, and landscaping duties. I got accustomed to no downtime.

I'd hang out with my varsity coaches whenever I could, absorbing wisdom about the sport and life from professionals who'd been there and possessed the fierce vibrational mindset to which I gravitated. I'd observe, innovate, and design moves that were then named after me. Moves that were sometimes Hail Mary in nature, but that's the point: risk and reward. You always want to be unpredictable to your opponent. The Phillips-Head Screwdriver was my finest move. I'd look at what others are doing and see room for innovation and application in my own repertoire.

Wrestling confirmed the idea that you only lose if you stay down when attacked. The moment you rise from the ground in the face of adversity, you've already made a valiant statement. I would see some wrestlers forfeit a match if they decided they'd lose to inflate their win-loss ratios for better rankings. I understood the logic. But I wanted to go up against these so-called monsters. In the worst-case scenario, I'd learn something valuable and take my game to the next level. The dopamine spike from the prospect of upsetting the rankings and scorecards from the league of coaches underestimating me was pure upside. In tournament locker rooms, I'd hear other team coaches talking about me and telling other coaches: "Don't sell that guy short. My guy did last month and was put on his face during the first 30 seconds." Most of the time, I ended up winning, anyway. Fear is a complete misallocation of scarce resources. The ingenuity is that most so-called monsters aren't accustomed or prepared to be met by ferocity, so they're at a distinct psychological disadvantage. Whenever I wrestled an opponent, it was always a projection. I was fighting everything about myself that I didn't like, which afforded me physical and mental strength, resilience, and violence of action that many, including my coach, would remark on as unnatural and pathological.

In wrestling, it's just you and your opponent. There's no way to hide your mistakes or lack of preparation. It's purely gladiatorial. It's marked by planning moves, then executing with complete violence of action, devoid of indecision. The mental evolution prepared me for the challenges I'd soon find myself facing. It's also a combat sport where you learn fast that no one is coming to your rescue. Victory is dependent on your mentality, especially when running on fumes up against a vicious adversary. You're so dehydrated and malnourished from dropping weight and maintaining that weight all season long while performing at your best that you live with migraines and your immune system crashes, and you fight through colds and chronic pain for yourself, but more importantly, because you're a valuable member of a team bigger than yourself. You fight on.

In my senior year, I was graced with the title of Most Improved Wrestler. It taught me that I could make huge leaps of progress in short time spans, which was an attribute I'd need abundantly following graduation. The mindset also permeated across the academic spectrum. I was bestowed a presidential award for outstanding academic achievement for my prowess in advanced U.S. history. Once again, I projected everything bad anyone had ever said about me or anyone who'd ever sold me short and applied it to the competition at hand. I knew no one else would push me. It was on me to not leave myself behind and show up every day demanding excellence from myself.

Months prior to graduation, I'd contemplated my next step. My father was a corporate lawyer, Major in Army Judge Advocate General (JAG), former FBI agent, and a Department of Defense Employee.

Chapter 1: Rebellion

My older brother was moving into his third year at West Point. My Uncle Charles was a firefighter. I grew up around firefighters my whole life, and I'd been heavily considering the fire academy. I made the decision to enlist in the Marine Corps and branch out, opting to be a Marine Rifleman with the idea that I'd defer pursuing the Fire Academy for post-military enlistment.

CHAPTER 2:
KILL! CHARLIE COMPANY SCHOOL OF INFANTRY

2nd Platoon, January 2006

Twelve weeks of Marine Boot Camp at Parris Island over the scorching South Carolina summer months of July, August, and September had ended months earlier. I matriculated to the Marine School of Infantry (SOI) deep in the frigid forests of North Carolina.

We stood at crisp attention on the two lines running down port and starboard side of the squad bay. We were being prepared for rapid and imminent combat deployments to the Middle East by seasoned combat veteran instructors. They'd have us scream "Kill!" over and over in perfect unison as one cohesive unit. This would take place for dozens of repetitions at any given time. This was the industry we found ourselves in and before we knew it, business would be flourishing.

We spent most of the eight weeks in the field, far away from the garrison and the barracks. The biggest constructs that were instilled throughout those eight weeks were the unimaginable consequences of abandoning the perimeter given the enemy our nation was confronted with vanquishing. One of the most intimidating things about Marine Corps Infantry School and Fleet Marine Force is hiking. It's a psychological crucible and prepares troops for extended combat patrols with substantial amounts of gear. In Infantry School, you're loaded up with gear and weaponry, so you must help each other stand up after laying down on top of your pack to secure it while horizontal or another technique, depending on the extent of the gear. We'd go for 20-mile hikes at night, deep in the wilderness of NC. We'd be on the verge of collapse 70 percent of the way through, but no one would take breaks during quick halts because we knew there'd be no way to get back up with that level of gear and inflammation. Your arms went numb from the weight of the pack, which had cut off circulation hours earlier.

Our feet would bubble up and form one big, white blister by the time we'd finish. The next morning, we'd have to walk on eggshells to the chow hall out of fear of popping the entire blister that was our feet. It was universal. After weeks of hiking, it was time for defense week.

Defense Week in the Marine School of Infantry is the most arduous phase of training before graduating and matriculating to the Fleet Marine Force. It consists of silently inserting as a platoon into the NC wilderness and establishing a 360-degree perimeter. Two-man teams then carve out foxholes along the perimeter, establishing interlocking fields of fire to ensure no enemy probe breaches the perimeter and compromises the integrity.

Ron Reid and I were half our fire team and assigned to one foxhole. Next to us was Hertzberg. Months later, Hertzberg would be the first KIA from our class while our units deployed to Al Anbar Province, Iraq. Reid and I had completed boot camp together months earlier.

Sleep was prohibited for the entire week of perimeter security. Instructors would silently insert themselves while slithering up to stu-

Chapter 2: Kill!! Charlie Compnay School of Infantry

dent foxholes overnight and conduct reconnaissance. Via night-vision goggles, they waited for their prey—anyone who'd fallen asleep. They'd come up from behind, silently covering the mouth of the unsuspecting student, and drag them off without a word or any commotion.

These were the instructors assigned to prepare me for the Fleet Marine Force and the rapid deployment that would commence a few months post-graduation. One morning, when dawn vanquished twilight, we noticed a foxhole empty and wondered what had happened to PFC Carlton. Then, we were summoned a hundred yards away at the tactical operations center where instructors had set up camp.

It was late January. The ground was covered with frost from the bone-chilling NC winter. The windchill was something I'd learn not to underestimate after that week. Bright lights arrayed and illuminated their captured prey with hands in bondage behind his back, simulating a makeshift terrorist video studio, a hallmark of their viral beheadings.

He was ordered to repeat his name and social security number over and over with a terrified demeanor for effect, orders from the instructors to avoid hazing punishment for being the first prey. I remember the moment vividly because it was chillingly choreographed to simulate the enemy we were up against.

The instructor had a knife prepared and screamed a notorious religious phrase being deployed by our Islamic Fanatic enemy before randomly lunging mid-sentence while the student was in bewildered recitation. I recall vividly the looks, sensations, and faces of my fellow classmates. It was the moment the mission started to hit home. Nothing, in all honesty, could prepare me for the upcoming deployment and corresponding savagery. Short of loss of life and real emotion.

The First General Order

The look on Private Carlton's face in that simulation was seared into our brains and SGT Jakle and SGT Lockhart had done their job. The instructors' last words were to the effect of, "This is what happens when you fall asleep. This isn't a video game. It's Game Over. This is what happens when you leave a man behind, leave the perimeter exposed, or abandon your post without being properly relieved." That week was about drilling the fundamental value of always maintaining a secure perimeter and never moving anywhere short of two-man teams or relief. The Fifth General Order cannot be violated, or the entire unit is compromised. You never leave your post until properly relieved. You always hold the line. If you move forward, you do so as a cohesive unit.

Charlie Company SOI was one of the tightest cohorts I'd ever been a member of up to this point. Some of the instructors were notorious for abuse. One day, for no reason whatsoever, the largest of the instructors grabbed me by my throat and lifted me clear off my feet up against the wall. One night, we were back in garrison in the barracks, standing uniformly up and down port and starboard sides of the squad bay. Something happened. It got so bad that an instructor started yelling, "If you can't take it, or don't want to, when lights go out in 30 minutes, leave your ID and gear on your racks, and get the fuck out and don't come back!" I don't think they anticipated how literally it would translate, but I was glad because if someone couldn't stand the abuse for the sake of their brothers, it was better they bowed out now and didn't take up a valuable space any longer with the enemy we were tasked with annihilating. We'd all spent our first year of school watching the towers fall and American men and women leaping to their deaths on a Tuesday morning at the office to avoid being burned alive by the towering inferno.

Chapter 2: Kill!! Charlie Compnay School of Infantry

When we woke up, there were ten racks with IDs and issued gear neatly arrayed. The instructors lined us up outside in the courtyard. For the next two or three days, we didn't sleep. When the buses came to take us to our assigned units in the Fleet Marine Force Marines, the guys were delirious. The unit commanders couldn't get appropriate responses from any of us. Typically, on the day of graduation, when unit commanders arrive to escort their new unit members, everyone is supposed to be well rested. We were all detoured.

Upon Infantry School graduation, our class was divided into two different cohorts and assigned to separate units that would both deploy and operate on either side of The Euphrates River from each other.

I went to 2/8, while Reid and Herzberg went to 3/2. I would later link back up with two of my SOI classmates in 2nd Squad and step into history in a way none of us anticipated. Ron would later go on to Marine Corps Enlisted Program, then OCS, and lead Marines on the officer. (While Ron was going through the MCEP program, he used my JAG prosecution as a case study for his oral and written presentation before gaining his commission. It was that process that sparked the inspiration to draft this book.)

The buses unloaded us at a building, and we were all escorted to a classroom where investigators briefed us on the situation and allegations and put official blank government statement forms in front of each of us. Some started writing voraciously. I rolled mine into a ball and tossed it in the basket. I knew there was a context for which those instructors weren't being given credit. I thought to myself: In combat when some terrorist was trying to sneak up behind me and slice my throat, did I want the investigators, a few guys giving statements alleging abuse, or the instructors who knew the enemy we were facing and the lengths they were willing to go to win their objectives?

Friends turned to me and said, "Phillips, why aren't you of all people writing something? After what they did to you!" They were referring to some physical and emotional abuse that one instructor in particular who fixated on a couple of us was notorious for delivering. I just grinned and said it's going to get a whole lot worse soon, and if someone honors the Fifth General Order now, it's a personal choice, and there's no judgment to be assigned. There were two instructors I couldn't stand, and they made life hell for eight weeks just to make themselves feel cool. However, the other instructors took my mindset to the next level with great training and mentorship. Two months later, we were all made aware that at least two instructors were convicted at court-martial. That eight weeks forged one of the tightest Marine Infantry Classes. No matter what training or abuse they threw our way, whether in garrison or in the wilderness, at night, all that could be heard was 2nd Platoon laughing hysterically and taunting the instructors that even the other instructors didn't like. They had done their job. Brotherhood.

CHAPTER 3:
UMBRELLA CORPORATION: GOLF COMPANY

3rd Squad Fleet Marine Force, 2nd Battalion, 8th Marine Regiment

Arriving at The Fleet Marine Force amidst a raging two-front war is one of the most intimidating experiences. By the Grace of God, I was assigned to the most proficient squad leader and tactician in the Battalion, Corporal Nicholas Rapavi and 3rd Squad. Seasoned veteran of the unit's prior deployment to Afghanistan. I was further blessed to be assigned to the Fire team with teammates LCPL Hite and LCPL Derrick. Supremely fortuitous was the supplemental and synergistic blessing of having LT Cameron Browne assigned as 2nd Platoon Leader. I was the odd one out, and the platoon was at maximum capacity for upcoming combat deployment, so from Infantry school to deployment, I slept on the ground.

It was a welcome trade-off for top-tier mentorship and another evolution that prepared me mentally. It wasn't about sleeping on the ground as much as it was about the corresponding mentality that accompanied the habitat. It made me increasingly grateful for what I had. I focused on the positives. We spent most of the time sleeping in the field and beside live-fire ranges and training in the Mojave Desert in California to gain unit cohesion, which was what LT Browne drilled into our platoon from day one, while CPL Rapavi focused on fundamental small unit warfare tactics. We did everything together. Especially on squad level. Then, as a platoon.

The joke in Golf Company 2nd Platoon was Phillip's a virgin. I showed up on day one of the Fleet Marine Force. A senior Marine from my assigned squad asked several of us if we were virgins. I was the only one who answered in the affirmative. Anyone in Golf Company knows I've never been the type who feels any need whatsoever to lie or misrepresent myself. I was there to earn my place and protect my fellow Marines. Losing my virginity wasn't something that was at the top of my priority list at 18. That wasn't my mission. The way I saw it, American youth were sacrificing everything they had and more to the most atrocious degree. I also didn't drink or smoke.

For 2nd Platoon, as a result, I was appointed designated driver. When anyone would go out drinking on the weekends when we weren't conducting field ops, they'd leave their keys and call hours later, even at 3 am. It was my job to be on standby. There was no clocking out. You were always training in some respect. But as a result, I learned and absorbed more than your average junior Marine by being around the unit's top-tier talent. Senior guys took me to beach parties, and I learned and absorbed everything. Knowledge, experience, mindset. Sometimes, I felt stupid. But it's because I was around top-tier talent and learning new and advanced concepts every single day.

Over the next few months, our platoon leader and squad leaders drilled topics into us centered around the principles and fundamentals of warfare: fire and maneuver. Also known as "suppression and flanking." Topics centered around the critical elements of speed, communication, and complete and overwhelming violence of action. No margin for hesitation or self-doubt. CPL Rapavi would have us out all night miles in the cold forest, leapfrogging across open clearings outside the urban training mock city. We'd repeat the drills until we understood the imperative and unforgiving nature of maneuver without suppression. When suppression stops, the unit gets overrun. Fire superiority is the lifeline of mission completion and unit survival. This tactical mentorship would save my life in combat when I was reassigned from rifleman to light machine gunner and turret gunner.

He briefed us on the fact that our upcoming deployment was going to be unlike any deployment in the unit's history. At the time, I assumed it was due to his intuitive brilliance and prior combat experience and distinction. I eventually realized that along with those traits, he had a mentor who now stood among the top-tier elite part of the military.

Admittedly, even from my military pedigree, I had no idea just how elite. I simply knew, like my revered squad leader, that they were operators, and their energy introduced itself with no need for further elaboration. Those individuals would, on a small handful of occasions, visit the squad in the barracks for Q&A. One topic that was over my head at the time, but not completely since I was vaguely familiar with the movie, was what the elite operator referred to abstractly as the *Umbrella Corporation*. I didn't grasp the authenticity and severity of the lesson, and there was little elaboration. It centered around the illusion of what we're indoctrinated to believe as opposed to what really happens. The members of that small band from the prior Afghanistan deployment saw things overseas that allegedly rarely added up. I'd just turned 19 in the barracks. Nothing to celebrate. We barely had enough time to train and prepare.

Weeks before we deployed, the operator came one final time to take our platoon through CQB while we were training at the urban training grounds on base. I remember it vividly because he was trying to instill elite CQB tactics and methodology, and the Company Commander was acting as if he was going to win the war all by himself. However, he misallocated most of the time fearmongering and verbally projecting the consequences should any Marine violate the escalatory rules of engagement that were becoming progressively convoluted and unclear along with the devolving mission in Iraq and domestic disfavor. He'd also severely downplayed the combat operational tempo we were about to encounter, which was a strange sensation as it stood in direct contrast with the mindset my squad leaders, team leaders, and elite operators were drilling into my mind. We went through the mock structure room to room on live-fire drill and, I believe, frag grenades. I remember standing outside of the structure while other cohorts were engaging indoors. Watching Special Operators and Senior NCO gunfighters was more than just observing them give tips. It was about being inspired and mentally galvanized. It made me want to elevate my game. I began aspiring to aim for the Marine Recon Program while on deployment, and that added mentality when everyone was tired, which allowed me the energy to volunteer for missions and working parties and absorb all the top-tier mentorship from guys like CPL Rapavi. That's the mental stimulus that follows great leadership. They inspire you to be, do, and strive for more every moment—especially when you're running on fumes and the next guy is dropping out from a six-to-eight-hour day foot patrol in 120-degree heat exhaustion, and you're in jeopardy of doing

Chapter 3: Umbrella Corporation: Golf Company

the same. But then a voice and image in your mind defiantly declares: NO. I'm not leaving. Game On, not Game Over.

That was my introduction to the *Umbrella Corporation*. Lack of clarity for some odd reason was being deployed on a level and degree that didn't compute at a time when it was critical for leadership to bolster confidence to make the right calls decisively in high-stakes no margin-of-error scenarios. And incompetence alone, even to a 19-year-old, just didn't complete the puzzle for why we were being mind-fucked. The unit commander's unhealthy fixation towards CPL Rapavi was universally known. He was optimized with confidence, tactical knowledge, and experience. He naturally enjoyed the flattery and would confide that when we got overseas, the Company Commander was going to take orders from him. In retrospect, that was an inspiring and equally disturbing prospect. But I was 19. And the Captain kept downplaying combat operations so we'd all board the upcoming flight to the Middle East as if Marines were threatening to go AWOL or UA. It's clear in retrospect he was taking decree from up the ladder of command, and for some reason, that was the directive circulating.

It was as if the company leadership was just trying to get trigger-pullers overseas. At one point, the Company Commander said, "I've been over there. It's nothing. The most that's going to happen is a 155-artillery shell will land a few miles away. With a loud bang." I remember the informal speech because it was a Sunday, and he'd raced to the barracks. The Marine in the room to my right had an hour earlier died from alcohol, swallowing his own commit while unconscious. The room was cordoned off with crime scene tape. The Commander pulled Marines out in front of the barracks and went on a slurry-word tirade about what idiots we were and how Marines feared the upcoming deployment and were trying to escape combat. He then called out the Marine to my right about an incident a week prior where he was injured while surfing at the beach while wearing his GI Boots and wasn't going to deploy.

The atmosphere made no sense because most of Golf Company were eager to apply the company motto against all foreign enemies of America: terminate with extreme prejudice. But still, he insisted on downplaying the upcoming deployment. Standing there, I knew something was off. In retrospect, I don't think the Marine who died from alcohol poisoning was the only one intoxicated. If it weren't for CPL Rapavi, an unnamed operator and a scout sniper who would stop by the barracks room, I wouldn't have taken the situation seriously, but due to top-secret clearances, he was able to brief our squad leader on current geographic dynamics. CPL Rapavi used to make fun of the Company Commander, saying he should've never been our commander and that the Marine Corps was starting to let anyone through officer candidate school (OCS) due to the war on two fronts. These were the subsets of officers no one wanted to address. They were guys who wanted to be officers but had no place or qualifications. Then they permeated the ranks while leaving a trail of body bags in their wake with none the wiser. Meanwhile, the Officer Corps seldom cannibalizes its own, just like the Vatican hierarchy. Guys like Golf Company Commander seek out easy academic degrees just to qualify for Officer Candidate School (OCS). The invoice for that circumvention is then passed to enlisted subordinates under the burden of their commands and incompetence.

My squad leader had been verbally aware of how many Marines Golf Company Commanders stood to get killed and wounded along the way. I listened attentively. With guys like CPL Rapavi and the other squad leaders and team leaders, we stood a chance. That was the consolation. The Company Commander tended to defer and submit to Rapavi, which resonated as strange, but I was just thankful to be learning from top-tier operators and absorbing everything I could in a condensed period. Lessons like being decisive and never second-guessing your gut instincts. If you hesitate in high-stakes environments, you'll have an eternity to reflect on it, or one of your friends will.

CHAPTER 4:
SINK OR SWIM

On about July 30th, 2006, we were preparing to deploy to Iraq. We weren't trained extensively in 3D urban terrain which would comprise our upcoming Area of Operations. We'd spent most of our training running up and down sloped ranges like Mount Sir-abaci. Range 400, 410, and Lima 6 were among the most challenging live fire maneuvers.

Ammunition seemed finite, so we performed minimal live-fire maneuvers. We did minimal work with night vision optics and almost zero training with vehicles, let alone navigating 3D environments with vehicles through narrow urban terrain. We were going to have to learn a lot in a brief period when we stepped foot in-country. That's where the bond and confidence factors come into play and manifest in quickly acclimating to a foreign Area of Operations (AO).

Looking to senior NCOs and trusting their experience was key. What we lacked in specific training and high-tech gear we compensated for in bonding through PT and Field Ops and occasional off-base recon assignments at the local exotic dancing venues with specific mental tasks to ensure we were always vigilant and could recall salient details with precision no matter how dim the lighting. We all lived together and shared cramped rooms. We learned about nonverbal languages and idiosyncrasies—the subjective sounds of a teammate's approaching feet, which, in combat, is oftentimes the difference between life and death. In urban warfare, you're surrounded by high ground perpetually and don't have the luxury of being able to focus on panoramic views. You must know where a teammate is by the imperceptible sound of their feet 20 yards behind at night, in addition to their infrared laser pointing past you in the distance, designating zones of coverage and painting potential targets without even their knowledge. This was no joke.

    I realized all this extremely quickly upon arriving at The Fleet and under the tutelage of the 3rd Squad and 2nd Platoon Commander. I was terrified at the prospect of not performing to my best and being responsible for a teammate getting killed or wounded. It's the weight of the world. It makes you take things seriously. We were warned of the consequences of not taking a shot overseas and a teammate paying the price for that indecision. In 3rd Squad, it was unnecessarily implied that if that ever happened, you were dropped from the squad immediately. Completely understandable. This wasn't a game. There was no redo. It was game over. I told Nick he'd never have to worry about me not acting decisively. I'd rather be judged by 12 than have one of my comrades be carried by six out of some liberal idealism that has no place on the battlefield against a savage enemy. If my brothers were alive after the gun smoke settled, I couldn't care less how many bodies there were. We were being prepared for rapid deployment against an enemy who, by intel reports, were doing unthinkable things to soldiers. I knew this war was going to be polarizing enough and knew I had to keep my paradigm as simple and fundamental as possible.

    It was strange, but the Company Commander not only didn't instill confidence leading up to deployment, which is imperative for

Chapter 4: Sink or Swim

an unknown objective because it can be transferred to any mission that arises overseas, but he'd take great lengths to instill panic about the prospect of making the wrong decision overseas and perceivably contending with the Geneva Convention which states in detail how a military force is expected to treat enemy combatants—though the Geneva Convention only applies to an enemy who identifies himself as an enemy combatant, not one that hides among civilian populations. A month before deployment, he gave another fear-mongering speech outside the base theater after an intel lecture. The talk about his drinking problem was well-known. There was an apathy about him. He gave no inspirational speeches. Just threats.

In hindsight, it made me even more grateful for how violently accurate Charlie Company Infantry School Class Instructors and Corporal Nicholas Rapavi and LT Browne had been in preparing us for the battlefield. It was strange having a Company Commander determined to intimidate us at a pivotal juncture where confidence needed to be abundant. LT Browne was a great Platoon Commander because he commanded the respect of all but incisively realized the value of squad leaders as the backbone of small unit warfare and what we'd soon come to know as hunter-killer tactics.

Pre-Deployment Leave: Arlington, Massachusetts: July 4th, 2006

I spent two weeks on leave with my family back in my hometown before deploying to the Middle East. My final day of pre-deployment leave had arrived. My parents threw a big cookout with cake for my extended family and my high school friends. Towards the end, we were taking pictures together, and my friend said something that never left me: "This feels morbid. It's like people are planning on you not returning." There was a distinct sense of posterity. But it was necessary. That was the job I signed up for and the mission I was tasked with. I had no idea what I'd be walking into, and people wanted pictures in the event anything happened. Those words hit home. I started to have anxiety about what operating in the peak desert heat as a Marine rifleman was going to be. Being a junior infantry Marine, you get so much pressure put on you physically. It was natural to wonder what that type of battlefield was going to be like. I recall being nervous the last day before leaving back to base and then immediately en route to Iraq. Miss Daily, my neighbor up the hill and mentor, pulled me aside and said something that changed my paradigm in an instant. They were the words that I needed to hear from company command leadership, but which never came. Words that only the wisdom of an 84-year-old Catholic woman who had experienced a lifetime could provide.

She said: "I want you to listen to me carefully, Jonathan. This is an enemy unlike any other. There are spiritual forces at work. Be bold. And always remember: God forgives sinners first. Don't hesitate. Ever. There's no time. Act." That sweet, incisive angel prepared me for deployment more than any officer I served under ever came close. Later, I'd reflect on how she had more guts and fortitude at 84 than my Company Commander. I would've followed that woman over him any day of the week. Whoever the Umbrella Corporation was. Miss Daily was old-school catholic and violently opposed.

It was the evening before I was to return to base for immediate deployment. I was sitting on the cement doorstep with my mom. She asked me if I was nervous. I lied and said no, but I had no idea what we were walking into, and that didn't feel right, in the least, from a command standpoint. Something was off. It wasn't that Marines were

Chapter 4: Sink or Swim

scared. There was just a ton of distrust for the company command by this point, for good reason. The Company Commander had already been actively plotting to rid 2nd Platoon of our extraordinary Platoon Commander. At that moment, I reflected and simplified things. I promised myself two things. No matter how bad things got, I'd never violate the Fifth General Order or leave any Marine behind. Those were the only non-variables I could guarantee to myself or anyone else.

There was a complete lack of preparation at the company level. No instructions except a fear-mongering threat campaign. They didn't even tell us to put salt in our water to prevent dehydration. We were clueless. So, I made myself watch movies like *Blackhawk Down* and *The Last Castle* to mentally prepare. We were on our own, deploying to a foreign battlefield. There were no instructions on acclimation and how to prepare for desert warfare. I was lucky to have gone through Paris Island (Boot Camp), South Carolina, during the peak summer months as it prepared me on some primitive level with mentorship in how to optimize myself in the summer heat. While at home during pre-deployment leave, I'd make myself sit in the sweltering sauna for an hour a day like in high school wrestling because that was the level of initiative that I needed to exhibit.

My mom came into my bedroom at 3 am. I hadn't slept a wink. So many things were going through my mind. She told me it was time. I kissed my dog Shadow goodbye and tried to stifle the emotion, knowing she had no idea once again where I was going and that it must've felt like I was abandoning her. I threw on my backpack, and my parents drove me to the airport. My mom had worked for Delta Airlines for a decade, so I was well-versed in navigating airports. But this time was different. I couldn't let my mom see me as vulnerable because she was in remission from cancer, and in my mind, any added stress could change that. Deploying to combat was already taking its toll on her, though she never let it show. That was her nature. I looked back over my shoulder before heading towards security one last time, fast enough to obscure any emotion but slow enough to savor one final look.

Back at Camp Lejeune, NC.

CPL Rapavi came into the room with the saddest look I've ever seen. He said, "Prepare your will," solemnly. I asked him why. With two weeks left to deploy, the Company Commander waited to change our entire company and all the squads. Unlike the other companies who had done so many months prior, the Golf Company Commander must've had other more pressing issues, like recycling beer cans, and waited until we had two weeks left before operating in an unknown Area of Operations and hostile territory. When training for war, it's imperative that you train with the same teams. You develop verbal and nonverbal communication modalities.

I was thriving as a junior Marine in 3rd Squad and learning and absorbing at a rapid pace, according to CPL Rapavi and his team leaders. Excellent in all areas under 3rd Squad's leadership and ferocity. One more wrench in the socket. Adapt and overcome. No complaints. Utility player mindset.

You live and breathe around the same teammates 24-7. It's what makes The Marine Rifle Squad so lethal. This was who the Company Commander was. Zero proactivity. Only threats. He did nothing until someone forced him to act. The incompetent Company Commander waited until after a month of Combined Arms training (CAX) in the mountains of the Mohave Desert. That's some of the most intense training for desert warfare that is saved for the last crucible

Chapter 4: Sink or Swim

before deploying to combat. Two weeks before combat deployment, the Company Commander held a random lottery and reshuffled the deck with the results. Seven months of intense training and bonding to just throw dice against the wall for life-or-death decisions.

Mohave Desert Pre-Deployment Training – 3rd Squad during Combined Arms Training (CAX) Left to Right: LCPL Memphis Hite, LCPL Jonathan Phillips, LCPL Timothy Derrick, CPL Ryan Cavey, LCPL Howard March

LT Brown said, "We were the last company to switch our operating structure. Other companies had switched to four platoon concepts. Golf Company was the last to pick up on that. So, we had to make some adjustments as far as readjusting people in squads, bringing in people who, at one point in time, were attached to Weapons Platoon. We had some new guys come to the team. I was deeply concerned that he was breaking up the squad that had been working together, training together, that he was disrupting the unity, the information flow that we had going in 2nd Platoon. It was a big concern I expressed to the Company Commander. It's like changing the sheet or music in the middle of the performance. You never do that. But we had to. We were forced to make that adjustment. We made it. And we had to understand the implications of that and make do."

The First General Order

Most people would have quit and gone AWOL with that level of misfortune right before combat. Not my style. I realized that I was going to have to be my own team leader, and my iPod was going to be my trusted subordinate. I went to the Blackhawk store off base and made the decision to spend all the money I had left after the iPod acquisition and bought the best pair of combat boots available so I could be tactically proficient and deploy all that CPL Rapavi and CPL Cavey had taught me in 3rd Squad even though I was reassigned. Those boots would save my lifetime after time. I was fast.

SGT Reagan immediately reiterated that I was being assigned to the least respected team leader in the company and said, "Good luck, man…" and smiled sadistically. It was no secret. I knew I was going to have to lead myself while continuing to absorb mentorship from the top-tier Marines and corpsmen. To mentally come to terms with the possible death sentence, I suddenly started thinking about post-deployment goals like recon indoctrination since I was being passed around by the Company Commander like a bowling ball. I put on a smile, suited up, and reminded myself of the Fifth General Order. CPL Neal, my new team leader, was infamous for being the only Marine to fall out of a patrol on the prior deployment and would be the only Marine in Golf Company to faint on a combat patrol weeks later in Iraq. Ironically, CPL Rapavi's squad was on QRF and had to be dispatched to evacuate him.

I boarded the plane, barely knowing the leadership in 2nd Squad, let alone knowing their operating styles. It was going to be an uphill battle to earn a place while everyone had reputations already well established. That's what CPL Rapavi meant when he said to prepare my final will. The only solace was knowing the excellent gunfighters that comprised the backbone of Golf Company: SSGT, Best-man,

Chapter 4: Sink or Swim

Ybarra, SSGT Rivers, SGT Nichols, SGT Jefferson, SGT Diaz, SGT Tirado, SGT Patrocinio, CPL Rapavi, CPL Payne, CPL Santiago, CPL Reagan, CPL Bates, CPL Boyd, CPL Aucoin, CPL Cavey, CPL Smallwood, CPL Kenny, LCPL Copeland, and LCPL Panza.

Golf Company was also graced with some of the Navy's most exceptional FMF combat corpsmen: Doc Strotz, Solbach, Feller, Mackinnon, Harrington, Tyler, Jerez, O'Gara, Burdick, and Kiraly. Having these medical savants with us enabled extraordinary feats of confidence. When the area descended into chaos, and the command passed a decree that required all hands-on deck, the confidence derived from these exceptional lifesavers would mean the difference between action versus inaction and between life and death.

CHAPTER 5:
TALE OF TWO CITIES: FOB RIVIERA

August 4th, 2006

"The mission of the Marine Rifle Squad is to locate, close-width, and destroy the enemy by fire and maneuver and or repel enemy ambush."

2/8 Golf Company Motto

The First General Order

The first thing our company command did when we arrived was transfer our platoon leader and platoon SGT to another assignment, leaving us even more discombobulated than a week prior when he changed up the entire company. The second thing he did was line each one of us up against a wall to have our death photo taken for a future memorial PR portrait. They called us in one by one and had us smile for the camera so that when we were killed, they could use it for PR and tell our families a patriotic tale. That was the level of prioritization that encapsulated Golf Company Commander and 1st SGT. They waited until the last second to do everything. Photos that could've been taken months earlier were now taking up precious downtime between missions. We were up against a diabolical enemy, and they wanted to push the psychological aspect of convincing teenagers they were heading towards death.

We'd been in the country for a little over six weeks. The dehydrating effect and lack of air conditioning had begun to take a toll, given the high operational tempo. Enemy engagement had been relatively light, but the combat tempo was nonstop. We barely had sufficient troops to secure the Area of Operations (AO). Our platoon was on rotating shifts. Dismounted components were responsible for two six-to-eight-hour foot patrols daily, with one daylight and the other nocturnal through night-vision optics and infrared lasers. Golf Company's 3rd Platoon, led by phenomenal platoon leader LT Durham, took several casualties at OP-Phoenix when a suicide vehicle-borne IED (SVBIED) dump truck rammed into a house filled with 3rd Platoon Marines and detonated. Second Platoon was QRF and spent a week reinforcing the perimeter and fortifying the observation post, only to have Gold Company Commander order us to dismantle the observation post because it made no strategic sense.

Chapter 5: Tale of Two Cities

He had a way of making things up along the way capriciously. I remember sitting in a ditch when we initially arrived and reinforced the perimeter. I was two feet away from the torso of the suicide bomber. That was my introduction to death.

The mounted component was responsible for vehicle-mounted operations and running Quick Reaction Force (QRF) for the dismounted contingent. The third component was on rest, though that simply implied fortifying the FOB and Observation Post set-up on the rooftop of the nearby Iraqi Police Compound. There was no rest.

Morale was running low as mission clarity was nonexistent, and command leadership was ambivalent at best. The commander never gave speeches and only offered anecdotal threats about the consequences of violating the rules of engagement and making him look bad. Early on deployment, he kept escalating the absurd threats. It was the calm before the storm. He threatened to withhold survivor death benefits to our families beneficiaries should we be killed and our bodies be discovered without our dog tags. The fear was of friendly repercussions superseding enemy engagement. The mental calculator kept indicating: Error.

2nd Squad junior room was called the boot room because it had more junior Marines than any other room. Because of that, it was even more of a brotherhood. Tempers flared at times, but it was mostly the funniest time of my life. No matter how tired we were from around-the-clock operations, there was laughter. Senior Marines used to come over after eight-hour missions and tell us to shut up. My bunk mate was LCP Steven Johnson (Georgia). Looking back, it was the calm before the storm and the best days of my life. Absolute tale of two cities. The jocularity and camaraderie between LCPL Steven Johnson, LCPL John Hale, LCPL Hector Soto, LCPL Michael Parcels, "Doc"

Arthur Solbach, and myself when not running operations was something no enemy could ever vanquish. Absolute lions. We operated with no sleep for those first six weeks, and combat hadn't even commenced.

Left to Right — LCPL Brent Mheule, LCPL Jonathan Phillips, LCPL Stephen Johnson at FOB Riviera shortly before bridge ambush.

In those initial desert months of 24-7 operations, I was most impressed with LCPL Johnson and LCPL Soto, who were light machine gunners and had the burden of lugging around the most gear and ammo while conducting two eight-hour foot patrols a day and then mission preparation and compound fortification between that. During this time, the most valuable commodities were Crystal Light and the infamous Tang, which Hale always had a way of procuring. I'd gaze at it on his shelf across from my rack, thinking about what I could barter for just a teaspoon of that pure liquid gold. Hale was also mechanically inclined and was able to get the old A/C working

Chapter 5: Tale of Two Cities

every now and then until it would die from the strain of desert heat. The squad leader NCO room had full-blowing perpetual A/C, and I assume that was the reason we were given the room we were. We adapted and offset the detriment with jokes. It was hell. But looking back, after what was to come, it was pure heaven. We had each other, and we had youth on our side.

Lance Corporal Jonathan Phillips manning the machine gun from Observation Post (OP) 286 upon arrival in Iraq

We barely had a functioning A/C. We had lukewarm bottles of water and stocked up on Crystal Ice Packets before we deployed because that wasn't stuff command provided. If not, all the water would have depleted our nonexistent electrolytes. What I wouldn't do to return to that phase. Youthful. Naive. Optimistic. Enthusiastic. We got two hours of sleep at night because combat hadn't started. We were so forcibly hydrated in those two hours that night that we would keep empty water bottles in bed with us. We'd be so fatigued we couldn't make it downstairs, and getting an hour of sleep was an operational imperative for sustainability and mental acuity. We would wake up throughout that one-to-two hours and urinate in the plastic bottles before rolling over and drifting back to sleep. Eventually, I realized I wasn't even consciously doing it. I'd just wake up next to a full yellow plastic bottle.

LCPL Jonathan Phillips at OP-Phoenix reinforcing 3rd Platoon after dump truck packed with explosives drove into observation post. Holding steering wheel from suicide vehicle.

Chapter 5: Tale of Two Cities

LCPL Jonathan Phillips manning machine gun atop Observation Post (OP) 286

Most can't fathom that level of exhaustion. There'd been no training or classes in preparation. There were times I'd piss myself in bed. That's how intense the operational tempo was. You just didn't have the energy to reach for that empty water bottle, or you already used it earlier, so it was full. There'd be no energy to rise to go find another, and you needed that precious hour or two of sleep for continued operational viability. Our A/C only worked 10 percent of the time and only because LCPL Hale was great at fixing things. The summer heat and operational tempo sucked the life out of us. At that time, I wasn't even a light machine gunner like LCPL Hector Soto, LCPL Stephen Johnson, LCPL Steven Jackson, LCPL Memphis Hite, and LCPL David Washington. Those guys had to operate with all that weight under those conditions. I don't know how they did it. Complete lions.

The First General Order

The peak desert heat and operational tempo were inducing delirium. One night, SGT Reagan tackled one of the team leaders in the makeshift galley. He at least had the room with a fully-functioning A/C.

I was assigned the least desirable tasks because I was now the most junior member of the squad by no choice of my own. One of my designated jobs was to find a way to jump from the vehicles and retract the collapsible barrier re-mount vehicle in record time to limit operational liability—especially when returning from missions, as that's the most precarious point for attack. Like in wrestling, I innovated and found ways to reduce time and drag. One day, a Coordinated Air and Ground (CAG) Captain called "Toad," who was attached to Golf Company, tagged along. He turned to the team leader, and as I got back in the vehicle seconds later, he said, "How'd he do that so fast?" The team leader just smiled and said, "That's Phillips, Sir." That was the mentality. Whatever the currently assigned job was, I made sure to learn it inside and out for complete optimization. Then, when someone was killed or wounded, you were thrust into a completely new job like light machine gunner and repeated the process but deployed the same mentality in doing so. Rifleman, Aid and Litter Team, Light Machine Gunner Dismount, Turret Gunner, etc. Whatever the job required. Complete utility player mentality. You go where you're needed and don't complain.

Because of the intense heat and operational tempo, we'd wear warm-weather slick, form-fitting T-shirts and underwear by Under Armor Brand sold at Base Camp. The gear would stick adhesively to our skin. Between running around-the-clock combat operations in the desert summer heat and not showering for many months, the shirts made it practical to keep everything where it should be and facilitate throwing on gear instantly while precluding abrasive chaffing. We were told that the enemy was engineering and deploying specially engineered IEDs intended to torture American and Coalition service members and force them out of their vehicles.

We were also told that a Marine in another unit wearing Under Armor form-fitting T-shirts and underwear had been engulfed by an IED designed for that purpose. When the corpsman went to remove the underwear during triage, the Marine's genitals came off with it. We were hereby instructed to discontinue form-fitting Under Armor gear. I went and vomited. The sentiment was universal. The looks on everyone else's faces were identical. The Department of Defense doesn't publicize this intelligence, so the American People don't get the full context of the depravity American Troops, especially youth, were exposed to daily. The Department of Defense omits a whole lot to maintain recruiting quotas and a steady supply of service members for the front lines. Even writing this, I'm struck with nausea and rage and the inclination to fall in line with that disingenuous omissive campaign. But sometimes silence should be a capital crime.

Thunderstorm

I was standing at the top of the stairwell of a deserted 2nd deck, hunched over the banister, looking down at the open semi-spiral and staring at the radio operator's desk at its base. It was pitch black. Suddenly, an explosion so powerful the percussion rocked the compound like only the most violent thunder and lightning storm could. In the dim light, the dust from the walls and ceiling shook free from the decrepit structure in a cry of rebellious emancipation. CPL Santiago, the leader he is, had gotten out of his vehicle patrol 80 yards away from my position to open the gate to spare his men exposure. He stepped on a pressure plate IED that an insurgent had somehow pulled up and buried unbeknownst to perimeter security.

Company commander had been returning many guys to the front line and forcing guys who were cooks and motor transport to take over certain jobs. They'd then make wounded Marines return to the front line and designate them as "light duty" status but would stick them on rooftop or perimeter security. There was no justifiable reason an insurgent would've been able to drive up, sneak out, and bury a pressure plate IED day or night with the interlocking fields of fire and night vision and thermal optics we had. The command would intentionally stick people they deemed less than dependable on rooftops and perimeter security, as if perimeter security wasn't important or was a linear job. CPL Santiago, one of the top knights of Golf Company, lost both legs, several fingers, and part of his arm. Doc Feller worked on him and stabilized him while the Blackhawk was en route. Santiago was one of the fiercest guys in Golf Company. Doc Fellers was in a league of extraordinary combat corpsmen.

I've never seen CPL Rapavi display the eyes he did the next day as he came and sat next to me on the couch in the lower-level galley/TV room. It was like his eyes changed. He stared forward through the television. He said, "He was my best friend. They're going to pay." I followed the declarative statement with a declarative question: "What do you need from me, CPL?"

Chapter 5: Tale of Two Cities

September 24th, 2006

We lost our first comrade. Lance Corporal Howard March was struck by a sniper bullet to the throat while Corporal Rapavi's 3rd Squad was conducting daylight dismounted foot patrol. March and I served together in 3rd Squad until I was reassigned.

The sniper reloaded and shot CPL Rapavi in the abdomen. The bullet struck his ammo magazine, preventing further penetration. The 2nd Squad, led by CPL Reagan, was Quick Reaction Force (QRF) and began clearing houses on the other side parallel with 3rd Squad. I identified a military-age male casually beside a bush between our pause and 3rd Squad clearing houses. Through my scope, he was just standing there as if he was smoking a cigarette as the firefight was going off, trying to appear casual during a gunfight, partially obscuring himself by the bush. I called off the shot before execution and was given orders to stand down due to the possibility of crossfire. The Company Commander was attached to our squad and his threats had done their job. The impact would only get worse.

March was a beloved member of Golf Company and was always jovial and uplifting to unit morale, which is one of the most lethal weapons a unit can possess, along with competent leadership and confidence. He was hilarious. He was the one who drove me to the airport for pre-deployment leave before deployment. LCPL David Washington and March were best friends and inseparable. Washington was devastated, and it took all SGT Nichols had to keep him from hunting down anyone who knew anything or had information on the assassin. I would've tagged along. March was the type of individual who was always down to help someone. He drove me to the airport when heading home on pre-deployment leave, and the ride was longer than anyone could afford for cab fare since it was far from base. One day, March was here, and the next, he wasn't. It made even less sense because the company leadership acted like it was all anecdotal. We'd soon discover that losing March was just the beginning of the historical Sunni uprising and Civil War that had now commenced with no warning with the Islamic observance of Ramadan. Late September 2006 was the start of the most brutal military campaign of the Iraq War.

We were scheduled to return to Base Camp in about ten days for a memorial service. Platoon SGT SSGT Bestman called us into the cramped, dusty hallway of 2nd deck at Hotel Riviera and informed us March had died en route to Base Camp hospital. He told us this changed everything. The enemy had now just drawn first blood, and he'd back us in whatever action was necessary for counterattack. SSGT knew the stakes. You let an enemy get away with that, and its open season on the unit. He had a soft spot for March, though he tried to hide it. He was a great, jovial guy who kept morale boosted. He was attacked without cause.

Days later, I was sitting in the open galley on the first deck down the hall from the command operations center (COC), watching TV. At this point, FOB Riviera was quiet because most platoons and squads were outsourced to external observation posts or internal perimeter and rooftop security. I heard a commotion and intuitively knew it was Corporal Rapavi's signature no-BS voice. He was livid, and his roaring tonality echoed down the hall of the lower deck.

As he dressed down the Company Commander, I instantly knew something was off for two reasons. First, Corporal Rapavi never fucked around, especially not when it came to troop welfare. Secondly, the ground commander turned instantly submissive: "Whoa whoa

Chapter 5: Tale of Two Cities

whoa…you misunderstood!" he said, attempting to placate an enlisted subordinate.

Corporal Rapavi later expounded that the commander wanted his squad to continue conducting exaggeratedly slow dismounted foot patrols with the objective of giving the enemy sniper operating in our AO more soft targets, making the sniper "extremely comfortable operating in the AO." It was a pure escalation of insanity.

He wanted the enemy to be extremely comfortable in their lethal confidence while he was extremely comfortable and safe. He spied his wife stateside from the confines of the command operations center back at FOB Riviera. People were beginning to take note of escalating absurdities.

At this time, all who served in Golf Company knew unequivocally that the true company leadership consisted of a tight band of NCOs and Staff NCOs: SSGT Rivers, SSGT Ybarra, SSGT Bestman, SGT Nichols, SGT Jefferson, SGT Jacobs, SGT Diaz, Corporal Rapavi, CPL Reagan, Corporal Santiago, CPL Cavey, CPL Bates, CPL Smallwood, CPL Patrocinio, and CPL Tirado.

These were the Marines who stood on the wall separating the company command from the lower enlisted. Gunny Rowe's infamous operating motto was: "Mission Objective Priority One: Troop Welfare Always." They were intertwined. That's how it's supposed to be. You only sacrifice for reasonable upside. These were the seasoned knights of Golf Company and the Battalion. With them, we would have defeated the entire country and been home for dinner should the rules of engagement shackles and incompetent command have been removed.

The Company Commander had an utter disgust and emasculation for 1st Platoon Commander (LT Gregory Baxter), 2nd Platoon Commander (LT Browne), and 3rd Platoon Commander (LT Frank

Durham). This insecurity induced existential issues. The Company Commander cared more about dominating them than protecting Golf Company and dominating the Area of Operations (AO). It was asymmetrically adversarial. The commander kept the platoon leaders he disliked due to emasculation out of the loop from sensitive intelligence. It was well beyond appropriate levels of command compartmentalization.

I was sitting on a makeshift bench across from LT Browne outside the sandbag hut that comprised the smoke deck when the Company Commander came out. That was LT Browne: always preparing for missions with Marines and sailors as the sole priority. Until then, everything was peaceful and contemplative. It was the calm before the storm as far as combat operations were concerned.

LT Browne was reading a book on leadership and tactics. The Commander ripped the book out of his hand while scoffing and said, "Let me see this." He laughed while looking at it to make his disdain clear about what he thought of the Platoon Commander before flinging the book back at LT in a desperate display of false dominance. Six weeks earlier, when we'd arrived in the country, he had transferred LT Browne to the Iraqi Army outside 2/8 out of pure hate and emasculation, but LT Browne found a way to get back to Golf Company as no one, especially not some jackal imitating an officer, was going to take his platoon and men away from him. That's the fierce leader he is. It's one of the only reasons I'm alive right now and escaped the snare of the Company Commander. That's who the Company Commander is. That was how far he was willing to go to undercut Golf Company enlisted, just to ruin leaders and men superior to him. For those six weeks, SSGT Ybarra had to step in as 2nd Platoon's acting Platoon Commander. The Company Commander had also reassigned our Platoon SGT, SSGT Bestman, along with LT Browne for those first six weeks until high command ordered that they be restored to the platoon they'd trained and bonded with while preparing for combat deployment. They were deprived of six weeks of vital familiarity with the Area of Operations and had to adapt and sink or swim. The Company Commander had tried to undercut the Fifth General Order and had once again failed miserably. Golf Company Lions don't get separated from the pack. But the surcharge of consequences would be passed on to 2nd Platoon, nonetheless.

Any commander who would attack a subordinate officer, let alone a great one, in front of a junior enlisted Marine intuitively knows he is pathological at worst and incompetent and unbecoming at best. I nearly lunged in defense, taking one for the company to replace him right there to preserve the integrity and stop the madness while junior officers could then step up and fill the power vacuum and lead. The ship was sinking fast with Captain Broekhuizen at the helm.

We had no idea how much we were about to need their leadership and ferocity because the Islamic observance of Ramadan had just commenced, which would initiate the uprising and Civil War later known as the Hornet's Nest. Violence and carnage would be the daily menu, and appetites were ravenous. Ramadan 2006 was the date the enemy commenced their violent offensive meant to induce all-out sectarian strife and ambush American troops in the most barbaric forms. The phase of violence, evil, and historical bloodshed that would force Washington to usher in the infamous "Surge" Campaign was, at this very moment, underway—we just didn't know it. The Uprising was in the beginning days of commencement. The area would descend into an all-out civil war between the Sunni and Shiites and would engulf the entire region in violence and death. We were in the heart of the Sunni Triangle. We didn't know it, but the Pentagon had intel knowing a threat was coming because of the infamous Samara Mosque Bombing months earlier. As a result, Baghdad's " Green Zone" was beefed up to protect the Capital and all the military, diplomatic, and intelligence personnel.

New York Times Article highlighting the capture and mutilation of American youth but omitting the full extent to torture by AQI.

Chapter 5: Tale of Two Cities

Left to Right: LCPL November Romeo and LCPL Jonathan Phillips

When many of the indispensable knights were later knocked off the chessboard either by death, incapacitation, or Involuntary Dismissal, Golf Company enlisted were left with a weak company-level command, and the burden of commands became progressively disturbing. That's how the commander put the Pentagon at risk. He would transfer out and involuntarily dismiss any leader perceived as a threat to his career. The war wasn't a priority for him. He was looking much more forward. It would become a daily crucible to protect each other until our unit was properly relieved and the Fifth General Order was faithfully fulfilled. Nothing else made much sense. I don't just mean protection from the enemy. All logic was dissipating. The reality became progressively polarizing. Who were friendlies versus hostiles would soon be anyone's guess, and sectarian and tribal alliances seemed fluid. The enemy was given free rein to murder while conventional forces were under perpetual duress daily with the fear of violating the asymmetrical rules of engagement (ROEs) that exponentially emboldened the enemy. The enemy would use harassing tactics to exploit this. They knew every time they engaged a position, our adrenaline would spike and drain our mental faculties, depriving us of even more sleep. They knew which hours to exploit. They weren't foolish. Not from a conventional viewpoint, at least.

It's hard to describe just how many minutes are in a day in combat or how long each minute feels when operating under a command determined to inflate itself at all costs. It's a form of walking on eggshells incomprehensible to most. Every step, decision, and direction is scrutinized. There was never any upside. Only downside and potential repercussions.

Days later, we were briefed at squad level, which was passed down from company command. They'd received actionable intelligence reports from above indicating there was an active enemy plot to capture a Marine alive to torture on Al-Jazeera for the world to see. The actionable intel reported that in the minds of the insurgency, it would equate to a substantial morale boost and victory because Marines operate under the ethos "No Marine left behind." Also, it was made clear that the enemy had already successfully captured and tortured individuals from the Army, leaving the Marines as the ultimate status symbol for the terrorists. We were told that only months earlier, Army soldiers had been captured and castrated alive before being found stuffed in a trunk with their testicles in their mouths for U.S. forces to find. This was not your average enemy, and these were not your average times. The Pentagon knew we were under heightened stress against diabolical opposition. Falling into enemy hands was not an option.

Chapter 5: Tale of Two Cities

Squad leaders briefed subordinates on the non-negotiable nature of being captured. At the time, it seemed like the institution was more worried about its tradition and reputation and not our individual welfare. I ruminated about why else they would hamstring us by impossible rules of engagement meant to put the insurgency at a distinct advantage, perpetually putting the fear of God into us about being court-martialed and incarcerated, meanwhile claiming they were recommending suicide versus torture because they were concerned for our wellbeing. But that had become the polarizing logic. The Umbrella Corporation was at work high above my pay grade. Company Commander ensured that he didn't brief us on the live torture and mutilation of American Troops in Iraq before we left for deployment, even though he clearly had those intel briefings from two months prior. In hindsight, it's clear why his whole focus was getting trigger pullers overseas, downplaying combat operations. The Pentagon knew a bloody campaign was en route stemming from that torture and the infamous mosque bombing that had been a complex attack engineered to induce all-out civil war between the Sunni and Shiite populations.

It didn't help the situation that the Bush Administration was becoming increasingly controversial for its enhanced interrogation program. This war was shady. No other way to articulate it. I'm not saying whether I disagree with the tactics, just that the conventional forces were being held to a disgusting and untenably contrarian standard in contrast to special operations and central intelligence agencies, who were given carte blanche operational rein.

We were given a tutorial and instructed on how to tactically prep frag grenades and how to stack on gear for rapid deployment. We were shown how to administer a thin layer of loose black electrical tape around the ordinance to protect against inadvertent deployment yet could be removed in a split second and engaged. We were instructed directly to detonate should the moment arise when it was perceived that our squad was in the process of being overrun. I recall mentally noting that I found the implications self-serving by command, but I had zero intention of being taken alive or allowing one of my brothers to be. During this briefing, 2nd Squad was given a tutorial by an external NCO attached from the Battalion. We received lessons on a new collapsible, shoulder-fired light assault weapon (LAW) that was being rolled out and added to mounted patrols for additional small unit protection. They knew something big was coming without telling us directly. I don't know why I was so intimidated by operating those, but when you're a junior Marine in combat, you're just trying your best to absorb information, protect your fellow Marines, and not screw up. There's zero margin for error. Things like radio communication and explosive ordinances are intimidating foreign languages at that point.

CHAPTER 6:
BAPTISM OF TERROR

October 6th, 2006—Two Days Later

Pre-mission briefing was wrapped up, and we were given a scheduled countdown. We went back to our assigned gear room and began with our pre-mission ritual and gear check. Hydration. Weapons inspection. Caffeine. Precision music blaring to tap back into the carnivorous mindset necessary to cross the Line of Departure (LOD) each mission physically and psychologically. During this ceremonial ritual, all jocular dynamics ceased prior to commencing gear prep. The margin for error operating outside the wire, especially in a 3D urban terrain environment, was nonexistent at best and unforgiving at worst. Zero jocularity. We were gearing up to hunt. The mental LOD was, by this point, breached. The next step before leaving the wire was the smoke deck for ceremonial fraternal cigarettes. I always abstained.

I knew my personality. Once I go down a road, I'm all in. It would've been a dead-end vice. I could do more for the pack by being as tactically proficient as possible.

The day was sunny. The temperature was starting to abate, so there was a natural morale boost and optimism, even if merely grateful for the reprieve and restore our bodies. The patrol exited the FOB

Compound and took a route running parallel to the Euphrates River. We later approached a short, narrow bridge crossing a canal that ran perpendicular to the ancient and biblical body of water, which held secrets of time that were only imaginable to the living.

The lead vehicle crossed the bridge successfully. I was in one of the two interior trucks, just approaching the end of the bridge and linking up with the lead vehicle. At the same time, the rear vehicle was making its way onto the bridge from the other side and entering what would soon be realized as the kill zone.

The explosion detonated directly underneath the vehicle in precision detonation, resulting in a completely catastrophic kill and commencing U-shaped ambush. The Explosive Ordinance Disposal (EOD) team later described the bomb as five 155mm artillery shells. They were flanked by a ring of propane tanks for maximum accelerant to engulf and force occupants to exit the vehicle to be captured or killed.

In what must have been milliseconds, the turret and turret gunner were launched somewhere off the bridge. We had no idea where or that it was even in the canal due to chaos and zero visibility, which made matters more precarious because we weren't leaving a brother behind. Dead or alive. Unacceptable. If necessary, this would be our final resting place. Together. In unison. Only days later would Marine Recon Divers, under the cover of darkness, locate the turret and Marine at the bottom of the canal and retrieve LCPL Johnson's body. Corporal Payne lay dead and motionless on the bridge, having been ejected from the vehicle but somehow seemed otherwise unaffected by the explosion.

When I got out of my gun truck, he was just there at my feet. LCPL Muehle and I linked up and moved toward the crash site while

Chapter 6: Baptism of Terror

suppressing the long grass and a vehicle that had been trailing the now burning vehicle out of fear that it was a secondary IED.

At the same time, vehicle NCO was somehow pulling himself out of a vehicle that had no doors and no discernible characteristics other than fire and was thrown on its side, making the pull and fall completely vertical in nature. He was severely burnt and completely incoherent from major traumatic brain injury and instinctively able to extricate himself. One of the best team leaders I ever knew. As he walked out, his 203mm grenades were on fire. I wasn't raised to stand on the curb while survivors burned in the house, so I engaged. I frantically patted down the five or six 203mm grenades affixed to his chest, thinking we were surely done right there and then.

Someone who I couldn't identify at first (LCPL John Hale, Louisiana) was engulfed in flames, lying next to a heap of junk overturned. He was surrounded by what I recall was a 90-degree ring of fire trapping him between the crash site and the bridge railing. We were under constant enemy fire while stuck in the kill zone as we tried to extricate the Marine from fire. He was attempting to scream "Help me" though the diabolical propane IED had done its job, making it increasingly impossible due to inhalation. His throat was charred. But he was screaming for help at the same time. I never recovered from this moment. The fact that Hale wasn't in shock is a testament to how tough and indefatigable he was. He also had unlimited energy and kindness.

The First General Order

Bridge Ambush Recreation

Ambush Explosion from bridge crash site
seen miles away by Marines at OP Matilda

Chapter 6: Baptism of Terror

Continued Observation of bridge ambush from Marines at OP-Matilda.

I lowered my head so the heat from the furnace was partially blocked by my Kevlar helmet enough to get close to Hale and get him far enough away quickly. I pulled him just far enough away from the fire towards the railing with bare hands by grabbing the strap on his flak jacket. My original squad leader had taught us this maneuver while training at Mojave Viper in California, except the training exercise was for the purpose of clearing houses. When someone gets shot in the doorway, the guy behind him needs to instantly grab the loop and drag the Marine backward so other Marines can keep engaging forward through the structure while getting aid to the wounded Marine. Admittedly, I was disoriented at the crash site and was solely determined to get Hale down the embankment to the Euphrates River on the other side of the railing. It was the only thing I could think of to help him. So, I just sucked up the heat and fumes and pulled him towards the edge where the water was.

Muehle was able to get a pair of gloves and pull Hale the remainder of the way along the railing so that the squad leader and corpsman could tend to him, as well as maintain a 360-degree view of the ambush and direct each of us in assigned duties. To make matters worse, we were along the Euphrates River, and on both sides of the canal crossing and beginning and end of the bridge was an abundance of densely populated tall grass areas and several berms making the perfect kill zone for insurgents to close in to engage and capture Marines while vulnerably trying to extricate our Marine. Insurgents knew by intel reports that Marines don't leave Marines behind. Period. It's unacceptable. Our defining ethos was now our greatest vulnerability. I was dispatched to run and retrieve the stretcher from the vehicle as rounds were impacting around me. I couldn't get the stretcher to engage and lock, so three of us had to get Hale on the stretcher, and one of us had to hold the bottom.

> "Shortly after noon, we were preparing to conduct a vehicle-mounted security patrol. During our equipment checks, we discovered a malfunction in the inter-squad radios. John's team leader could hear me, but I couldn't hear him. Because of this, I had to rearrange the order of movement for the patrol. Because of the radios, I placed them in the second position so our turret gunners could utilize hand and arm signals. Once the problem was resolved, we began our patrol. About thirty minutes into the patrol, we were crossing a bridge across the Trout Canal on ASR Lobster. After the first three vehicles had crossed the bridge, the insurgents initiated a U-shaped ambush on our patrol by setting off an IED propelled by fuel underneath the last vehicle. Destroyed is not a good word. Someone later asked if the burning heap of metal was a suicide bomber vehicle. It was that mangled. We have one dead Marine lying right beside John's vehicle, one Marine trying to walk out of the fire, one Marine blown some-

Chapter 6: Baptism of Terror

where into the canal. And our close friend and Iraqi interpreter lying in a dozen pieces all around. Head here, arm and torso there, fingers and toes everywhere. That is only the beginning. We spent the better part of the next hour fighting through the ambush, in which we were stuck in the kill zone and virtually surrounded. And at the same time, we must evacuate our friends which we successfully accomplished with the selfless bravery of Jonathan Phillips. Jon was able to do something that neither I nor his team leader could do by ourselves. The vehicle was burning so hot we couldn't close enough to the Marine inside the fire. We tried pouring water, but it only seemed to fuel the flames. Jon, without thought of self, grabbed a hold of the Marine's burning flak jacket and pulled him free of the fire, burning his hands in the process."

CPL Stephen Reagan

There was a building off to the other side that gave perfect cover and high ground for an enemy to unleash suppressive fire while using the opposing side's tall grass and berms as defilade to potentially spring forth and flank from. The structure had a bunch of small stucco windows, which made firing easy but hard to return. CPL Sellers deployed numerous rounds from 203mm grenade launchers to nullify the threat.

The enemy had destroyed an entire gun truck, placing our squad in a precarious position. We now had one less machine gun in the fight to keep the enemy from closing in on us. Because of the wounded Marines at the crash site, the surviving dismounted Marines were focused on retrieving wounded Marines and suppressing fire intermittently to compensate for the lost machine gun. That meant that the remaining two turret machine gunners had no Marines to assist with reloading ammunition, placing a greater burden of proficiency on them. The entire squad was put to the test in one of the most extreme forms of teamwork.

While responding to enemy fire and trying to extricate my fellow Marine from the crash site, I heard RTO screaming that comms were knocked out from blast percussion. The squad leader made the call to initiate the pre-established distress signal to all available units in the area as we were rapidly depleting ammunition, and we weren't going to leave any Marine behind. It was of the question. Lance Corporal Parcels and another turret gunner were providing excellent suppression and fire superiority, each suppressing targets in coordination with each other throughout the entire ambush, doing their best to maintain a 360-degree field of fire, though impeded by several surrounding berms. I could not imagine being a squad leader in that engagement and maintaining a 360-degree paradigm. I was too focused on single tasks like suppression and crash site extraction and ensuring I wasn't at risk of enemy capture. I suddenly saw and heard the unmistakable profile of a white-star cluster distress signal, which was deployed by the NCO at that precarious point.

At that same point, I took an intuitive hint and removed the frag grenade from the pouch and the thin layer of electrical tape, then prepped a grenade for rapid deployment. We were able to extract the Marine from the fire and onto a stretcher. I don't know how long it was later when 3rd Platoon, led by SSGT Alfred Rivers, was the first responding unit to reach the ambush point and reinforce the perimeter after being re-tasked into Quick Reaction Force (QRF). Squad remained behind to brief the arriving QRF contingent and ensure no Marine was left behind. He did a superb job leading and defeating enemy ambush.

Chapter 6: Baptism of Terror

I was not comfortable leaving the crash site with fellow Marine (LCPL Stephen Johnson) MIA, and I made that clear. I left because Doc Solbach needed help in the back of the medevac vehicle. The vehicle's up-armored back hatch had been experiencing issues, and it could not be secured. If someone else had jumped into the back of the high-back vehicle, I would've stayed back at the bridge with the squad leader and QRF element as they secured it. I wasn't ok with leaving my squad leader. It's not how we were trained. But there's no way Doc would've been able to triage the two wounded Marines, hold trachea, and hold the back hatch closed the entire ride. He would've fallen out when the vehicles were at max speed. It was a predicament, but I acted decisively with the factors I was presented with. In my head, I planned on getting right back out there with an instant turn-around after getting the wounded to the Landing Zone.

About 45 seconds later, we exited the crash site to get Hale to the LZ at FOB Riviera. At this point, Doc had administered a tracheotomy like a true professional under unthinkable circumstances and chaos, which allowed the burning Marine to breathe and communicate. The Marine was not in shock, which placed me in a morally existential position between what I should do versus what was allowed, given that his chances of survival in any form were attenuating exponentially, and the torture was unlike anything I'd ever seen. Hale was the toughest Marine I ever saw up until the end. Doc had me holding the trachea in place with one hand and securing the swinging back hatch with the other so he could assist the other wounded NCO. Somehow, LCPL Hale, being the toughest guy I knew, was able to do his best to communicate to me at what angle he needed me to hold the trachea whenever it would shift or I would be flung because the back hatch would open due to the speeding vehicle and nearly take my right arm with it

Time was of the absolute essence. Suddenly, Company Commander MB arrived with his Personal Security Detail (PSD) and halted our convoy. I was irate. I stood up in the back of the open medevac Humvee. When I realized we'd stopped, I transferred custody of the trachea to Doc and stood vertically, towering over the back of the vehicle. What I saw enraged me. Company Commander Mark Broekhuizen stared at us and the bridge like a deer in headlights. Nonverbal. I said something to the effect of "Get the fuck out of the way," called him a piece of shit, and told him to go worry about the rules of engagement. He never said a word. At that point, he backed off, and we moved. The squad leader had stayed back on the bridge with SSGT Rivers' QRF Squad to ensure LCPL Johnson wasn't left behind. He was willing to hold up a medivac just to look like he was in control yet offering nothing profitable per his nature. At this time, LCPL Muehle was driving our vehicle, and I could hear him screaming and crying to let us pass.

> "I can't think about a time in my life when I was so unsure of living from one minute to the next, from the moments being quiet and still to a sudden to a sudden ambush. There was so much uncertainty in each minute. The only time I really felt safe was when I was fighting back against the enemy alongside my squad of brave Marines, and the gunfire distracted my mind from the uncertainty. Out of all the close calls I had on the Iraq deployment, I can remember a Marine who was there during some of the toughest of times. That Marine, the author of this book,

Chapter 6: Baptism of Terror

Jonathan Phillips, was an amazing team member and close friend and brother. There are several occasions when I vividly remember that without his help, I would not be where I am today.

The most memorable occasion was a life-changing event for the both of us. We were on a vehicle patrol on the outskirts of town. Eight kilometers North-West of Fallujah. As we were on patrol, we came to an area that was infamous for ambushes and Al Qaeda activity. The road led to one of Saddam Hussein's properties. The dirt road was narrow, with tall, heavy grass along both sides of the road and an abandoned building lay off in the distance. Each of our vehicles slowly advanced down the road. Then, a large bang went off. One of our vehicles was hit. After that, all hell broke loose. I remember hearing gunfire and the general direction of fire. I remember being in the back of the medivac vehicle and receiving the casualties. It was surreal. Phillips was with me the whole time; we were both talking to the injured Marine the whole time, desperately trying to keep him conscious. We heard a voice from the mortally wounded Marine. It was difficult to hear him due to the extent of his injuries. One thing I hold dear to my memory to this day is hearing him say: I wanna go home. We hauled ass back to our patrol base, where further, in-depth care was initiated. Time was ticking before the helicopter was scheduled to arrive. As soon as it touched down, we laid him on the stretcher and carried him out to the helicopter.

I was talking to him the entire time. Later, I came to find out that would be the last time I would talk to my friend again."

HM3 "Doc" Arthur Solbach, USN

Let there be zero equivocation – LCPL John Hale wasn't merely killed — he was tortured and burned to death over the course of an hour, which was exactly what the diabolical enemy had intended. If God hadn't intervened and allocated the strength and fortune necessary to fight through that ambush until QRF arrived, they would've captured as many Marines as possible and amplified that torture after dragging off any residual life. This was the enemy we were up against. They wanted us on Al-Jazeera being tortured and beheaded for our families and the world to see.

Back at FOB Riviera

Let no one equivocate the extent of that ambush or the ensuing combat operations following. That was the opening days of The Sunni Uprising and Sectarian Violence in The Sunni Triangle. It had been planned for months before and set in motion comprehensively across the AO—what would later be coined The Hornets' Nest.

My brain was never the same. None of our brains were. That wasn't just another ambush. LT Browne, CPL Rapavi, and CPL Bates had to restrain me physically and psychologically after getting back from the ambush as I kept trying to go back out. It was CPL Rapavi, my initial squad leader and mentor, who would keep me sane from there on out. He'd come to my rack, and we'd watch movies like *Flags of Our Fathers* on the small TV someone had procured, and he'd bring chocolate pretzels. Acts like that are the difference between san-

Chapter 6: Baptism of Terror

ity and madness. Small windows of human contact and camaraderie. He knew me since the first day I arrived in The Fleet and had known who I was prior to the ambush, which, in retrospect, was a Godsend. I attribute CPL Rapavi with keeping my mind going in combat and not drifting off. LT came, and I vividly recalled the Biblical story of Job, which I'd never heard before. That story calmed me down and changed my paradigm because I was losing it. What the enemy had done to Hale needed to be met with a statement, primarily because of the pain he'd experienced. Secondly, I knew, even semi-coherent with rage, that to allow that enemy to escape immediate and declarative retribution would make it open season on U.S. Forces. When they tortured and killed Hale, they'd crossed the Rubicon many times over. They'd fucked with the wrong dudes.

My brain couldn't accept that someone took a spot meant for my teammates and me at the last second. I was also afraid. Terrified of being tortured. That day changed me no matter how far I ran from it. Anyone who calls me trigger-happy after that day can tell it to Hale's family. For me, it made it easier to bring the fight to the enemy with an offensive vs. defensive mindset. Sitting idly by, waiting to be picked off, captured, and tortured, wasn't something I cared to engage in. We didn't have a Company Commander or company 1st SGT who was going to protect us at any juncture. Did they save us on the bridge after they'd had Intel reports about an active plot to capture a Marine alive? Of course not. It was going to be on me to protect my fellow Marines and vice versa. Any other bodies on the ground were simply collateral damage. I didn't start the war.

Later that night, in the room abutting the Command Operations Center (COC), I stayed paralyzed, kneeling next to the body bag that contained the NCO. The evanescence didn't compute. I just stayed

The First General Order

there to make sure there was no loneliness for either of us. We were a squad. One moment, he was alive, and the next, he wasn't. His final fire watch had ended, and his duty was faithfully fulfilled.

Even in death, I struggled to abdicate the bond of camaraderie in that dusty, dank room next to the COC, enveloped in a generic body bag as he was. I was consummately numb and filled with antipathy toward our adversary, who had now drawn first blood. That was the moment the mission became real. You never leave a man behind. I knew he wouldn't leave us behind. It's the unyielding covenant that forges an unbreakable bond. It's the Fifth General Order. That's the distinct difference of being a Marine gunfighter. He had fought to go on this deployment and had been afforded every opportunity to stay home and tend to his family. But he made it clear that we were his family. He had arrived in-country just weeks earlier after fighting assiduously to deploy. I recall what a reunion it was on both sides to have an experienced teammate back in the fold when he'd arrived with a sea bag and M16-A2 rifle ready to terminate with extreme prejudice. That's the caliber that Golf Company bred ubiquitously. Absolute lions. No way I was leaving the frontline anything short of unconsciousness and unable to resist. That was how we were recruited and trained to hold the line at all costs. We took whatever personal problems we had and stuffed them down. No one separated us from our brothers and left them a man short. No one violated the Fifth General Order.

Somewhere within the span of the hour following the ambush, while one of our Marine brothers was still marked as MIA though the canal and ambush area had been secured and rescue operations were underway by recon divers, there was suddenly a heated altercation on the lower level of FOB Riviera between Company 1st SGT Reginald

Chapter 6: Baptism of Terror

Robinson and SGT Johnson. First, SGT Robinson walked into the galley casually and apathetically and asked SGT Johnson, "So, what's for dinner?" SGT Johnson rightfully lost his composure as any great Marine in his right mind would. This was the type of company-level command leadership we in Golf Company had—to everyone's detriment.

A brief time later, I was still in complete shock and barely able to stand up. All the adrenaline had been dumped and depleted, and now came the invoice with a vengeance. I felt like a diabetic in need of insulin. I was dry heaving uncontrollably, coughing up black bile from the crash site, diesel, and propane, which would last for two weeks before attenuating. But sleep wasn't an option.

We were ordered to pack up the gear and personal effects of fallen comrades to be shipped back to Base Camp. To make matters worse, the memorial service for LCPL March killed the prior week was still green-lit, and we had two hours to sleep before heading back to Base Camp via platoon convoy on top of everything. 2/8 Battalion Commander was notorious for his endless desire for photo ops depicting him as a phenomenal tactical and mournful leader. However, he issued no inspirational speeches or morale boosters. But the moment he could get a photo op and capitalize on PR, that guy morphed into a stoic leader in the optical sense.

Unfortunately for us, he was about to have an abundance of grieving photo opportunities. I just wish he had focused as much time on tactical operations far behind enemy lines while living at Base Camp in one of the most luxurious living situations as he had ensured his tear ducts were fully operational and poised to move up the hierarchy ladder. He was there to capitalize not on the terrain but the byproduct of it. I never once saw him come out to FOB Riviera besides the time he came to grab CPL Payne's body and get a photo op. That was one of the problems with this war: The officers and senior enlisted back at Base Camp had more lavish situations than they did back in the States. It was a war of careerism. Here we were, grieving at a memorial service for our fallen brother, and our minds were preoccupied with combat operations awaiting. They also ruminated on the three more fallen who would be grieved at the next memorial after more combat operations. It was likely that even more would be killed between now and then.

CHAPTER 7:
BURN THE BOATS: SHARPEN THE WOOD

Base Camp—Memorial Service

I was battling demons in the form of guilt. I was accustomed to downplaying emotions and was optimistic by default. The truth of the matter was that seeing Lance Corporal Hale agonize broke something inside of me. He was the purest human being I've ever come across and held no hate in his authentic heart, which made it more brutal. Even if it wasn't someone so pure, make no mistake about it: that kid was tortured to death by the enemy. They hadn't merely drawn first blood.

I felt inherently guilty and couldn't relinquish that burden. He had taken my place in the vehicle lineup, and the level of agony he suffered was unthinkable. I was filled with self-hatred as I would find myself ruminating and being glad it wasn't me who was tortured. The prospect scared me to my core. The fact that someone else incurred it amplified the feeling astronomically.

I was angry for many reasons. The premeditation. I wanted to end the suffering. I had known what the right call was and let my fear of potential consequences outweigh my action. No one trains you for a moral case study like that. No one wants to make that call. You must do what needs to be done even though no one wants to do it. It's the weight of the world.

Everything in my gut wanted to end the unnecessary suffering that demonstrably felt like an eternity for the recipient. I failed that day by not decisively putting a stop to the suffering with morphine. Many would've pawned it off, saying that's not your call to make. It's anyone's call to make at that point when your brother is in agony with no chance of survival. It was a moral imperative, and anyone there, including myself, would've desperately reached for a euphoric reprieve at that moment. That failure haunted me and galvanized me to come back and show up every day and volunteer for whatever mission was mounting up.

Courage doesn't come with an infinite supply. It's manifested in the form of crusades. Micro and macro. Each time a brother was killed or wounded, I faced two choices: leave them one less experienced gunfighter or deploy that pain to honor the fallen by persisting. Burn the boats because there's no option after what the enemy did to my brothers. I'll either vanquish the enemy or perish, cursing them with my dying breath. In the waning days of deployment, a man who has my reverence told me something that is etched in my mind. Staff SGT Ybarra said, "We fight now and grieve later." I think that's why the constant memorial services interspersed between combat operations amplified the inability to compartmentalize the mission at hand. That's among the many differentials of modern warfare and the problematic cognitive dissonance of conducting memorial services interspersed with combat and grieving. As a result, I minimized calling home as an ardent attempt at compartmentalization, among others. My iPod became the comrade that the enemy was in-

Chapter 7: Burn the Boats: Sharpen the Wood

capable of killing. It provided the best chance to keep my mind from lingering towards things over there that simply didn't add up, like the mission confusion, in-cohesive strategy, and command backstabbing.

At this time, following the terrorist ambush, I found my speech impediment flaring up for the first time in many years. It's a horrible feeling, especially when you can't make sense of it and have no way of hiding it or keeping it concealed. So, in my mind, I did the practical thing: I began talking less and observing more to offset the deficit and make it look reasonable, given the environmental hazards. I became faster at engaging targets when ambushed. Some people, at times, saw me talking while cleaning my weapon system. That was the only time where I could get words out in private. I knew I had to verbalize stuff, or it would fester in my mind. It was a cathartic mechanism, given the overwhelming casualty ratio and loss of life. Something on that bridge affected me mentally and neurologically, and my speech impediment aggressively flared up. My only practical recourse was to talk only when spoken to and matter of fatly. Mostly Yes and No answers.

Around this point, the Battalion Medical Officer (M.O.) LT Douglas Pugliese began actively prescribing Ambien to several Marines, including me, while participating in combat operations. Not long after, the Department of Defense and Department of Veterans Affairs discontinued prescribing the substance due to the side effects they were observing. People were waking up and driving across state lines late at night without knowledge of how they'd arrived. He began prescribing several Marines at FOB Riviera Ambien under the guise of smoking cessation while operating far behind enemy lines. This is just one horrendous thing they were prescribing to front-line troops, along with the endless palates of high-energy caffeine drinks and soda.

Memorial Service Tribute for Lance Corporal Howard March

Chapter 7: Burn the Boats: Sharpen the Wood

Battalion M.O. asked some rudimentary questions geared towards getting me back to the fight, and I was completely and collaboratively on board priority-wise. Plus, there was no way I was going to stay back at Base Camp and enjoy decent food and rest while my comrades were being engaged in heavy combat operations. Being on Ambien back at Base Camp was one of the most terrifying realities. I was alone and without direction, wandering around our trailers, which were now deserted. If not for a Marine from 2/8 Fox Company, with whom I attended School of Infantry, taking me into his room and keeping an eye on me, I don't want to speculate what would've happened. I'm not proud to admit it, but I was bad off. That ambush cannot be understated. But that was how Golf Company Command operated. It was on the enlisted Marines to figure out the war in every respect under the burden of commands with zero upside. Consummate predicaments. Nineteen years old and forced to make decisions that 40-year-old commanders deferred. It was a surreal baptism into maturity. But that's what leaders do. They step up and butt-stroke excuses and adversity in the face.

Cleared by the Battalion psych. Absolute relief. When confronted between being isolated in a deserted mortuary with the spirits of what used to be and reuniting with your family, combat becomes a celebratory matter. I later realized he had disingenuously indemnified himself and 2/8 and Golf Company Commander by annotating the medical record saying that I was being returned to the front line under the guise that I would be put on light duty and would be "initially kept close to FOB Riviera." That was the mechanism the Navy and Marine Corps were using to perpetuate the labor premium as far as notational purposes. It was clearly disingenuous because I would be in a firefight the very next day and almost shot in the head by a sniper lying in wait. This was not the line of work or industry where one got vacation time or convalescent leave. I did whatever was asked of me to protect my fellow Marines and Navy Corpsmen, many of whom I graduated SOI with. We were brothers. Absolute Lions. I was given a bag of Ambien by a Medical Officer and hitched a seven-ton transport back late one night under the cover of darkness to link back up with a squad at Hotel Riviera. Never was I once kept off operations or from volunteering for optional operations where volunteers were coming up short. Nor was I ever kept back at FOB Riviera.

Base Camp (Camp Fallujah) Memorial Service for Marines Killed in Action During October 6th Bridge Ambush

Chapter 7: Burn the Boats: Sharpen the Wood

Name (Last, First MI): Phillips, Jonathan Andrew	**Patient I.D. / SSN:**
Past Medical Hx: ☒ None	**Current Medications List**
Notes:	none

Hx of Present Illness: 19 y/o USMC LCPL referred to Combat Stress Clinic by medical officer for his unit for eval for combat stress/SI. LCPL was involved in IED attack yesterday in which vehicle behind him was incinerated and 3 Marines were killed, to include turret gunner whose body was not found. LCPL tried to pull body out of vehicle while returning fire and medical record states there were reports that he made suicidal statements. LCPL denies this and states everyone was shouting and screaming at that time. M.O. states LCPL made statements to effect that "I don't know why we are here" and "Why are we doing this." HM3 Ogara, corpsman with unit, states unit has suffered several losses over past few weeks and LCPL has exhibited declining military bearing during that time and made derogatory comments about Iraqis. He states this contrasts with LCPL's initial attitude upon coming to Iraq in July when he was joking and everyone enjoyed being around him. LCPL denies SI, any hx of SI or self-harm, and denies any family h/o suicide. He states he has had variable sleep during deployment as they are frequently awoken at odd times to go on missions. He also reports decreased appetite with 15-lb weight loss since arrival in theater in July, which he states most other Marines have experienced as well. He denies changes in energy or concentration and says when he has had down time in theater he has been able to enjoy exercising and listening to music. He reports increased "situational awareness" since arriving in theater and denies sx of avoidance, stating he calls home once a week and feels very close to his unit. States he feels hopeful about his future after deployment, but does not feel positive about remainder of deployment and does not want to stay in Marines.

Mental Status Exam

Appearance & Behavior: ☒ Within Normal Limits	**MSE Notes:**
Eye Contact / Speech: ☒ Good eye contact, normal speech.	
Motor: ☒ No psychomotor agitation or retardation	
Mood: ☐ Stated mood was "angry"	
Affect: was restricted	
Thought Processes: ☒ Linear, logical and goal directed.	
Thought Content: ☒ No suicidal ideation, intent or plan ☒ No homicidal ideation, intent or plan ☒ No evidence of psychosis.	
Cognition: ☒ Alert & Oriented to person, place, time, situation. ☒ Concentration Intact. Intelligence estimated to be **Memory:** ☒ Intact for immediate, long and short term memory.	
Judgment: ☒ Intact	
Insight: ☒ Intact	
Impulse Control: ☒ Intact	

Psychiatric Diagnosis	Combat Stress
Axis I: Bereavement, r/o Acute Stress Disorder	☐ Not Applicable ☐ Combat Stress
Axis II: No Diagnosis	☐ Operational Stress ☐ Light
Axis III: No Diagnosis	☒ Heavy
Axis IV: Occupational problems	**Axis IV or Misc. Stressors:**
Axis V: GAF (Current) – 51-60 Moderate symptoms	
Axis V: GAF (Past Yr) – 0 Inadequate information	

Formulation: 19 y/o USMC LCPL referred for eval for possible statements about SI made in context of fellow Marines being killed by IED in vehicle behind him during mission yesterday. LCPL reports being angry about what happened but denies SI and has no personal or family h/o SI or psychiatric illness. May meet criteria for Acute Stress Disorder if sx persist beyond two days and further hx indicates he is exhibiting sx of dissociation and re-experiencing.

Treatment Plan

Goals/Medications/Interventions:	Goals/Medications/Interventions ☒ Informed Consent Given
1. Rec Marine stay inside wire until f/u on 09OCT.	4.
2. Ambien 10 mg, 1/2-1 tab po qhs prn insomnia #2 RF0.	5.
3. F/u with this provider on 09OCT06 at 0900 for further eval.	6.

Disposition

Duty Status: ☒ Light Duty x 2 day(s) ☐ Return To Duty/Fit for full duty ☐ Rec Medevac out of Theater	**Safety:** ☒ At low risk for harm to self or others at this time ☐ At high risk for harm to self or others, precautions listed below. **Precautions:**
Limitations: Rec Marine stay inside wire until f/u appt on 09OCT.	

Provider Signature: *Eden Temko*	
Psych Tech Name (Printed or Typed):	**Date/Time:** 09OCT06
Provider Name (Printed or Typed): E. Temko D.O. LT, MC, USNR	

OSD(HA) Trauma Registry Form / Navy-Marine Corps CTR – Psychiatry (02 Jun 2006)

Base Camp (Camp Fallujah) Medical Notes pertaining to evaluation of LCPL Jonathan Phillips

Pugliese, who had removed him from his FOB. The following was information comes from Dr. Pugliese's report: The patient was involved in a combined IED SVDIED complex attack on 06 October 2006. He pulled a badly burned marine out of a flaming vehicle. He stated at that time that the last few weeks leading up to him being seen by Mental Health had been accompanied by him feeling decreased pleasure in things, a decreased appetite, mild difficulty sleeping, other marines had commented on his decreased military bearing, and he had various concerns about not knowing what his mission was in Iraq. He was also involved in a QRF, for a marine who was killed, the week prior to being seen on 07 October and at that time he had some suspicion of Iraqi civilians and also made comments about not caring about them as well as making disrespectful comments about the Iraqi interpreters close by. He denied any suicidal or homicidal ideation. He denied any depressive symptoms. He denied any history of suicide. He stated he had no history of mental health problems in his family. He had a glazed-over look on his face per the report. He had some survivor guilt about recent IED that had claimed one friend's life. He initially refused to leave the area on October 6th, 2006, because they couldn't find Lance Corporal Johnson's body. He was sent to his first mental health visit on October 7th, 2007 with the diagnosis of RULE OUT COMBAT STRESS and RULE OUT DYSTHYMIA. The patient was to follow-up at 1400 with Dr. Temko at Fallujah per the note by Douglas J. Pugliese. Dr. Temko's note reports the patient was referred to Combat Stress Clinic by a medical officer for his unit for an evaluation for combat stress and suicidal ideation. At the time he made several

Base Camp (Camp Fallujah) Medical Notes by Battalion Medical Officer Douglas Pugliese pertaining to LCPL Jonathan Phillips.

Chapter 7: Burn the Boats: Sharpen the Wood

Name (Last, First MI): Phillips, Jonathan Andrew
Patient I.D. / SSN: [redacted]
Past Medical Hx: ☒ None
Current Medications List: none
Notes:

Hx of Present Illness: 19 y/o USMC LCPL here for f/u. States he took Ambien 10 mg (had recommended 1/2 to 1 tab) two nights ago and slept well but felt somewhat overly sedated so did not take last night and did not sleep well last night. He partially attributes latter to sharing room with multiple other Marines. Says rest of his unit left for FOB Saturday after memorial service, which he describes as a difficult experience. He has stayed at Camp Fallujah with members from 2/8 who are here taking classes and he states he doesn't like being separated from his peers further forward. Does describe recurring thoughts of Friday's events and did not want to talk about them. Reported some increase in restlessness and feelings of derealization. Stated he ate yesterday and "hung around" without doing much. Denies feelings of SI/HI and stated he would not be a liability to his unit.

Mental Status Exam

Appearance & Behavior: ☒ Within Normal Limits
Eye Contact / Speech: ☒ Good eye contact, normal speech.
Motor: ☒ No psychomotor agitation or retardation
Mood: ☐ Stated mood was "I don't know"
Affect: was restricted
Thought Processes: ☒ Linear, logical and goal directed.
Thought Content: ☒ No suicidal ideation, intent or plan
☒ No homicidal ideation, intent or plan
☒ No evidence of psychosis.
Cognition:
☒ Alert & Oriented to person, place, time, situation.
☒ Concentration intact. Intelligence estimated to be
Memory: ☒ Intact for immediate, long and short term memory.
Judgment: ☒ Intact
Insight: ☒ Intact
Impulse Control: ☒ Intact

MSE Notes: LCPL was guarded during interview with sparing speech.

Psychiatric Diagnosis
Axis I: Bereavement, Acute Stress Disorder (provisional)
Axis II: No Diagnosis
Axis III: No Diagnosis
Axis IV: Occupational problems
Axis V: GAF (Current) – 51-60 Moderate symptoms
Axis V: GAF (Past Yr) – 0 Inadequate information

Combat Stress
☐ Not Applicable
☐ Operational Stress
☐ Combat Stress
☐ Light
☒ Heavy

Axis IV or Misc. Stressors:

Formulation: 19 y/o USMC LCPL with symptoms of Acute Stress Disorder in context of seeing deaths of his fellow Marines 3 days ago. LCPL is eager to return to his unit. Discussion with Marine's medical officer indicates squad and command are eager to have him back and are supportive. In keeping with PIES philosophy (proximity, immediacy, expectancy, simplicity), feel returning LCPL is less pathologizing and more helpful at this point then keeping him back at Camp Fallujah.

Treatment Plan
Goals/Medications/Interventions:
1. LCPL cleared to RTD (unit will initially keep him close to FOB)
2. Marine declines medication at this time.
3. F/u with this provider on 21OCT06 at 1300 for re-eval.

Goals/Medications/Interventions: ☒ Informed Consent Given
4.
5.
6.

Disposition
Duty Status: ☐ Light Duty x ___ day(s)   ☒ Return To Duty/Fit for full duty
☐ Rec Medevac out of Theater
Limitations: No limitations at this time. LCPL cleared to return to unit.

Safety: ☒ At low risk for harm to self or others at this time
☐ At high risk for harm to self or others, precautions listed below.
Precautions:

Provider Signature:
Psych Tech Name (Printed or Typed):
Provider Name (Printed or Typed): E. Temko D.O. LT, MC, USNR
Date/Time: 09OCT06

OSD(HA) Trauma Registry Form / Navy-Marine Corps CTR – Psychiatry (02 Jan 2006)

Base Camp (Camp Fallujah) Naval Officer starting prescriptive campaign of controversial hypnotic (Ambien) to LCPL Jonathan Phillips and other marines following horrific bridge ambush

The First General Order

MEDICAL RECORD	CHRONOLOGICAL RECORD OF MEDICAL CARE
DATE	SYMPTOMS, DIAGNOSIS, TREATMENT TREATING ORGANIZATION (Sign each entry)

06 OCT 2006 — 2/8 Golf Co BAS

Pt involved in pulling fellow marines out of burning HMMWV after IED attack. Pt says that he is "fine" but on scene he had to directed to leave. He was noted to be very agitated on scene. Upon returning to OP he made a statement that he was suicidal but denies it upon talking to me. He doesn't want to seek care but needs to discuss his feelings.

A/P: Marine c̄ suicidal ideations
1) Put watch on pt. tonight
2) Return to South Camp

R. ADAM KOLIT, MD
LT/MC/USN

7 Oct 2006 — 2/8 BAS - Iraq

19 yr old Marine presents to BAS this AM upon request of his squad leader, platoon SNCO, and lead line corpsmen for his company as well as the MO out at his FOB. Was involved in combined IED/SVBIED SAF complex attack yesterday. Pulled (over →)

Patient: Phillips, Jonathan
LCPL/USMC

Base Camp (Camp Fallujah) Medical Notes from Battalion
Medical Officer pertaining to LCPL Jonathan Phillips

Chapter 7: Burn the Boats: Sharpen the Wood

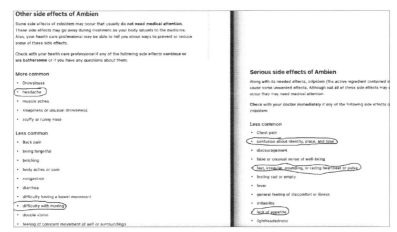

Healthline Article detailing the side effects of Ambien

Ambien side effects

Zolpidem may cause a severe allergic reaction. Stop taking Ambien and get emergency medical help if you have **signs of an allergic reaction**: hives; difficulty breathing; swelling of your face, lips, tongue, or throat.

Report any new or worsening symptoms to your doctor, such as: depression, anxiety, aggression, agitation, confusion, unusual thoughts, hallucinations, memory problems, changes in personality, risk-taking behavior, decreased inhibitions, no fear of danger, or thoughts of suicide or hurting yourself.

Stop using this medicine and call your doctor at once if you have:

- chest pain, fast or irregular heartbeat, feeling short of breath;
- trouble breathing or swallowing; or
- feeling like you might pass out.

The sedative effect of Ambien may be stronger in older adults.

Dizziness or severe drowsiness can cause falls, accidents, or severe injuries.

Common Ambien side effects may include:

- daytime drowsiness, dizziness, weakness, feeling "drugged" or light-headed;
- tired feeling, loss of coordination;
- stuffy nose, dry mouth, nose or throat irritation;
- nausea, constipation, diarrhea, upset stomach; or
- headache, muscle pain.

This is not a complete list of side effects and others may occur. Call your doctor for medical advice about side effects. You may report side effects to FDA at 1-800-FDA-1088.

Healthline Artcile detailing the side effects of Ambien

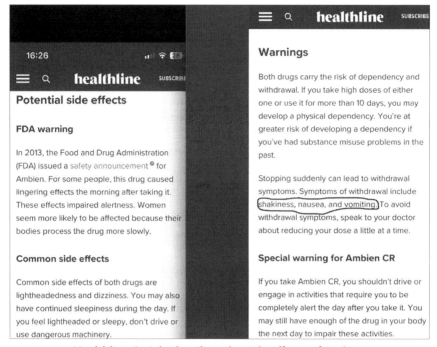

Healthline Article detailing the side effects of Ambien

After the Bridge Ambush, everything changed. The M.O., who was a dermatologist, started prescribing hypnotics—which are intended to produce hypnosis and induce sleep, among other objectives—to what I later realized were more Marines than just I. Everyone in that ambush, especially the crash site extraction, was never the same. It's important to emphasize this. It wasn't just some ambush. I wish it was. It would be much easier existentially. The ambush and torture of LCPL Hale, the propulsion of LCPL Johnson, and the attempted

Chapter 7: Burn the Boats: Sharpen the Wood

capture of live U.S. Marines were beyond horrific and personal. Dr. Douglas Pulgiese started prescribing a drug he had no qualification to prescribe. The more the morale fell, the more he prescribed. The morale and mental health of the 2nd Squad went down daily, especially with each subsequent combat engagement.

I was admittedly affected by the carnage. But I wasn't the only one. Brent, too. And SGT Reagan, who suddenly became fixated on saying the most vitriolic and sexual aspersions to me, intended to take me off my game. CPL Rapavi would make it clear that I was off-limits. If he was alive, I was ok. But the fact was that the bridge changed everything. What happened on that bridge affected all of us. It affected me. I could tell there was a power dynamic forming that I didn't want to be a part of. SGT Reagan became fixated on throwing whatever he could at me to make me ring the bell and violate the Fifth General Order. But no matter what he threw at me or said to me, I wasn't abandoning my duties. I don't even think he was aware of the things he said at times. I just know the treatment was entirely asymmetrical, and no one else in 2nd Squad was subjected to it by a long shot. Ever.

For reasons unclear and controversial, I was not permitted to be reassigned to another squad or platoon when I knew there were plenty who would eagerly accept me. LCPL Jackson would've taken me on his team, along with LCPL Derrick, my original teammate. LCPL Jackson and LCPL Derrick were already discussing how they wanted me for team leader billet for Jackson's future squad should I opt out of Recon Indoctrination. That camaraderie was the only cognitive dissonance standing between me and recon pursuit. I loved those guys. The more I refused to ring the bell, the more of a physical reaction SGT Reagan sought from me. One that never came. So,

The First General Order

I spoke only when spoken to, cleaned my rifle, and listened to my iPod. CPL Rapavi was my lifeline at this point, and I owe him in every way.

SGT Reagan is on record saying he didn't want me after the bridge ambush but instead promoted me to saw gunner to pick up the slack for the four squad members who perished, and I was awarded a certificate of commendation from Battalion. The Medical Officer noted the squad's eagerness to have me back after the bridge ambush, and I was eager to get back. Never complained. I kept finding myself in firefights, and no matter what I did, it was perceived as wrong by the squad leader to the point other squads started noticing and intervening. If we took enemy contact and I laid down suppressive fire, he'd harass me no matter what. It was clear that if I had done the opposite, he'd harass me for that all the same. My reactions weren't the problem. Medication and deference by the Company Commander were the issue.

At that time, I had no idea anyone else was on Ambien. I assumed I was the only one prescribed and felt like an outcast. I didn't know that dermatologists weren't licensed to issue psychiatric medication. I was 19. The drugs were messing up the dynamic. We were acting in ways that we weren't even aware of. Marines said I was screaming in my sleep, and I didn't believe them because there was no proof. I didn't believe them because SGT Reagan had gotten in the habit of saying so many patently false things about me that veracity went out the window, which was an added psychological predicament beyond mere combat. It probably just depended on which days we took the pills and which days we experienced withdrawals. The squad leader would say things I could almost tell he never meant and would perpetuate

Chapter 7: Burn the Boats: Sharpen the Wood

rumors he knew had been debunked by other squad leaders. Add to that the pallets of high-caffeinated energy drinks command inundated us with. I would become distant and only speak when spoken to. I lived on my iPod and walked to the rhythm of songs like "Glycerin" by the band Bush. Some songs were toxic, like "This is War," but at the same time, several of us listened religiously for different reasons, especially during the pre-mission stage. The songs reminded us of the reality of the stakes and gave us the mentality to sustain the necessary level of compartmentalized apathy. The dynamic we found ourselves in was no joke whatsoever. Life got real in an instant, starting in late September, and progressed exponentially weekly.

Certificate of Commendation awarded to LCPL Jonathan Phillips

October 14th, 2006

The day was about 100 degrees, which was a reprieve by this point. The squad was conducting a dismounted security patrol on foot. LCPL Muehle was Point Man. We were newly assigned to the same team as his fire team, which was wiped out during the ambush. The two of us reached the end of the long alleyway with a narrow path running perpendicular to the alley. It was a dead-end because the alleyway ran straight into a wall five yards on the opposite side of the dusty quasi-street. Squad leaders used the terrain to conduct a tactical security pause. We were operating nonverbally by this point. Everyone interspersed throughout the alleyway lined by residential courtyards and three-story urban structures took cover. There was nowhere to hide, as always. This was the reality.

LCPL Muehle took the right side of the alley wall, poking out slightly to maintain view. I took the left side. Utilizing cross coverage, I knelt and took aim down the right side, covering the avenue of approach. He covered the blind spot behind me to the left.

Moments later, the ear-splitting round deployed from the high caliber bolt-action sniper rifle, striking him in the shoulder and causing a massive wound. I don't know why, nor will I ever, but he must've been a more appealing or softer target because I was directly facing the sniper head-on to the degree that the moment I heard the rifle unveil its hate, I had a complete line of sight as to his position. Brent was holding an M-4 Service rifle, which has a significantly smaller profile and enables greater agility. The downside is a sniper has a larger profile on you. I was carrying a light machine gun across my chest with a full 200-round drum, so even though I was looking directly at the sniper, it covered a great amount of my body mass, especially as I was tactically kneeling, and my frame was condensed.

Chapter 7: Burn the Boats: Sharpen the Wood

Muehle must've exposed his shoulder a fraction more from his flak jacket. That's my best guess. The sniper in wait had a full profile on me. Maybe I tucked my chin, inadvertently covering my vulnerable arteries. More likely, I was looking directly at the sniper, and he may not have had a shot at any of my main extremities since I was kneeling and protected by gear and a large automatic weapon. He was aiming for a classic neck kill shot but ended up striking Brent's shoulder. A high caliber sniper rifle report is terrifying. It's a paralytic agent. I had trained myself cerebrally by this point to automatically move and shoot at the mere sound of a gunshot or explosion. I made it my default mode so that there was no contemplation of boldness or lack thereof. It was the mechanism of action that Corporal Rapavi had ingrained in me: "Shoot and move, cover to cover, repeat. Don't think." Search, assess, move, and kill (SAMK). Repeat.

Muehle fell backward but not far enough to be fully behind the wall and free of the sniper's line of sight. Still in the tactical kneeling position, I became the lone Point Man by default. By this time, I had completely memorized the Psalm 91 bandanna underneath my Kevlar helmet that Lance Corporal Stephen Johnson's mother had gracefully bestowed each of us to always wear. Johnson's death a few days earlier took the spiritual incantation to a new level of boldness. Without Mrs. Johnson's gift, I don't think I would've survived deployment. That incantation gave me a level of innate strength that others around me can attest to. It had a supernatural effect.

Tactically kneeling, I racked my M249 Light Machine Gun, stood up, and walked out into the open towards the only possible sniper position to draw fire and suppress the position at the same time. It was another alleyway leading to the marketplace at the end. There was nowhere to hide unless I wanted to remain back in the other alleyway with the squad. But I needed to cover Muehle's egress and the avenue of approach from the marketplace in case the sniper was the decoy and suicide vehicle-borne IED (S-VBIED) was the real operation. The same had happened a month earlier at OP-Phoenix, where the dump truck nearly wiped out LT Durham's 3rd Platoon after an initial small arms diversion.

My instinct had been to deploy a frag grenade behind me to cover my blindside. I was isolated without any teammates by this point, as they were securing the alley and the opposite avenue of approach. The alley behind me had a curve, severing line of sight to what was on the other side of the bend. I also wanted to deploy a frag grenade for a subsidiary psychological effect while Muehle was being dragged into a secure courtyard to amplify my presence and mindset. I found myself exposed and isolated, suppressing Muehle's egress, and I wasn't going to attenuate suppression or give the sniper my backside, so I took my chances engaging and not letting up. I told myself that it was game, but at the same time, game over wasn't an option for myself or fellow Marines and sailors, which enabled me the necessary fortitude during those crucibles.

It also became a form of micro-competition for me. That's what kept me going when my stomach was empty of nutrients, and my sleep barometer was zero. Acceptance breeds courage at that point. I was operating in that environment day in and day out under the very real reality of some of the most devastating injuries I've ever seen in a psychological battle no one prepares you for and everyone confronts subjectively. For me, living in constant fear is a death sentence. So, I would find ways to look forward to the action and prospect of victory in microforms. When a sniper opened, I'd say this is going to go one of two ways. Either I'm dead, and I won't feel it, or I'm going to confront the sniper and ensure he doesn't get a second shot off. It became a mental game for seven months.

Quick Reaction Force arrived in vehicles to evacuate the wounded. Around that moment, a grenade was tossed over a courtyard wall approximately 15 yards away near the open-backed medevac vehicle. The dismounted squad ceased security pause and began operating house-to-house clearing structures in the vicinity.

CHAPTER 8:
FRESHMAN JSOC

Iraqi Police Station

I was seen by the Battalion Medical Officer. Medication was refilled. It was conveyed that the Company Commander merely wanted to check the boxes and needed me to say I was fine. I didn't need a rationale as my main priority was always to get away from the fake intellectuals and get back to the front line where Golf Company was fighting an evil adversary. I didn't even want to be at the Base Camp memorial services, which served no purpose but the opportunity for PR photoshoots for officers who used them to justify their upcoming promotions.

My subjective way of honoring fallen brothers was to be back on the front line and actively engaging and doing my small part. Another reason I didn't feel comfortable being back in garrison with the level of detached careerism from senior and mid-level officers and enlisted who were living a life of luxury involving routine exercise, beautiful dining venues, and many other recreational amenities, including constant phone and email communication with families back home. Many of these officers were completely detached and filled with antipathy and emasculated any junior enlisted Marines who would come back to the chow hall disheveled with a thousand-mile stare while they only had five minutes to get a warm meal for the first time in three months and their convoy was heading back out in five minutes. It made them question themselves morally.

Back on the Front Line

We had to transport a prisoner to Base Camp. My teammate and I had five minutes to grab food in the chow line and devour it. We looked and felt like hell. Hadn't slept in weeks. As we sat down, we saw what turned out to be a Marine SGT Major run across the chow hall from his luxurious and mundane warm meal. He ran up to our two-man table and started berating my teammate for his lack of fresh shave and the broken zipper on his flight suit that was so stiff and starched from sweat and blood that it was no longer functional. For a moment, I was in shock. Not the paralytic type of shock. The type of shock where you take a deep breath as you start seeing red because in your lap resides an M249 Saw ready for rapid deployment against what is clearly an adversary.

This was the hierarchical absurdity that encapsulated the Iraq War. There was zero incentive to win the war because too many mid-level and high-level personnel were living extremely luxurious existences, climbing the career ladder while calling themselves patriots. To win or end the war precipitously would've meant the gravy train would've derailed and run off the tracks into a ditch of reality. American youth were being used as mere bodies and subjected to being tortured alive by an evil opponent, but the moment they got a rare chance at a five-minute warm meal or reprieve, they were expendable to the industrial meat grinder. To me, that's what the Umbrella Corporation came to existentially represent. We were the umbrella while it was downpouring, flanked by thunder and lightning. The moment the sun came out, the umbrella was closed, and it was irrelevant and discarded like a mere expendable instrument set out on the curb like a weekly trash collection.

Iraqi Police Compound

One of Golf Company Observation Posts (OP) was on the rooftop of the police station, which made zero tactical sense because it was barely 70 yards away from FOB Riviera, connected by a narrow corridor named "Sniper Alley." It was a single-story compound surrounded by higher vantage points all around it, affording little, if any, geographic value. FOB Riviera was five stories high and graced with panoramic rooftop views of the entire Area of Operations, which was why there were multiple observation posts situated up there.

Iraqi Police Station Compound – North Post Machine Gun Bunker

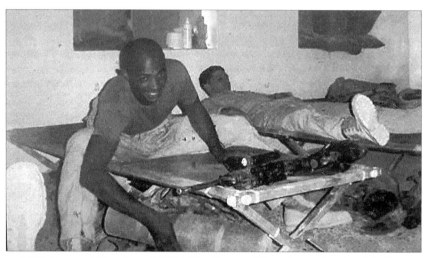

LCPL Howard March and CPL Mike Romeo (Pseudonym) at Iraqi Police Station Compound between Combat Operations.

CPL Nicholas "Nick" Rapavi aka "Claymore" at Iraqi Police Station delivering pre-mission briefing to 3rd squad

Chapter 8: Freshman JSOC

At the station, there was a lack of sovereignty, autonomy, and mission clarity between the Marine, Army National Guard, and Iraqi Police contingents. We were babysitters for the IP contingent, though in no way trained, equipped, or even verbally briefed for that amalgamated and polarizing dynamic.

When we initially arrived in-theater, there was a great U.S. Army Military Police contingent consisting of about seven men running the Iraqi Police Station. They were all-around superb guys and extremely competent. When the civil war erupted, one of the Marines with SGT Nichols' 1st squad became injured and pinned down by an IED approximately 50 meters from the Iraqi Police Compound. The Iraqi Police refused to take their trucks, retrieve the wounded Marine, and reinforce 1st squad outside the perimeter. An Army Staff SGT from the Iraqi Police Station had less than cordial words with the Iraqi Police at the station, took the keys from the IPs, and raced the Iraqi Police pickup truck down the street without escort to retrieve the wounded Marine while rooftop observation posts provided overwatch. We shared everything. We ran external operations, and they ran internal. They'd have food available at times since they had an industrial heater to prepare stuff, and the group meals would bring much welcome camaraderie on top of calories and nutrients from 24-7 combat operations in the desert summer heat. These would soon become known as the good old days of Teamwork. We were far behind enemy lines against a diabolical opponent, and it was imperative that we worked together for our safety and the mission at hand. Protecting each other would soon be the only clear mission, and even that wasn't verbalized by company command.

It was common and spoken knowledge of what a substantial liability to operational security and tactical awareness the Iraqi Police were. It was a taboo subject for the command. They rarely ever left the compound to conduct any sort of external operations whatsoever, which, quite frankly, was preferable, as the risk of infiltration and threat to operational security was exorbitant. They didn't have night vision gear, nor was the coalition leadership willing to supply them with such gear because they knew they were dirty at worst and unmotivated at best.

> "The Iraq deployment was my third and final tour. Leading up to it, I felt different that I had on previous deployments. It wasn't that I didn't feel prepared – I was more prepared than ever – but there was a sense of doubt. Our Rules of Engagement (ROEs) were strict, almost as if our hands were tied behind our backs. It felt like our Commanding Officer (C.O.) and senior leadership weren't on the same page, and the idea of "winning hearts and minds" wasn't a viable military strategy for winning the war."
>
> CPL Jay Boyd

It was a tactical and operational liability in an already polarized 3D urban battlefield. Their tactical training was nonexistent, although American Forces had been in Iraq for nearly four years of intense warfare and forced protection by this juncture. It became mentally problematic that so many Marines were perishing daily to protect their compound, yet they took a backseat even though it was their nation and locality. They refused to help fill sandbags to help us fortify their compound. Our platoon filled, stacked, and relocated so many sandbags that the rooftop around the courtyard began caving in.

There was a universal sense by this point that the previous four years of American bloodshed hadn't produced a police force with a prospect of ever taking over—let alone one that showed up for anything more than collecting cash paychecks. It was a mess. Washington, from a ground perspective, didn't know what to do, and the Iraqi Police, by this point, showed no signs of incubation. There was plenty of empirical responsibility to go around. You didn't need to look far for a culprit. But that didn't change the fact that we found ourselves in a completely lethal, chaotic dynamic.

Very rarely had they left the Police Compound, and on the *extremely* rare occasions they did, it was solely to conduct "lightning" nighttime mounted patrols in pickup trucks where they'd return two minutes later and re-enter the compound. The Army Police Contingent at the station prohibited them from leaving the compound on random stunts. Not that it was hard because they barely ever were willing to leave, which only served to exacerbate the substantial liability across the spectrum of perimeter and operational security. It would've been prudent to simply assign the Iraqi Police work around the station because the quasi-amalgamation, combined with a lack of mission clarity and unmotivated nature, was a liability for the Marines, sailors, and soldiers defending, fortifying, and conducting external operations from the compound.

A few of the Marines were talking with two of the Iraqi Policeman, an Army National Guardsman, and an interpreter. The Iraqi Policeman were conveying that AQI and ISIS were actively moving in and seizing the area. At the time, I didn't really have the mental or emotional bandwidth to understand as it seemed well above my compartmentalized pay grade. The Iraqi Police knew more than us, and there existed immense information asymmetry even from a lance corporal's viewpoint. The Company Commander certainly knew more than us. Because our extraordinary Iraqi Interpreter was blown to a thousand pieces on bridge 2nd Squad, we no longer had the benefit of foreign translation. The prior interpreter was one of the best Iraqis I ever knew. I loved that dude. We all did. He was absolute family. He was so trusted and beloved that he was given a sidearm to amalgamate him as an auxiliary gunfighter and protect himself while outside the wire. He would teach us Arabic and tutor us during the little downtime we had on the smoke deck. Losing him was a huge blow. He had been the bridge between our culture and theirs and brought the invaluable trait of diversity to our small unit. LT Browne and he had struck up a rapport the moment they met. Energy never lies. We were extremely protective of him.

Marines occupied the North and South Post rooftop Observation Post Bunkers at the Iraqi Police Station. North Post overlooked the marketplace where I'd eventually have the final firefight of deployment. The Butcher had his rack positioned in front of North Post on the other side of the parking lot of the Iraqi Police Station. He'd butcher rams right in front of the post, then lined the heads with horns in a straight line looking backward, which was directly at North Post field of fire. It was psychological warfare. The sight, smell, and sound once again cut deep, sending shockwaves of the different reality that I suddenly found myself in. No matter how hard I try to forget them, I see those five, horned heads in a perfect line, looking at me for hours and hours while behind the machine gun. In hindsight, I realize they weren't the only ones being led to the slaughter. We were comrades in that respect.

When the uprising commenced three weeks earlier, the Civil War plunged the Sunni Triangle into a kill zone. The exceptional Army Contingent that we'd bonded with was relieved with a fresh contingent of the Army National Guard team. They were replaced with a

Chapter 8: Freshman JSOC

new Army National Guard Group. Right off the bat, things were off. By that point, Golf Company had lost so many killed and wounded and were running on fumes. The small, maybe seven-man National Guard contingent was all wrong. They weren't trained tactically, but moreover, they lacked the combat mindset necessary to operate in an environment like that. The Army and Army National Guard Leadership barely briefed the new contingent. They merely showed up one day and took over.

The inexperienced, naive, and resentful Army National Guard Contingent showed up like a new sheriff. They changed all the Tactical and Technical Procedures (TTPs). IPs would show up and leave from their shifts at will wearing ski masks with little if any security protocol. There was a perpetual threat of infiltration. It was chaos. Meanwhile, the Army National Guard contingent was listening to a different sheet of music, not taking the reality we found ourselves in seriously, having only recently arrived in-country and overly idealistic with the wrong indoctrinated mindset for this type of enemy, warfare, and 3D urban terrain. There was no company command doing anything to lead, organize, and clarify responsibilities or grant authority or autonomy. It was a fucked-up freshman JSOC without any dominant leadership by Golf Company Command.

Among the parceled-out National Guard contingent, there was a sense of liberalism, yet they knew nothing about the volatile Area of Operations to warrant such views and moral superiority. Moreover, they were, for some reason, emasculated by the Marine infantry even though their safety was ensured under the blanket of our protection by our internal and external operations. They got no intelligence training about the AO from the contingent they received and opted out of having the Marines, who knew every street and threat by this point, take the lead and mentor them. They were angry at us because they hadn't been mentored by the prior Army contingent for two weeks as the Marine Corps SOP dictated. Immediately, they became extremely insecure and tried to establish an arrogant and illogical dominance that was unwarranted and lethal. To draw a line in the sand, they installed a padlock on the food pantry that the prior contingent had openly shared due to our symbiotic and synergistic teamwork and offsetting resources.

We were all in it together. They started telling us we needed to come and ask for their permission every time we wanted something from the pantry. An effective Company Commander ensures that everyone underneath his leadership is clear on their individual responsibilities so that they can execute them.

To make matters worse, whether it was part of their institutional training or what, the non-Marine contingent had this obsession with running a pristine-looking compound, even though it was externally surrounded by trash and shit and syringes. This was instantly problematic because many Marines smoke cigarettes incessantly, and their priorities didn't, nor should they've, focused on maintaining a clean dirt courtyard. We were enduring round-the-clock combat operations and sustaining progressively high and escalating casualties without the luxury of replacements. Each time someone left the battlefield from death, wounds, or mental health injuries, the workload that was originally spread thin as is over the assigned Area of Operations had to be redistributed over each Marine and sailor. Golf Company sustained the vast majority of 2/8 Battalion casualties. Furthermore, the 2nd Platoon, for some reason, sustained 90 percent of all Golf Company casualties due to the specific AO and terrain. The non-Marine contingent were probably great soldiers who, for whatever reason,

Chapter 8: Freshman JSOC

were placed into the absolute wrong role and mission. They probably would've done exceptional in garrison. The Company Commander didn't manage any of this chaos. I don't blame the Army National Guard contingent. They were in over their head, cut off, and parceled out by their command to amalgamate within Golf Company AO. It was the Marine Commander's job to run a cohesive unit and AO.

The guardsmen began trying to organize, corral, and subjugate us to stand in line and walk with them across the courtyard to ensure it was free of litter and discarded cigarettes. Combat was so intense by this point that the conflicting mindsets were toxic to the atmosphere. When we had a moment of downtime it couldn't be disturbed by walking on eggshells. Casualties were continuing to mount exponentially, and their behavior kept intensifying. This was another dimension that, on top of extremely high combat operational tempo, was adversely contributing to troop welfare and mental health. Golf Company Command never intervened, which, by that point, was standard operating procedure per their leadership model.

The volatile dynamic with the Iraqi Policemen progressively couldn't be trusted. They were forbidden from entering the coalition side of the compound. We began to remove the Velcro name tags affixed to our flight suits out of operational security, uncertainty, and intuition after several incidents. The South-East rooftop bunker that belonged to them was only staffed intermittently at best.

There was a complex dynamic at that compound. Every day, you felt like you were sleeping next to the enemy who wanted to castrate you or give information that would lead to your capture. When I wasn't on missions, patrols, standing post on the rooftop, or on working parties, sleep was nonexistent because you had to practically sleep with one eye open. We weren't trained in any way for that level of quasi-amalgamation. There was no officer leadership at the compound. It was the taboo observation post in the Area of Operations (AO). Everyone knew, but there was a silence driven by fear of talking about it. It was like we just wanted to do our duty and then keep rotating out of the Iraqi Police Station mentality. They'd refuse to leave the compound unless they knew an impending attack was in the works, and so they'd leave for just enough time to not be present.

Securing and fortifying the IP compound and preparing for constant missions and patrols while spread dangerously thin was a full-time job. We all had to stand even longer post shifts all throughout the days and nights every time we took another casualty and redistributed workload that had already been spread bone thin. Any downtime was spent cleaning weapons after every monotonous firefight to be ready for the next ambush. Sleep was next to impossible past an hour every week, and even then, we were jolted awake by an enemy ambush and harassment small arms fire to which we had to respond. We would not be able to go back to sleep for another week between being amped up with adrenaline during firefights and going back on post. Because of the level of casualties that we were taking, we barely had enough men to keep the two rooftop observation posts staffed at 24-7. There were only enough men to always have one junior Marine per the two posts. Second Squad leaders and team leaders didn't have to stand post unless there were extenuating circumstances, such as when the National Guard contingent went back to Base Camp to resupply.

By this point, few people in 2nd Squad talked to each other, and everyone was emotionally guarded because no one knew who would be killed or wounded next, and we had to be able to effectively do our jobs at the same time. I would typically be on posts overnight because I would volunteer for those shifts. I felt I could be of value in keeping my unit safe, and people knew I was highly reactive whenever we were ambushed. I don't know how the other Marines psychologically passed the time on the rooftop, but I developed a habit of talking out loud to pass the time but also to remain vigilant and reactive as I was scanning for threats or incongruencies through night vision goggles while drinking caffeine drinks. I would recite Psalm 91 scripture from the bandanna on my head. I would lightly sing a song to keep myself vigilant. When I wasn't on post or missions, I would listen to my iPod while cleaning my weapon. SGT Reagan would pounce on me no matter what I was doing.

The whole atmosphere was deeply disturbing. By this point, the loss of life and injuries and mental health in Golf Company had taken its toll. We were gunfighters with a task, and by this time, that mission had become increasingly about surviving until our unit was relieved. Whatever was going on in Washington and the national electoral priorities, they didn't seem to be concerned with the chaos 3,000 miles away that they'd brilliantly engineered, though they were placing insane rules of engagement and threats of imprisonment if violated. Marines lived daily with the terror of court martial should they make the wrong split-second calls in combat engagements out of fear of losing military benefits and being stigmatized as dishonorable. This added another stratified dimension to mental health. People surmise why the mental health problems in Iraq turned into an epidemic. Name one other war where troops were subjected to that level of combat, let alone 3D urban warfare, and threatened and hamstrung daily by the consequences of making the wrong decision as if the dynamic wasn't already overly volatile.

I don't blame the National Guardsmen. They were five to six guys, junior National Guardsmen. They were put in the wrong situation and Area of Operations by their command. They were at the mercy of Golf Company leadership. They felt outnumbered by the three rotating squads of twelve Marines and Squad Corpsmen because they were separated from their biological unit. But our safety and theirs were paramount, and we covered their duties whenever they wanted to go back to Base Camp, restock, shower, and get warm meals. Then they would show back up and sit in the COC and stay in safety with their liberal mentalities. So, they can blame their waistline, not us.

The blame rests with Golf Company Commander and whoever parceled them out of their biological unit to an outpost that they were ill-equipped for training-and-mentality-wise. The Golf Company Commander violated the principles and fundamentals of unit cohesion.

Golf Company had been supplied and inundated with high-energy caffeine beverages called "Rip-Its" for months. It was The Department of Defense's (DOD) answer to nonexistent sleep and re-distribution of duties following each additional casualty. More casualties, more caffeine. When ingested, the liquid sent a surge straight across the blood-brain batter. It's what civilians now consume as pre-workout energy drinks. This is another taboo subject that the DOD doesn't like acknowledging.

To sustain that level of combat tempo and rate of casualties, they flew in palates of energy drinks and soda for FOB Riviera and all the surrounding observation posts throughout the AO. We would drink them all through the night while conducting operations and pulling rooftop security in four-hour shifts when we weren't conducting external operations. In retrospect, it's clearer. Fatigue turns into depression, and your brain looks for something to galvanize it, even just to stand up, gear up, and get to the rooftop when ambushed. I remember feeling lazy in my mind and being angry at myself, and caffeine gave me a nominal edge.

Retrospectively, it was universal, and the inundation of energy drinks was the carrot on the stick for enlisted.

November 4th, 2006

Morale at this point was low due to three months of 24-7 combat operations, the September and October carnage brought by the Sunni Uprising, and the lack of mission clarity or campaign strategy. Without my Apple iPod, I wouldn't have been able to hang in there as long as I did. That was my way to shift my reality and escape the present one, even for a few minutes here and there—along with reciting Psalm 91 by memory. Allowing my mind to expand and see the hand played by fear and raise the ante before calling its bluff. Several other Marines would borrow it from time to time, as did LT Browne, and we would all take our solitude in the presence of a different reality, even just for a few moments. This was also another way that Golf Company's extraordinary Fleet Marine Force (FMF) Corpsman saved our lives and didn't get enough credit. Without Doc Solbach, Doc Jerez, Doc Strotz, and Doc Tyler, I'd have had little music on my iPod and wouldn't have had that outlet nor the ability to share it with fellow gunfighters. They always found a way to keep us in the fight. That iPod also enabled LT Browne to be the fierce leader he was when combat kept intensifying. Little moments of lyrical reprieve can make the difference between life and death for subordinates. He was sharp throughout.

I was on the rooftop of the Iraqi Police Station one night, and another Marine passed on information that Defense Secretary Donald Rumsfeld had officially resigned after the horrific months of September and October and the amount of American and Coalition KIA and WIA that had marked the beginning of the Civil War. Up until this point, the Bush Administration had left us without a plan for two months while they played electoral politics in DC before securing reelection. Meanwhile, they took two months to decide on ushering in the Surge Campaign because American Forces were undermanned and being decimated by Sectarian Violence and inundated by an influx of foreign fighters—both Al Qaeda in Iraq (AQI) and Islamic State in Syria (ISIS). Throughout this time of indecision, Washington installed treasonous rules of engagement while they played politics 3,000 miles away.

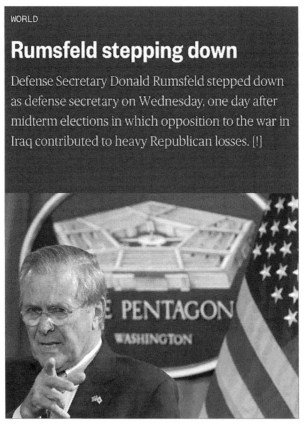

World News Artcile where Defense Secretary Donald Rumsfeld Resigns mid bloody Iraqi Civil War due to political calamity

Their war and handling of it had become exorbitantly controversial. No weapons of mass destruction were found. The Iraqi populace showed little interest in military incubation. And American casualties only continued to rise along with the fighting.

Stay the Fuck Away from My Marines!

One of the finest and most experienced Staff NCOS of Golf Company had fallen, not by the insurgents but by Company Commander and Company 1st SGT, just when we needed top-tier talent and enlisted leadership the most. The shady and universally unliked Iraqi interpreter "Leo" was sitting on the smoke deck with the Company Commander. He relayed to the officer that he was out with 3rd Platoon led by SSGT Rivers and that there was an incident. One of the Marines had taken a righteous shot, and SSGT Rivers wholeheartedly backed him up, but he hadn't reported it back to command in time. The entire squad of Marines was called into the office by 1st SGT Reginald Robinson, who read the military equivalent of Miranda rights without the notification of SSGT Rivers. SSGT stormed into the room, declaring, "Everyone get the fuck out," and slammed the door, trapping the 1st SGT in the room with a real Marine—an old-school Marine who came up the ranks together with Gunny Rowe.

He told the 1st SGT he was crazy if he thought he was going to prosecute one of his Marines for making the right call all because they took the dishonest tale told by the interpreter who was aiming for increased favor from the Company Commander and higher pay. Once again, the Company Commander was emasculated, SSGT Rivers was relieved, and the rest of Golf Company paid with their lives and limbs. SSGT's career was over. Not only had the Golf

The First General Order

Company Commander delivered another gut-wrenching blow to our company, but now every Marine was living in increased fear of firing their weapon. As a result, the insurgency was becoming exponentially emboldened and stepping up attacks.

The Company Commander relieved one of the most combat-experienced and respected Staff NCOs we had and once again cut our feet out from beneath us, sacrificing numerous lives and injuries in the process, all to cling to his dissipating command power. In a historically devastating campaign, the loss of each experienced leader and gunfighter produced exorbitant detrimental ramifications. The company command, minus Gunny Rowe, cared more about inflating their own perceived power and future careers at the expense of the Marines and sailors under their command and pissed on The Fifth General Order at every critical juncture like a punchline.

Gunny Rowe was demonstrably well past his patience threshold. He was amid an existential moral crisis. He was a man who would go on to become SGT Major, but he would never do so at the expense of Marine's life. His anger kicked into high gear with the loss of SSGT Rivers. Gunny Rowe's tolerance threshold had long since been breached. There's only so much immorality an authentic leader can stand by and justify before action is constitutionally mandatory. Inaction at such a point produces its own verdict by default, and you become a prisoner of your conscience. The more time that passes, the more self-consuming it becomes—which is why decisiveness is the most important ingredient on any battlefield. An officer once gave us a brief on calling for air support. He drew a circle around the target and said the longer you hesitate to order the airstrike, the wider that circle becomes concerning collateral damage. Indecision is the great-

Chapter 8: Freshman JSOC

est assassin on a battlefield. An honorable mutiny was in the works, and we were all behind Gunny Rowe for a much-needed coup d'état.

"By October 2006, it finally hit me – I wasn't in Iraq for its citizens or the Shia population. I was there for Marines to my left and right. I couldn't understand how some Marines were terrified, or why one would drop to the ground, curled up in a ball, screaming – until I experienced what a genuine IED was. It's something you can't see, smell, or anticipate; a hidden enemy underground, strapped to a person, packed into a car, or stuffed into trash on the roadside.

Many deaths and injuries could've been prevented if we had stopped sending dismounted patrols out during the day or allowed Marines, who were physically and mentally out of the fight, to stay back at Base Camp. The intel was there – warnings from the CIA, 1st Brigade, and RCT 5 – urging us to be cautious, but no real support, direction, or resources followed. We were on our own, cut off from Baghdad and The Green Zone. We weren't deemed important enough. We were a bunch of kids without college degrees.

There was morally reprehensible attitude towards exploiting and punishing Marines, without ever asking or answering why. I was part of an enemy IED ambush and helped evacuate two badly wounded marines, both drenched in blood. After calling for a Blackhawk to rescue them, The Company Commander berated me. The next day, the wounded were sent back from Base Camp, their injuries dismissed as mere lacerations and concussions. Leadership wasn't focused on preserving life or honoring our brotherhood. It was terrifying being up against a savage enemy knowing our own command didn't have our backs or best interest at heart. We were nothing to them. Pawns – nothing more."

LCPL Alex Cruz

CHAPTER 9:
TESTUDO

November 24th, 2006

The "Testudo" (Latin for "tortoise") was a defensive formation used by Roman soldiers. In this formation, soldiers would align their shields to form a protective barrier resembling a tortoise's shell. The front row of soldiers held their shields forward, while those in the ranks behind them held their shields overhead, providing protection from arrows and other projectiles.

It was my shift on the North-Side Observation Post on the Iraqi Police compound rooftop. The day was sunny, and the air was crisp. Company Executive Officer (XO) Glenn Taylor had ordered CPL Rapavi's 3rd Squad to suit up. His orders were that a suspicious vehicle was ambiguously racing toward the Iraqi Police Station and was to be intercepted. I received the radio warning to be on the lookout while 3rd Squad was getting in the vehicles below me.

Instead of sending a junior Marine to open the movable barriers at the front gate, CPL Rapavi, less than 15 yards away, the consummate leader he was, led from the front and exposed himself to spare anyone else the liability. He walked slightly to the right of the observation post to retract the barrier.

The First General Order

I leaned forward and said, "Later, corporal," getting closer to the machine gun to stay ready just in case, so he knew I had him covered. He'd just retracted the barrier. My post had a U-shape vantage point of the marketplace to the middle left and a traffic circle to the right. I kept my eyes swiveling between the two points where CPL Rapavi, right below, was surveying as he sensed a threat and was about to engage. He knew intuitively it was all off. It was too eerily quiet. He was always playing offense, which is what he taught me. You don't wait for the enemy to attack

The suspicious vehicle never came anywhere in sight of the compound. But it was never supposed to. In the trunk of a car, aiming out the taillight of a sedan, was an insurgent sniper lying in wait to pull the snare on his prey.

My mentor slumped to the ground. There was no time to register, process, or grieve the monumental reality. It wasn't until a millisecond later that I heard the ear-shattering and terrifying sound from a bolt-action rifle reverberate throughout the desolate marketplace like the delayed sound of a home run at Fenway Park, except exponentially louder and more terrifying.

It was tactical in nature. CPL Rapavi had taught me from his days in Afghanistan that I was already hugging the machine gun and ready. I immediately began suppressing and shifting fire between the two vantage points with complete violence of action along with three turret-gunners down in the lower-level parking lot covering fire in coordination while one then two Marines retrieved Corporal Rapavi. I engaged in a 2nd position in the North-East that was under construction, which made a potential sniper position. I shifted fire slightly to the North to the beginning of the marketplace near the traffic circle that had another direct line of sight towards CPL Rapavi. Turret gunners

Chapter 9: Testudo

from the 3rd Squad were engaging vantage points to the North-West but were obstructed by a tall tower that had been in the parking lot that was separating their field of fire and mine, so we coordinated fire.

The enemy had no idea what they'd done or who they'd killed. I would've never left the front line before this day, but now it was merely a matter of game-on. Metaphorically speaking, he'd just erected a billboard emblazoned in graffiti with the term "The Fifth General Order" in flashing green lights. I was ready to die here for the prospect of engaging Corporal Nicholas Rapavi's killer. The Company Commander knew this. He knew I was Nick's protege and how I planned, more than ever, to consolidate and deploy every moment of wisdom, training, and tactical mindset that Nick was kind enough to bestow. From this day forward, Golf Company Commander prohibited all daylight dismounted foot patrols anywhere in the AO. If movement outside any compound was necessary during daylight hours, it would be done via vehicle convoy. No exceptions. You couldn't walk two feet outside the FOB wire without being gunned down immediately. We were pinned down. The only advantage we had was rooftop security with automatic weapons and the complete cover of darkness to wage war via night vision optics, thermal imaging, and infrared lasers for zone designation and target acquisition and engagement.

This day served to solidify any nonexistent questions of resolve for me. Losing one of the senior lifelines of the unit was a loss that even several officers acknowledged was a big victory for the enemy. The enemy was always smarter than the company command. By this point, Golf Company had now lost Corporals Rapavi (KIA) and Santiago (WIA), Payne (KIA), Regensburg (WIA), and many other NCOs. It changed the atmosphere of Golf Company in ways that are hard to describe. The only thing that bothered me more was the lack of counterattack our company command exhibited in the aftermath.

The enemy had knocked a knight off the chess board and there wasn't so much as a discernible countermove or proportionate, let alone disproportionate, response from company command. It was disturbing. I blamed myself for many years for this day. Maybe if I was looking out in the distance, Golf Company's foundation would still be alive. Maybe I could've seen something was off or that it was too quiet lambently and went on the proactive suppression offensive. But that's the thing. NCIS would've burned me. Everything over there was in terms of risk-loss. Zero upside. But I would've gone to prison for a decade if it meant Nick Rapavi lived. The atmosphere in Golf Company was already abysmal, but at least then, we had CPL Rapavi. The Company Commander deferred to him.

> "I knew the call that got Nick killed was a bad one. I argued with Nick about going out. When we got the orders, I told him it was another ghost mission. We were instructed by command to execute a mission to intercept a BOLO vehicle. The vehicle was supposed to come by the IP Station Compound and our posts never saw it. The intel said it was coming in our direction, and we were going to intercept it. As QRF was mounting up to roll out, there was a shot as Nick was opening the front gate and surveying the landscape for threats. My vehicle was then targeted in rapid succession, forcing the turret gunner to drop down. I thought my gunner had been shot. Peterman opened fire along with Phillips on above machine gun post. I got out of my vehicle and saw Nick on the ground. I ran to his side and immediately tried to

Chapter 9: Testudo

staunch the bleeding. At that moment, I became the de facto squad leader. My next mission as squad leader was to evaluate Nick and get everyone to safety. Nick was in the area being worked on well within 40 minutes from the time he was shot. Every second was critical. We had no clue there was a sniper until it was too late. We changed a lot of things when I became squad leader. We would drive during the day and walk at night. Our missions became shorter and more frequent. The intel squad leaders were later given from command following apprehension and interrogation that the sniper had shot from the center circle and shot from the taillight opening from the trunk."

Corporal Ryan Cavey

After this day, the atmosphere throughout the company never recovered. I counted down the days until relief came. I would never dishonor Nick and all the training and mentorship bestowed by leaving the front line. We'd just lost the best gunfighter and tactician in the Battalion, along with many other wounded, relieved of command, and killed-in-action leaders of Golf Company. The only Marine many wished would be killed, the Company Commander, was alive and well and filling up body bags day by day while inflating his career.

Subjective rumor was spread by SGT Reagan and quickly debunked about the level of suppressive fire as I responded to the enemy sniper and accusations of indiscriminate suppression while he was downstairs safely in the Command Operations Center (COC) away from the engagement. Every time I would do something textbook, corroborated by others, he would pounce. Other Marines caught on.

Every Marine in 3rd Squad quickly came to my aid and reiterated that I suppressed with other turret gunners, in textbook fashion, when Nick was shot. Regardless, SGT Reagan continued to aggressively perpetuate the myth. I was on the machine gun before the bullet was fired. Waiting. That was my original squad, and we were coordinated. There were only two vantage points, and I shifted between the two. If I had a grenade launcher or shoulder-fired rocket, I would've deployed those two, reloaded, and continued. I just lost my top mentor and protector, and now I had to explain my actions suppressing with all the other machine gunners

As I watched my friend and mentor fall to the ground that day, I vowed that no matter how unsure I was, I'd never hesitate to preemptively engage a viable target and not think twice. Offense saves lives. I would go to military prison for the rest of my life for violating the rules of engagement if it meant returning a fellow Marine or sailor to their loved ones back home. That's a sacred covenant.

Why I would be sent back for evaluation and subjected to psychological scrutiny for doing my job is beyond me, but that was the added strain that I had to asymmetrically carry on my back. Meanwhile, SGT Reagan, the Company Commander, and the Medical Officer continued to withhold information about Reagan being prescribed a controversial hypnotic under the guise of "smoking cessation" and all the tantrums he was continually exhibiting in front of myself and other senior Marines.

CPL Cavey, CPL Rapavi's second in command, assumed command of 3rd Squad for continuity and to continue executing combat operations now that Nick had fallen. Hours later, CPL Cavey's squad came back to the marketplace outside the IP Station to retrieve gear. No one wanted to go walk to the marketplace and expose themselves,

Chapter 9: Testudo

so SGT Reagan had me gladly bear hug all the gear and walk the 40-50 yards to the marketplace to hand it to CPL Cavey, who bravely and solemnly stood outside ECP. I gladly and defiantly walked slowly to make sure any enemy sniper realized there were guys who weren't even phased by their existence. I took my time. This was the pattern. When no one else volunteered or we were short on men due to exorbitant casualties, suddenly, I'd magically possess utility for SGT Reagan. The goodwill would rapidly attenuate immediately afterward. SGT Reagan would spread a malicious and immediately debunked lie and tell the Platoon Commander I was crazy and took unnecessary risks. I had to explain myself in ways that no other Marine had to. Every Marine came to my defense at the Iraqi Police Station.

Seven to ten days later, the 2nd Platoon headed back to Base Camp for another memorial service for CPL Rapavi.

I was sent for psychological evaluation due to the aspersions cast by SGT Reagan on everyone who wasn't present at the compound during the ambush, including LT Browne, about my actions suppressing fire on that observation post. No other Marine in that engagement had to answer a single question, nor should they have. He also sent me back, admitting that the reports by SGT Reagan were debunked after talking to several Marines and myself. When he'd come out to FOB Riviera, or when we'd be back at Base Camp, the Battalion M.O. would issue more Ambien below the radar, presumably on orders from Battalion due to the nonexistent morale on the ground in Gold Company's Area of Operations and the reports that Battalion was receiving about deteriorating condition and monumental casualties.

Indeed, my coping mechanism involved living in my own world. Nineteen years old, exposed to terrorist attacks and daily increasing small unit warfare, seven months of sleep deprivation, high caffeine, and pharmacologic hypnotics. Meanwhile, living under the threat of being burned and castrated alive and court-martialed under a command who saw enlisted warriors as inhuman pawns. There's no operating manual for that kind of alternate universe, just subjective survival.

Memorial Service for CPL Nicholas Paul Rapavi — Post November 24th

Chapter 9: Testudo

After I left the medical, the Company Commander, Medical Officer, and squad leader spread the word that I had outsmarted the doctors and told them what they wanted to hear to indemnify the command in keeping me on the front line and operating fiercely should there be any potential future fallout.

The signed litany of annotated medical notes from the Medical Officer reviewed by the Company Commander completely sheds the command's assertion that I was anything but entirely truthful to officers and doctors. They also withheld those records from my Platoon Commander, who was observing some of us in 2nd Squad acting strangely. I made it verbally declarative that no matter how much I had going on, I'd never violate the Fifth General Order. I was there to hold the line. We were Spartans. The insurgent sniper was later caught and hung in Baghdad. According to our commanding officers, the interrogators uncovered that he fired from the taillight of the sedan parked between the marketplace and the traffic circle—the two vantage points I had vigorously suppressed.

```
about him; particularly his increased quietness and withdrawn
behavior. The following was taken from Dr. Pugliese's report: He
had been seen by Lieutenant Temko in October for issues after an
IED blast that had killed three marines. He was also present
several weeks prior to that when Corporal Robari was killed by
sniper rifle. He had supposedly fired his weapon in the
direction of where the shot had come from and the Chain of
Command had difficulty getting him on his PRR to stop the
shooting. Also there were reports of him talking to his weapons
although some marines have stated he did that before he came to
Iraq. He told his treating psychiatrist that he was just not
sure why he was there in his office yesterday. He stated "I
guess for follow-up." His company had kept him behind the wire
the last two days. Prior to his being seen they had not taken
his weapon away. He denied suicidal ideation at that time. The
company's main concern at that time was what his reaction would
be during the next firefight. He reported no complaints to the
treating psychiatrist. He said he was sleeping well, no issues
at home. He stated "I just want to return to my platoon sir".
He was to follow-up with Dr. West that day at 14:30.
    He presented for a headache on 20 December 2006 which was
treated with Naprosyn and the patient given SIQ. He was then
brought in on 21 January 2007 after the incident in which the IP
was killed and seen by Dr. Pugliese. He was not found to be a
danger to himself or others at that time and Lance Corporal
Phillips was aware that he could see his general medical officer
at any time for further follow-up care.
```

Base Camp (Camp Fallujah) Medical Notes pertaining to Lance Corporal Jonathan Phillips.

"After September 11th, every Marine who signed up, especially those in the infantry, had one thought in mind: revenge for the attacks. It's astonishing how they teach you to excel in violence but don't prepare you to turn it off. Golf Company got exactly what they asked for, and more.

When we first arrived in our Area of Operations, only a select few weren't wide-eyed and scared. Those few had seen combat before; the rest of us had no idea what was about to unfold, including our chain of command. Golf Company was tasked with blocking the flow of weapons and IEDs into Fallujah. We quickly learned how tough and complex the fight would be to achieve our goal of stopping AQI insurgents from ambushing other Marines' units in the area. We stepped up our game. We took every necessary precaution to bring all our brothers back alive. It wasn't meant to be.

2/8 Golf Company took a lot of hits throughout that deployment, me included. Second Platoon bore the worst of it. They experienced our unit's first loss early on and continued to incur heavy casualties. We all lost close friends, whether a senior Marine who was a mentor or a junior Marine. It took a toll. Most people don't understand what it does to young men when the best leaders in your company are killed and dismembered. When they're gone, you wonder—if the best Marine we have got hit, what chance do I have? Your mind starts spinning in all directions.

Chapter 9: Testudo

What do you do? You keep your chin up and figure it out along the way. If you're injured, you put one foot in front of the other and fight on. If you survive, you become that leader for the next deployment. Phillips did that. He kept fighting. Marines were being tortured alive. It was all hands-on deck. The command asked for more and more, and he gave more and more. Then they threw him under the bus and smeared his name. They never thought in a million years he'd survive solitary confinement and come back to write about it. But he kept fighting."

LCPL Neil Carius (USMC)

SGT Reagan wanted me in his squad because others wanted me in theirs. They knew push came to shove; I wasn't a variable. SGT Reagan knew I'd thrive in someone else's squad under alternative leadership and wanted to maintain my effective suppression, or he would've, at the very least, promoted one of the three other squad riflemen to machine gunner and demoted me. I earned a reputation by that point as being fierce. Instead of acting decisively and relinquishing me to another hospitable squad, he tried to break me every second he could and cathartically take out his self-hatred on me. He was caught in the process several times by fellow Marines who were dangerously losing their patience with his vitriolic and unstable fixation on me.

It's absurd and weak to allege that anyone made SGT Reagan keep me in his squad and that he was precluded from transferring me to another squad where others were more than willing to utilize and absorb me.

No other squad leader was even remotely worried about me. If SGT Reagan legitimately felt that way, he would've transferred me immediately, which was his discretion and his alone. He's not some hostage being held for ransom. He never even broached the question of whether I was willing to be reassigned. In fact, LCPL Mike Silva, among other 3rd Squad Marines, can attest that I requested transfer back to CPL Rapavi's squad for nearly two months following the bridge ambush, whereby SGT Reagan denied the petitions. I kept petitioning because SGT Reagan's unhealthy anger towards me was dangerously affecting my mental health and squad morale. He wanted me standing post all day and night, running combat operations so he could sleep on Ambien. He knew if he relinquished me without replacement, he and the NCOs would be forced to stand post and sacrifice sleep. There was no way junior Marines could viably absorb more sleep deprivation and remain combat effective. Junior Marines were running combat operations, rotating off five-hour rooftop shifts. After the rooftop post, we were required to fill sandbags for 30 minutes on the rooftop to continually fortify the compound. If you got a minute of sleep after that, you were typically jolted awake by enemy ambush and had to gear up and engage the enemy. SGT Reagan's a guy who needs to compensate for indecision and inadequacy by finding someone to blame. He must've learned that leadership construct from the Company Commander.

CHAPTER 10:
THE MAD KING

OP-286 was an observation post about 80 yards from FOB Riviera. It was located atop a highway overpass. The highway was MSR-Mobile (Main Supply Route). It consisted of multiple machine-gun nests ready to engage and intercept threats coming off the highway off-ramp that could target FOB-Riviera or the Area of Operations.

One night, under the cover of darkness towards the end of deployment, the Company Commander requested two Marines from each squad for a mission. No one else volunteered, so I raised my hand to spare my teammates. I've always operated better when staying mentally and physically mobile. I also didn't ever see value in being paralyzed by fear, so I had a reputation to look forward to the possibility of engagements. Not out of bloodthirst. On the contrary. It was proactivity. Anticipatory. It seemed like the smartest psychological viewpoint to keep me sharp versus just sitting around complaining about how many days we had until we were headed home. I knew the enemy wasn't sitting around worrying about relief. My teammate from SOI and I were assigned to teams, thinking this was going to be a great op. We were told that we'd be heading out to OP-286. LCPL Kyle Mercado was assigned as my team leader for the operation.

The First General Order

When we got there, we were told that we'd be collecting trash from the side of the highway under the observation post because the commander wanted it to look "nice." Traffic was buzzing in North and Southbound directions on either side. He refused to even halt the traffic passing beside us only five yards away to ensure our safety. Another tell-tale sign that this operation was unwarranted and didn't even rate a priority status involving halting traffic to protect Marines from suicide vehicle-borne IEDs (S-VBIEDs). We were completely exposed and for no matter of operational significance.

Amidst the overwhelming loss of life that would soon force Washington to usher in the Surge Campaign, Golf Company Commander was having us collect trash next to unmitigated and free-flowing traffic in a filthy trash-infested country. Even the locals didn't care where they put it. MSR-Mobile was so dangerous at this time due to thousands of daisy-chained IEDs engineered by the influx of foreign fighters and bomb makers that every morning, the U.S. Military would deploy a specially equipped aircraft to buzz the highway with sensitive technology. Its purpose was to electronically detonate as many IEDs as it could to spare ground troops traveling by up-armored vehicle convoys. A guy to my left suddenly said "fuck" when he realized he stepped on something that felt like a baseball. It turned out to be an unexploded fragmentation grenade.

This was the night that the Company Commander branched into Mad King territory. It was also the night that I reached my tolerance threshold concerning the overwhelming and asinine loss of life. I renewed my vow that night to do whatever was necessary to protect myself and, more importantly, my fellow comrades, regardless of the consequences.

Chapter 10: The Mad King

The Company Commander was unequivocally sacrificing human lives for trash. I made the decision to aggressively protect myself and my fellow brothers, no matter the cost. After this night, Gunny Rowe would finally reach his tolerance threshold concerning the overwhelming lack of concern and needless command sacrifice of enlisted life for next to zero gain. He had been verbally constraining himself as much as possible, given the loss of faith in our company command for months. There's only so much diplomacy one can engage in, and that night, he and many others had reached that breaking point. Me included. The Company Commander was approaching the point of mutiny, and Gunny Rowe palpably sensed it. The event reminded me of the mad Roman emperor who forced his legionnaires to pick up seashells.

Base Camp: December 20th

I was sent back for psychological evaluation after the increasing escalation of Golf Company madness. The doctor refilled Ambien in a small plastic bag. He noted my diminishing physical health and the caffeine pills and said, "Do whatever you need to do, LCPL. We're almost home." Once again, combat stress was also marked as "heavy," and they let the rumors swell that I was "pulling a fast one."

Once again, doctors completely ruled out any psychosis or mania, debunking accusations by SGT Reagan. However, he continued to perpetuate rumors that I was misleading command leadership because they knew he was full of shit. The Navy doctors did another extensive evaluation and discounted SGT Reagan's accusation that any Marine felt unsafe around me and even noted their interviews with the other Marines in question.

Battalion Aid Notes displaying LCPL Phillips debilitating health and command's continued exploitation.

They also interviewed Marines and dismissed SGT Reagan's allegations that I was pathologically talking to my weapon versus just verbalizing while listening to my iPod, confirming that SGT Reagan was speaking for others and driving the biased narrative. If anyone legitimately felt less than completely safe around me, I would've been reassigned or ejected from the Area of Operations immediately. I was,

Chapter 10: The Mad King

however, the only Marine who had to be subjected to SGT Reagan's vitriolic tantrums and accusations, and that was absolutely putting exponential combat strain on me. No other Marine was subjected to anything like that. Senior Marines who began catching on and observing these tantrums were losing their patience with SGT Reagan. Between intense combat, high causalities, and drugs, we in 2nd Squad spoke little by this point. We all had our assigned duties and were emotionally protecting ourselves from being the next fallen man.

December 30th, 2006

On the night Saddam was transported to the gallows for execution, we were tasked with blocking the off-ramp from MSR Mobile, as I'm sure other units were along the convoy's route. Blackhawks were above, which was likely his mode of transport, while the ground convoy passed under the overpass directly below OP-286. After the mission, we regressed back to the IP Station. The IPs kept asking if they could go to the rooftop and unleash all their weapons in a celebratory fashion. I forget who the NCO was, but I recall many of them being visibly angry at even the mere question.

This is what this war had come down to. American families were being forced to sacrifice their loved ones while all the local "forces" wanted to do was play games while refusing to leave the compound, even when wounded Marines were pinned down 30 yards away. These guys didn't take anything seriously, which is great when you're playing with other peoples' lives as poker chips. Nothing invested. Nothing leveraged. Just a guaranteed cash salary. It was one more sign that things in this country would devolve the moment we regressed. The only question: How many American dead and wounded would valiantly uphold The Fifth General Order?

CHAPTER 11:
MUTINY: 20 DAYS PRIOR TO DEPLOYMENT'S END

The infamous Surge Campaign had commenced ten days earlier as Washington's response to the Civil War and the overwhelming loss of coalition life and wounded-in-action and bloodshed throughout the Sunni Triangle.

Around this time, a 3rd Squad was conducting vehicle mounted patrol down the road from the Iraqi Police Station and suffered a mobility kill. LCPL Mike Silva was the turret gunner and sustained a nasty concussion when hit by a roadside bomb while approaching the open Iraqi Marketplace that was deserted by this late hour. At the same time, 2nd Squad was conducting dismounted foot patrol operations about 50 yards back from the road in a residential neighborhood. We linked up with the immobilized convoy. The 3rd Squad team leader quickly assembled a team, including myself and another Marine, and tactically traced the detonation cord about 50 yards back to an abandoned house. We found ourselves cut off and out of line of sight from the 3rd and 2nd Squad back on the road. We were exposed in a perfect ambush position while approaching, with the three of us forming a horizontal line moving forward.

The team leader quickly assessed the situation and contemplated going on the offensive by launching a 203 mm grenade through the open window but had a bad intuitive feeling that we were walking into an ambush. By that time on that deployment, your gut was like a compass needle being pulled. The situation was all off. There was a level of quiet that had become a tell-tale sign of an impending gunfight. Even ambient nature goes quiet, which is an eerie feeling, even after you've become well accustomed to the sensation markers.

The team leader made the incisive call to egress, and we leapfrogged back to the convoy. By that point, most Golf Company members, especially NCOs, had lost all respect and confidence in Company Commander MB and Company. We were done taking chances with absolutely zero upside and infinite downside to our lives and duress of legal consequences. I recall an SGT in 3rd Platoon had been recently involved in a justifiably heated discussion between himself and Golf Company Commander outside the wire after a similar IED. The Company Commander had arrived on the scene and demanded to know why the SGT hadn't dispatched his rifle squad to manually trace the cord from bomb to origin. A yelling match commenced to maintain their distance. The Marines once again were reminded that the senior Noncommissioned Officers were the backbone and logical apparatus of Golf Company. Something just wasn't right with the Company Commander on a fundamental level. It even made me feel insane at the time because everything fell on the individual Marines to make decisions that were well above what we should need to contemplate.

Chapter 11: Mutiny: 20 Days Prior . . .

Righteous Mutiny: FOB Riviera

Around this same time, Company Gunnery SGT Rowe called all enlisted Marines and Navy Corpsmen who were present at FOB Riviera for an impromptu briefing in the makeshift open-area galley at FOB Rivera. He'd waited for the ideal opportunity. The officers were off on some trip back to Base Camp to get warm showers and hot meals, so he seized the opportunity to put a verbal decree in place to stop the madness of the Company Commander sacrificing us for no reasonable or profitable gain whatsoever.

He declaratively and emphatically stated, "Enough is enough!" The essence of the speech was that the madness needed to stop. We'd watched for over six months as our brothers had been killed and dismembered for a country that didn't even care about its own sovereignty. We had three weeks remaining, and regardless of what we did or didn't do, this war had been lost well above our pay grade. We had a duty to each other. Not one more letter to one more mother and father explaining that their child died with three weeks left in this campaign. If you had a shot, you had to take it! He didn't care how much the Company Commander or Company 1st SGT threatened with the fear of a court martial. They had their own agenda. And we had ours— to take care of each other. More than ever.

I thought to myself this was the one and only authentic speech given in Golf Company Command throughout the entire deployment. He said what needed to be said and put himself on the firing line if exposed. It was abundantly clear that this speech came on the heels of SSGT Rivers being betrayed by Company Commander, which was another crippling blow to Golf Company's senior enlisted leadership. He'd been recently relegated back to Base Camp and reassigned to H&S Company as a result. The command didn't have any justifiable evidence to court martial him, so they made sure the career was over and he'd never be promoted. To demote an SSGT, it had to come as an order from Congress, and the command had zero proof. So, they found another way to sideline him.

Gunny Rowe had been doing his best at diplomacy for the sake of protecting the enlisted the best he could, with racist sentiment against the Company Commander only increasing along with allegations of negligence.

Gunny would later call me on the phone after deployment's end when the front-page *Marine Times* piece came out following the court-martial. He confided in me that he held himself accountable for keeping quiet about the loss of company command confidence and deference. I assured him that wasn't true. The fact that he even called speaks to that truth. The night he gave that speech, he put his career on the line despite the potential consequences, which is congruent with the principle of courage and leadership. On that same phone call, he made it abundantly clear who the unequivocal war criminals of that deployment were, that everyone who served alongside those two individuals knew it, and that it certainly wasn't me. The phone call meant a lot to me, though it wasn't going to spare me the fate of continued humiliation or captivity that would be decided well above my head. The war was somehow only beginning and progressively escalating.

Gunny Rowe started aggressively trying to save the lives of enlistees and get us to the day we were relieved, or the troop surge began yielding dividends by dropping the hammer in Al Anbar and distributing additional labor across the Province. He started rotating and going out on patrols and missions with different squads to figure out how to optimize operations to preserve life in the weaning

Chapter 11: Mutiny: 20 Days Prior...

weeks of deployment. In the final weeks, Gunny Rowe was out on patrol with SGT Nichols, callsign "Nightmare," and 1st Squad. SGT Nichols had a unique and incisive strategy when conducting vehicle-mounted patrols. He was known to take off the beaten path roads that other squads avoided. While patrolling with Gunny Rowe, he did such a thing. He took a circuitous route and ended up coming out of a canal passageway that was barely navigable. When they came out of the canal passageway, they came up behind a suicide vehicle-borne IED (SVBIED) that was hunting their convoy. The vehicle exploded prematurely.

Had SGT Nichols not devoted innovative pathways to navigate, the vehicle would've found their patrol head-on where Gunny Rowe and SGT Nichols were in the lead vehicle. Gunny Rowe turned to SGT Nichols and said, "Your shortcut saved my life." That's how nasty that AO had become. If not for SGT Nichols' tactical sense and adaptation, Golf Company would have suffered the loss of our Company Gunnery SGT, which would have been an astronomical blow. SGT Nichols, unlike the 2nd Squad leadership, managed to prevent any killed-in-action and to absorb only two wounded-in-actions by being tactical, stealthy, and adaptive. SGT Nichols understood the name of the game, like CPL Rapavi and CPL Cavey.

Somewhere around this time, 2nd Squad was finishing a six-hour nighttime foot patrol after months of sleep deprivation and were re-entering the wire at Hotel Riviera. By the time you finish a six-hour combat foot patrol, especially at night, you're at the point where you're in jeopardy of collapsing if you don't get off your feet and hydrated while undergoing post-mission debriefing. The mentally daunting part about finishing those patrols was making it up the hotel staircase to 2nd deck while desiccated and loaded down with the amount of gear necessary to conduct combat operations behind enemy lines.

Nocturnal Combat Operations are a whole other crucible entirely. Though you're afforded the cover of darkness via night-vision optics, the margin of error and the physical and mental toll are amplified. Every step you make must be with precision, calculation, and skill lest you disturb the ambient environment. It's not like the movies where night-vision optics just look cool. They require a level of focus that drains you adrenally, and the extended period peering through the green paradigm signals your brain it's time to sleep, so you must constantly resist the counter-intuitive instinct.

To compound matters, the heavy and awkward night vision goggles drag your head downward as if you're tucking your chin. You must resist the temptation the entire operation while engaging your neck to tilt back and remain upright, neutral, and focused while ready to engage targets. The part that makes it worthwhile is the infrared laser strobes that everyone activates, which can only be seen by those with night vision goggles and scopes. The lasers allow everyone to designate zones and targets and decrease guesswork. At that point, you just must line up the target with a laser and pull the trigger while also having the benefit of knowing where everyone else's zone of fire is simultaneously. This was where we excelled. Nocturnally. In this foreign realm, the cover of darkness was our best ally. Long gone were the formative days when you prayed for the bedroom door to crack a sliver and radiate light from the other side. Here, we prayed for the cover of darkness. In this realm, even night light meant death and liability. The complete cover of darkness kept us alive and effective.

The most critical juncture of a mission is returning through the wire. The enemy doesn't attack you as you're commencing the op-

Chapter 11: Mutiny: 20 Days Prior . . .

eration because they know you're mentally motivated, hydrated, and ready for a gunfight. They wait until you're at your weakest and depleted across all domains. Our squad leader trained us to be aware of this and resist the temptation. It's a level of mental endurance that most can't comprehend. In those final precarious moments, you're forced to tap into a mental space after having already tapped into a mental space for six hours. Every patrol ending is like being up against the ropes in the 12th round and going on the counterattack.

As we entered friendly lines, I headed towards the smoke deck to funnel through the doorway and make the trek up the daunting staircase—the same staircase that Saddam had walked thousands of times while vacationing in his now decrepit small personal resort on the Riviera. There was only one problem. The Company Commander was standing there in the doorway, talking to someone and smoking a cigarette. He saw me, which was impossible to avoid, standing inches from him, eying me through peripherals, as I tried my hardest to stay vertical and silently and professionally subordinate while deferring action to him. That was a mistake on my part. Deferring action to him had been the folly of many. By this point, he should've been on the board of directors for whatever defense contractor was responsible for manufacturing body bags. He certainly sent enough business their way and was capable of scaling revenue further.

Twenty seconds later, I made one of the smartest calls of my life. After smelling the subtle but unmistakable scent of alcohol, like all those car rides as 2nd Platoon's designated driver, I backed up and took a seat on the makeshift bench comprising the smoke deck and got all the weight off my lower back from full combat load. As an Automatic Rifleman, I'd been responsible for carrying four ammo drums on me, in addition to a heavy-mounted scope and all the other gear and water. When you're in red-blooded kill mode, and someone behaves that way, the best course of action, if possible, is to just breathe, de-escalate, and walk away—luxuries nonexistent during firefights.

He was provoking a tired, pissed-off 19-year-old Marine standing there with a tactical machine gun, K-Bar, and two frag grenades. The implication was clear at the time from a vibrational standpoint. There was continued petty retribution for the bridge emasculation. Except I wasn't emasculated and prudently took a seat, thinking about what hydration and sleep were going to feel like. Moments later, SGT Reagan arrived and was not happy. He had no idea why I wasn't upstairs and thought I was being belligerent and violating post-mission established protocol. In his mind, once again, I was the bad guy. He told me to get upstairs and subsequently had an exchange with the commander while I waited at the base of the stairwell inside. Seconds later, the commander came through the door, mockingly and bizarrely stating, "Next time, tell me to move, Phillips! No, really!" while moving his head up and down like a bobblehead doll losing his mind. Challenging a tired, war-weary gunfighter was commensurate with his progressively escalating bizarre and lethal behavior. By that point on deployment, I was just trying to survive and persevere like the rest while being the most proficient saw gunner for the protection of myself and my fellow Marines. Even if that meant simply not drifting off to sleep or making bad calls.

Between his bizarre behavior, flushed red cheeks, and lack of reaction time seeing me standing there, my intuition said that he had access to alcohol or, in hindsight, was also on medication prescribed by the Medical Officer. His behavior was becoming increasingly absurd. There was a level of apathy and petty, passive-aggression to this individual that made it abundantly clear that there was something

Chapter 11: Mutiny: 20 Days Prior . . .

deeper going on. My combat instincts and intuition from my days as a sober designated driver were in high gear. But I had a job to do. If it wasn't for Psalm 91 and my St. Michael medallion, I don't know what would've happened. Once again, I was completely professional, demure, and subordinate. I wasn't going to let the biggest loser in Golf Company get me to violate The Fifth General Order so that he could take one more Marine who emasculated him off the line and leave my brothers to pay for the additional loss of manpower. Everyone pulls their weight. That's part of the sacred covenant.

Golf Company was responsible for most casualties in the Battalion; 2nd Platoon was further responsible for a quadrant of the AO, including the IP Station that, for whatever reason, absorbed 90 percent of company casualties, which, to this day, I still can't make sense of. The AO quadrant, especially surrounding the Iraqi Police Compound, was volatile, and the mission, for lack of a better term, was increasingly polarized.

Steve Jackson was one of the best mid-level Marines in the 2nd Platoon and was headed for squad leader. One night, the 2nd deck of FOB Riviera was empty. He walked by a room and overheard SGT Reagan inflicting one of his most vitriolic and disgusting denigrations that had become all too mundane. LCPL Jackson, the leader he is, said, "No fucking way you're saying that shit ever again. He's a good Marine. You're out of line!" Usually, SGT Reagan was good at provoking altercations in private without witnesses and deploying sexual accusations, which seemed like projections.

I told myself it was just like Infantry School. If I couldn't withstand the psychological abuse, I had no place being a Marine Rifleman. Neither did I let the complete asymmetry of the psychological attacks make me quit. If dealing with a petulant child was what was required to protect my fellow brothers, then that was the price of doing business in the industry I found myself immersed in. It merely indicated that SGT Reagan saw something in me he feared and, like a child, was throwing tantrums while refusing to relinquish me to another squad. He backed down immediately as he did to CPL Bates months earlier on the smoke deck. I've never forgotten the leadership and compassion that LCPL Jackson showed. The 1st squad, under SGT Nichols, never lost one Marine. They were superb with guys like Jackson, Nichols, Derrick, Smallwood, and Nunez. Derrick was the guy I'd leave my death letter with before missions. They were a family, just like 3rd Squad. Lions like Nick, Panza, Cavey, Silva, Hite, Vinny, Rick, and Matt were some of the finest Americans I've ever known.

SGT Reagan's behavior kept spiraling out of control. To take the focus off him, he made me a focal point by attacking me perpetually in the most disgusting and asymmetrical manner. He kept acting out of sorts. He progressively began boasting about the time our Platoon SGT, SSGT Bestman, caught him in the barracks with the book *Mein Kampf,* and SSGT was demonstrably livid. I thought it was disgusting since my grandfather, while hunting Nazis, was based out of the same prison where that repulsive and unintellectual book was drafted. SGT Reagan would also keep making random non-sequitur statements, saying, "Deny it till you die!" referring to never telling the truth unless you needed to. I just let him keep portraying me as the mentally deranged one and counting the days until I'd be away from his command. I was beginning to deduce that he wasn't aware of things he was saying or doing, or conversely, he had no idea that other people didn't find them rational or humorous. I find it sadly ironic that the Company Commander and Medical Officer had us both on the same hypnotic.

Chapter 11: Mutiny: 20 Days Prior . . .

Doc Solbach, one of my most respected comrades, and I were on post at 50 percent capacity. There's only one high seat—the active observation seat—and then a ground-level low seat for the Marine who can rest and read or keep the active observer company and be ready to respond, when need be, to enemy ambush on a moment's notice. It's impossible to sit in low chair while resting and be able to observe. There's no view. That's why you're allowed to read or sleep. If you're on highchair or on post by yourself, it's a different matter.

Reagan came up to the post unannounced, looking for a fight. I was casually reading a magazine. I didn't take the bait. I knew right away by his eyes and energy he was in one of his dark modes and looking for a soft target to provoke. He grabbed the *Maxim Magazine* and beautiful centerfold that LCPL Silva had graciously bestowed me and tossed it violently about 25 yards, for which I'll give him credit as far as range. It went far. I still owe Silva a refund. SGT Reagan sauntered off. He sent another Marine up to relieve me immediately.

Downstairs, SGT Reagan instructed me to leave my machine gun and directed me to the area near the bathroom. He had me on my knees, picking up cigarette butts for a couple of hours of hazing. No worries. This type of shifting had become mundane since the bridge ambush. It was sad because it caused a rift and made squad members uncomfortable. At times, I almost thought that leaving the squad was the best for them, considering this toxic adversarial provocation campaign, but even if I had to crawl on my knees to honor The Fifth General, that's how it was going to be. The Fifth General Order isn't a punchline. It's a core value and sacred covenant. Attitudes and moods are meant to shift according to one's environment, but core values are a matter of constitutionality. SGT Reagan, at one point, came out while another Marine was watching me on my knees. I could tell the initial hazing hadn't produced his intended reaction. He had his pistol, which was made unambiguous in nature, and demanded that I stand at attention and then transition to parade rest, which is hands behind your back with a professional demeanor. Once again, complete professional subordination and compliance. As a matter of official record, I never once, through seven months of provocation, ever raised my hand or even my voice to him to warrant such a venomous accusation that was close to being shot like a dog.

I blame Golf Company Commander, Battalion Medical Officer, and Assistant Battalion Commander for hijacking our minds for added utility at the expense of our dwindling sanity.

The official record demonstrates continued self-restraint and the level of obstacles I had to deal with behind the scenes on top of combat operations. The only one with a litany of explosions was SGT Reagan, ranging from tackling team leaders, vitriolic diatribes, and pulling his side arms on unarmed Marines. That's why he brought his pistol while hazing me: because he couldn't believe how quiet and subordinate, I was once again while being subjected to the most denigrating vitriol during another manufactured offense. I wanted to put him on the ground for his disgusting behavior, but The Fifth General Order and protecting my fellow brothers was the ultimate priority, not settling a petty score with a petulant aggressor. That's why I kept close to CPL Sellers. That's a gunfighter who knew the mission was higher than any one of us and knew how to protect Marines.

It got to the point where SGT Reagan was on the record saying I only spoke when spoken to. He's truthful on that account. Yet he'd never tell LT Browne all the fucked up sadistic behavior behind the scenes. I could palpably sense LT was becoming suspicious because he's one of the sharpest people I know. I was always

Chapter 11: Mutiny: 20 Days Prior...

100 percent subordinate and honest to him, even when SGT Reagan would antagonize me in front of him, yet never remove me or refuse to utilize me on combat operations. It was a sick power dynamic. At times, I wanted to tell LT about the sexual and vitriolic remarks SJR would cast behind the scenes, but like growing up tongue-tied in Massachusetts, I was raised to keep my mouth shut. The more I kept quiet, the angrier SGT Reagan became because he couldn't provoke a reaction. He couldn't get me to violate The Fifth General Order. Plus, I believed in the fundamentals of a chain of command. LT Browne had one of the toughest jobs in the Marine Corps as a 2nd Lieutenant, further compounded by how incompetent and spiteful the Golf Company Commander was towards him out of pure emasculation. I empathized in that respect. The way CPL Rapavi, through mentorship but really observation, trained me was to always respect chain of command, be conservative in speech, and use the appropriate channels of communication.

The higher up the chain of command, the more compartmentalization was necessary. The Medical Officer was prescribing pharmacological hypnotics and endorsing caffeine pills notated in the signed medical notes, and for my part, I didn't think that was something LT Browne needed to be informed of, as I expected the Medical Officer and Company Commander to brief Platoon Commanders in basic leadership form commensurate with chain of command. LT Browne could tell stuff was up with Reagan and me, and we never told him. We didn't think we were doing anything wrong but taking medical direction from the Battalion Medical Officer. SGT Reagan was a talented squad leader. He, like Brent and I, was used and medicated. We were barely hanging on. He was trying to survive while also preserving what was the remainder of his rapidly attenuating squad. Battalion Commander, Company Commander, and Battalion Medical Officers are guilty as sin.

Around this time, Doc Solbach was standing post on the rooftop of the Iraqi Police Compound on the South Post. He was ambushed in vicious attack by the enemy.

> "I was providing overwatch from the rooftop post of The Iraqi Police compound. The compound was centered between our patrol base and the beginning of the marketplace, and we had clear views of the main roads that would lead up to the police station and, eventually, FOB Riviera. I was on the rooftop post facing away from the main streets, overlooking the vast neighborhoods. I noticed the building directly across from the post had been undergoing construction. There was poor visibility into the dark room on the second floor. I sat there for quite some time, monitoring the neighborhood, scanning for suspicious activity. From the lower part of my field of vision, a cloud of smoke appeared. I heard a bang and felt a rattle. An RPG had been launched at the post. It came from the dark room where the construction had been taking place. I immediately jumped off the makeshift chair where I'd been sitting and took a low stance behind some sandbags. I began firing into the dark room. I heard high-pitched cracks impacting the post. Over the radio, I called in: 'I'm taking fire and firing back!' Phillips came to the rescue again. He was the first Marine to run upstairs and into the post. The firefight lasted several minutes. My weapon jammed, but Phillips kept engaging with a machine gun until the gunfire stopped. After the firefight,

Chapter 11: Mutiny: 20 Days Prior . . .

I was able to see what the post looked like. Several enemy rounds had come through the wooden corners of the post. Two to three bullets could be seen on the chair where my shoulder and neck were positioned. That's why I must emphasize that I might not be here writing this today if it weren't for Phillips' aggressive backup. If he hadn't had the courage to rush up to the post, fearlessly firing off as many rounds as he did, the firefight might have lasted longer, and the enemy may have had time to take better aim."

HM3 Navy Corpsman "Doc" Arthur Solbach

After the firefight was over, I was scolded and verbally reprimanded by SGT Reagan. He said he warned me about firing too aggressively. I just stood there and took the abuse. By this point, I'd learned to just take it. I found it odd that he didn't come up to the post until the firefight was completely over, at which point he judged and scolded me for engaging in a firefight that he wasn't even involved in, nor did he have any visual clue as to what had been going on with the targets landscape. It was just Doc and I up there like the team we were. No one else ran to the rooftop. Certainly not CPL Neil, our official team leader. Doc Solbach was a machine. The enemy could never touch him, no matter how hard they tried.

The New York Times

Bush Adds Troops in Bid to Secure Iraq

By David E. Sanger
Jan. 11, 2007

WASHINGTON, Jan. 10 — President Bush embraced a major tactical shift on Wednesday evening in the war in Iraq when he declared that the only way to quell sectarian violence there was to send more than 20,000 additional American troops into combat.

Yet in defying mounting pressure to begin troop withdrawals, the president reiterated his argument that the consequences of failure in Iraq were so high that the United States could not afford to lose.

In a speech to the nation, Mr. Bush conceded for the first time that there had not been enough American or Iraqi troops in Baghdad to halt the capital's descent over the past year into chaos. In documents released just before the speech, the White House acknowledged that his previous strategy was based on fundamentally flawed assumptions about the power of the shaky Iraqi government.

Mr. Bush gave no indication that the troop increase would be short-lived, describing his new strategy as an effort to "change America's course in Iraq," and he said that "we must expect more Iraqi and American casualties" in the course of more intensive round-the-clock patrols in some of Baghdad's most dangerous neighborhoods.

But Mr. Bush rekindled his argument that a withdrawal would doom to failure the American experiment in Iraq, touch off chaos throughout the Middle East, provide a launching pad for attacks in the United States, and embolden Iran to develop nuclear weapons.

New York Times Article announcing The Bush Administration's Troop Surge after months of leaving troops to fend for themselves

CHAPTER 12:
KILL ZONE

January 20th. IP Station

The new Secretary of Defense had ordered the infamous Troop Surge ten days earlier. It was a move to bail out the Bush Administration after the past four months of overwhelming violence and loss of life after having declared an end to all major combat operations on the aircraft carrier two years earlier. American Forces hadn't yet received the luxury of the first installment. They were undermanned, and weak company leadership provided no solace or excuse to gunfighters—so we did what lions do and went looking for food and targets at night to devour. Daylight was defensive operations, and nights were completely offensive. We operated in squad-level hunter-killer teams, set up ambushes, and conducted reconnaissance—Wolfpack tactics. We'd insert into a house, politely corral the occupants, and ensure their absolute safety and that of their house. Meanwhile, the assault team would head up to the rooftop, set up ambush points, and coordinate with other Wolfpacks doing the same at various locations throughout the AO. I would be sent to the roof with CPL Sellers and two other Marines. I'd then find a vantage point, deploy my bipods, and sit looking through mounted blurry night vision scope for hours.

The First General Order

Waiting. Then we'd egress and link back up with FOB Riviera or IP Station

At this point, the madness continued to escalate. Company Commander now introduced the prospect of Unit Stop Loss as part of Washington's newly developed Troop Surge. Part of their plan was the magic trick of avoiding sending the necessary number of troops for the Surge by involuntarily extending existing units preparing to head home who were walking dead by this point. Navy doctors and ground commanders were taking orders decreed from way above to keep everyone on the line, even if barely "ambulatory." That prospect took Golf Company from the verge of insanity but barely clinging to a state of utter demoralization. Being extended for another six months with that level of operational tempo and a company-level command hell-bent on sacrificing Marines for zero gain was the ultimate gut check.

Our unit continued to quantitatively and qualitatively attenuate with killed and wounded and Staff NCOs being forced into involuntary resignations. LT Browne, LT Durham, SSGT Ybarra, SSGT Bestman, and a host of senior NCOs were leaders I was willing to stay on the front line for and die if the grim reaper came for a 19-year-old Marine drunk on caffeine, his iPod playlist, and *Maxim* magazine centerfolds.

Sleep had been nonexistent for weeks. Everyone was on the verge of delirium due to the constantly increasing operational tempo compounded by the amount wounded and killed in action. And how overstretched we increasingly became with our Area of Operations (AO) as a result. I was grabbing a Rip-It caffeine drink with fellow Lance Corporal from SOI to get some liquid life in us before we headed back to FOB Riviera to rotate onto different mission statuses.

Chapter 12: Kill Zone

The dry heaving and vomiting had been increasing in severity, and I was amid another vomiting bout. My vision and ambulatory issues were worsening. Another searing migraine had hit me.

The Marines were verbally and demonstrably uncomfortable sleeping and operating out of The Iraqi Police Station (a mere 70 yards away from FOB Riviera, which had the towering vantage points) due to the AQI plot to capture a Marine and the chronic behavior exhibited by The Ips. We even began taking off our name tags. Then the small National Guard parcel showed up, had a liberal mentality in a violent Area of Operations, and started making Marines uncomfortable like we didn't warrant our experienced operational concerns

Whatever rough shape I was in was noted by the Medical Officer, Company Commander. Seeing my character and tenacity, my squad leader aggressively recommended me for Marine squad leadership and S.E.A.R. school, but I declined SEAR school out of my intention to attend the Recon Indoctrination Program and potentially MARSOC, which was in its infancy and recruiting from Recon Units. SGT Reagan vehemently recommended I attend the program, which was scheduled for a few weeks after we were returning stateside, based on my proficiency, drive, and refusal to quit.

Up to this point, my fitness evals notated "subordinance and executes orders violently." My plan was to go home, rest and recover, get my mind right, and show up for indoctrination qualification. LT Browne will verify all this, as well as my fitness reports that notated my subordinance and, as the top tier of my junior class, the characteristic leadership trait to "execute orders violently." I didn't know the nightmares I was having while I slept or the screaming fits. I did know, and the Medical Officer noticed and notated, that my coordination was diminished, and migraines were increasingly exacerbating my sensitivity to light. However, the Officer highlighted that I never exhibited any psychosis or mania. The command knew the searing migraines were getting so bad that I was perpetually vomiting and dry heaving from the nausea. I could barely walk.

LT Browne did everything right and briefed the Battalion M.O. and Company Commander, Battalion Command, and Navy Psychiatrist. But none of them ever revealed to him that they had me or other Marines under his command, including the squad leader, on pharmacological hypnotic agents. We were not even recalling half of what we did until reminded or questioned. I would walk by Sergeant Reagan in the halls at night. We were both semi-conscious, trying to stay moving to keep our thoughts from veering into what was happening around us. What Company and Battalion Leadership were actively doing to us was depraved. What they chose to do when the curtain fell was even more diabolical. The Company Commander can claim he didn't know what was going on within his company, which is empirically false, but even if it is true, it's a direct and unequivocal admission of his command failure and abject incompetence. He and the Navy docs were playing with pharmacological fire, all to exploit everyone for every ounce of life they could offer. They were selling out great Marines afterward. It's a spectrum of immorality, and the Geiger counter was off the charts

One Week Left in Deployment

Seven more days. If only I could survive this madness for seven more days. Then I could wake up from this bad dream and be back home mowing and watering my lawn in peace. But seven days is an eternity in this foreign realm. How had it come to this? Barely eleven months earlier, I'd graduated high school.

Chapter 12: Kill Zone

With one fucking week left and minutes away from finishing our 48-hour rotation without sleep and for reasons unclear, the Iraqi Police exited the compound to conduct one of their rare and notorious "lightning" vehicle-mounted patrols. They refused to give an official concrete reason for their exit and violation of operational security and, in official statements, stipulated driving to a hospital for "a baby" even though they had their emergency lights activated, eliminating cover of darkness that was our best friend and main advantage and underscoring the dangerous operational liability and tactical disregard that was typical. It was corruption at worst, command negligence and a PR stunt at best.

I was standing in the compound's open courtyard, looking at the night sky and counting the days until we left the front line. I had just grabbed a caffeinated beverage as we were about to depart the compound and be relieved by the next rotating squad. Enemy gunfire broke the silence. I geared up rapidly and was the first one to make it to the rooftop. Insurgents quickly ambushed the IP Station from multiple directions. As I made it to the top of the stairwell, a hail of enemy gunfire came within inches. Someone was firing from an elevated position. There was no other way to see over the short rooftop walls at that angle, making the direction and muzzle flashes easier to get a bead on. I remember my mind instantly visualizing and anticipating the feeling of whether one of those projectiles should impact my flesh and bone and create a highway throughout my body. I think anticipating it was my default mechanism for courage. If I could anticipate how bad it was, it wouldn't hurt as much.

It makes you question everything about yourself and life in an instant. I immediately dropped to my knee, went condition-one with a light machine gun, and stood back up. I began gliding forward, engaging the exact direction while moving ahead to the North-West portion of the roof wall about twenty yards away, suppressing while other Marines charged up the stairs and got into position.

Once against the short wall, I quickly set up shop, deploying bipods for precision suppression, leaned in, and began engaging targets with complete violence of action, establishing fire superiority via machine-gun mounted night-vision scope. I first engaged small arms fire to the North-West at a structure that rose above our compound. By this time, several other Marines were able to reach the rooftop and were arrayed along the wall, suppressing targets. The other saw gunner, LCPL Hector Soto, somewhere to my left at the end, was focusing on the Western Avenue of approach and didn't have a machine-gun mounted night-vision scope, so he suppressed targets with his ambient light while I focused on specific areas to the North-East and the avenue of approach. Keep in mind there's no set plan. We had a great strategy. I had the night vision scope, and he could engage and suppress targets at will with the precision of an M-16, which is why the M249 Light Machine Gun is one of the most versatile, lethal, and effective weapons.

Every ambush is different but possesses the same underlying variable of volatility. It's all intuition and nonverbal communication. We'd been accustomed to insurgent tactics by this point, and I was making not to fall for a North-West diversion while dismounted or while a suicide vehicle approached the compound from the North-East traffic circle. I also covered the marketplace with night vision scope, looking for the smaller details or flanking elements.

Chapter 12: Kill Zone

LCPL Jonathan Phillips

Two minutes later, the lightning patrol returned with their police emergency lights flashing during what was an extremely short lull in the action. As they were about 100 yards out, LCPL Parcels and I looked at each other's and simultaneously said, "You have got to be fucking kidding me." This was the perpetual rationale as to why we didn't want to work with these shady foreign forces and were counting down the excruciating seconds in the week that we had left before egressing from this shady war. The Company Commander wanted nothing to do with anything. It literally fell to lance corporals.

The Iraqi Police Patrol approached with their flashing lights destroying the cover of darkness and stopped between our position and where seconds earlier we had been receiving fire from several directions. They were between our position and the marketplace, which was 50 yards. The Army National Guard Contingent had ignorantly blocked the Entry Control Point (ECP) to the compound with their truck, even though there were already sufficient movable barriers in place from the U.S. and prior National Guard Collaboration, but the new contingent wanted to assert dominance over the Marines even though it was Golf Company's Area of Operations, and we were well-versed in the application of violence and defensive operations and tactics. They came into our AO midway through the historical Civil War, didn't receive any integration from their predecessor, and arrogantly demanded that everyone yield to them and their liberal thoughts and feelings. Why the COC, who was in radio contact with the Iraqi Police patrol, didn't order them to push through the kill box and drive away is beyond me.

Insurgents recommenced attack. The Iraqi Police chose to dismount in the kill box from North-West to North-East. They dismounted and ran all over the place towards the North-West while engaging insurgents by their own statements.

The attack recommenced. We all began suppressing targets on the North side while the South Side machine-gun nest suppressed targets on the opposite side and Western edge of the rooftop.

The vehicle convoy that should've never left the compound was between us and the enemy on both sides, as well as the South side of the compound. FOB Riviera Entry Control Point (ECP) medium-machine gun was engaging targets on the street at the far end of their field of fire, which was near us down Sniper Alley. At the same

Chapter 12: Kill Zone

time, FOB Riviera Rooftop machine-gun bunker was engaging targets closer to the North-East.

Controversial Firefight in question.
Graphic Recreation of nighttime rooftop ambush.

Instead of pushing through the kill zone to circumvent the National Guard Vehicle blocking reentry point and driving onward past the station, the Iraqi Police (IP) did the worst thing they could've done dismounted. In the middle of a complex ambush. Great. They scurried in the opposite direction of the truck column towards the safety of the ground-level compound wall in our direction on the other side of the parking lot so they'd be safe under the umbrella of our fire superiority. Why SGT Reagan and the Army National Guard Downstairs in the Command Operations Center (COC) didn't order the patrol to push through to prevent Marines on the rooftop from being endangered is another reason the chaotic amalgamation at the compound and power dynamic had reached a fever pitch. Once again, it was on lance corporals to make life-and-death decisions with no upside.

Anyone experienced in nocturnal engagements in an urban environment knows the odds are already volatile and dicey as is. Using night vision optics, let alone subpar gear, is hard enough searching, differentiating, and engaging targets without the interference of flashing emergency lights drowning out night vision and chasing away ambient light. Everyone was yelling and designating. I was lightly singing a song to myself, keeping myself sharp and focused as much as possible.

I was focused on the front of the column (North-East). The other Marines to my left were focusing towards the middle and left (North-West) while the Army National Guard was focusing on the South and South-East. I was scanning, traversing, and suppressing through night vision scope, keeping an eye on the North-East Entry Control Point (ECP) and traffic circle. Fifteen yards forward of the lead flashing vehicle, I caught a target profile running towards the vehicle column that by this point was deserted all the way towards the back by the Iraqi Police who'd made the foolish folly to stop and dismount, then run the other direction during the ambush.

It was enough to make out an incongruent profile. It was nowhere near the other dismounted Iraqi Policeman running in the opposite direction. I was intuitively taking note of where the FOB Riviera rooftop machine gun was engaging, as they had the elevated position, including the enemy. It's a move called "Talking Guns," where automatic weapons communicate with each other silently and intuitively. As I looked through my scope, I saw that the target matched the insurgent profile running right to left (east to west), which was

Chapter 12: Kill Zone

my zone and sector at the time at a point between the marketplace and the median and covering the North-East traffic circle as well as the critical Entry Control Point to the IP Compound that had been sabotaged due to petty pride. I had less than a millisecond. I didn't hesitate, just like I'd been committed since the bridge ambush.

I didn't have peripheral vision as I was the only one with a machine-gun-mounted night vision scope while everyone else was going off muzzle flashes and tracer rounds, seeing them with their naked eyes and peripheral vision. I didn't stop engaging until I was sure my zone and sector were green lit and clear and that the Entry Control Point was free of any threat approaching the compound. I sawed from light to left—the same direction the individual was running—and I ended up strafing the police vehicle. I didn't care about the vehicle. It was nothing but a distraction and liability. After months of operating hunter-killer ambush teams, I was the quasi-designated sharpshooter as to Automatic Rifleman. Others opted for less weight and collapsible buttstocks for their light machine guns. There are pros and cons to each. Everyone has their part and specific gear to make the squad as lethal as possible. For instance, I didn't have a sidearm as most military machine gunners are supposed to have in case there's a weapon malfunction, or they're forced to reload in a close quarter battle with an enemy rushing your position. I didn't have a rifle-mounted grenade launcher, etc.

Subpar night vision optics, flashing red and blue emergency lights, tracer rounds from friendly and enemy positions on all sides, while sleep-deprived and sustained by high caffeine and controversial hypnotic—add to those untrained foreign forces running in multiple directions and admittedly engaging insurgents running up on them, according to official statements. In the firefight, I wasn't concerned about that choice. It was decisive. I was providing cover for the Iraqi Policemen who were well towards the left and who had, for whatever reason, left their comrade isolated and cut off from them.

When you're confined to a night vision scope, you must focus on your night vision and keep your other eye closed for focus. The black rubber round piece that suctions to your temple prohibits vision outside the scope. In the Marine infantry, we're trained to master three fundamental principles: Fire & Maneuver, Fire Superiority, and the construct of Eyes, Muzzle, Target (EMT). When I'm in a firefight using a rifle or light machine gun, wherever my eye goes, my muzzle follows. That way, the moment you acquire a target in a firefight, your reaction is automatic and cerebral since there's no need for hesitation. There's no time for delayed reaction or indecision. Only life or death.

I had one eye isolated through night vision scope, searching for targets. The moment my eye caught a profile, the muzzle was ready to engage. You don't stop engaging until the target is eliminated or until they reach cover and leave your zone and field of fire. In a complex nighttime firefight, every source of fire, tracer rounds, flashing emergency lights, muzzle flash, infrared laser designators, yelling out targets, and shifting fire all catch and draw your attention when close to your field of fire. You have milliseconds to react or be eternally apologetic for yourself or your fallen comrade who pays the invoice for the indecision or error. The instant you see tracers or lights flashing and an individual running towards the flashing lights who shouldn't be doing so, it's cerebral target acquisition and engagement. The ground-level machine gun bunker and rooftop bunker at FOB Riviera were doing exactly what Gunny Rowe had ordered. They saw multiple targets and engaged. No hesitation. No more bullshit. Until these points, the ground-level and rooftop bunkers had never engaged

Chapter 12: Kill Zone

targets. No one was listening to the Golf Company Commander by this point, nor allowing any more fellow Marines to needlessly perish. It was a professionally active, necessary, and defiant mutiny—a "No Marine left behind" ethos.

No one ever thought for one second on the rooftop that an Iraqi Policeman was hit. Why? Because it made zero sense as to where the target was running toward the back of the column and to the IP Station wall well before this point—which intuitively made anyone even near the middle, let alone ahead of that flashing vehicle column, running towards the column from an opposite direction, hostile in intent and fair game. We were only made aware that an IP was missing when someone came up to the rooftop after the firefight and told us an IP was MIA. We were all aware that there were friendlies down there. That wasn't the variable. The variable was the chaos on the North-Western and North-Eastern sides and target differentiation. They stopped and dismounted in the middle of a kill zone and ran in multiple directions. They left their comrade alone, and for whatever reason, that comrade chose to isolate himself in all the confusion.

If it had been a Marine contingent on the street in the middle of an ambush, they would've pushed through the kill zone, immediately freeing up the rooftop field of fire. The Army National Guard unit spent their time eating and watching DVDs inside, and regardless of what they claimed, they were not training the Iraqi Police Force. Official statements indicate that the Iraqi Police Lieutenant in the vehicle patrol was radioing back and forth with the Command Operations Center (COC) downstairs at one point. Why the National Guard didn't radio the vehicle patrol to push through the kill zone versus stop and dismount is unresolved to this day, but judgment has no place in an urban nighttime firefight. That should go both ways.

The First General Order

The range was about 50 yards. I was looking through a subpar green night vision scope, trying to stay focused with all the gunfire and yelling. There were IPs running in different directions, insurgents wearing similar attire running from cover to cover engaging, flashing sirens, and FOB Riviera engaging targets. Meanwhile, I was trying to keep it together for one more week of hell after I'd stayed on the line like I was told and happily agreed to my personal detriment. These are the moments The Fifth General Order matters the most. When you're in the thick of it. Game Time.

After I engaged the target, the National Guard NCO at some point yelled, "Cease fire; there are friendlies down there." I was in no mood for an inexperienced, idealistic dude telling me what we all knew while I'd watched him eating down in the COC and watching DVDs for the past month. The issues of Iraqi Police weren't the variable at stake. The million-dollar question was target differentiation, as the target I engaged was nowhere near anyone else. He was running towards the front of the vehicle column, indicating that he was running towards the other Iraqi Policemen, who were, by this point, all towards the back of the column and against the wall of our compound. Without taking my eye off my scope while searching for additional threats, I flippantly replied, "Yeah? Well, at least Marines aren't the only ones dying!" as I continued to scan without any hesitation like Gunny Rowe had verbally decreed

When there was a lull in the firefight, the Army National Guard, with radio, received all clear that all IPs were accounted for. Parcels and I exchanged looks. I knew it was the right call because the target was distinct. Sometime later, there was a radio transmission saying there was an Iraqi Policeman suddenly missing in action (MIA), which just added to the escalating absurdity.

Chapter 12: Kill Zone

Unlike the way LT Brown had fundamentally trained us, there was zero-unit cohesion at the IP Station. There were three different foreign and domestic units, all with separate and unclear priorities and degrees of training. It was the same type of casual deference and disregard for tactical procedures by the Company Commander that threw all the squads into disarray a week prior to commencing deployment. He did *nothing* until the moment he was forced to. There was zero proactivity, which is a vital prerequisite to leadership. He wasn't even a Monday morning quarterback. He was all the way to Thursday judging the Monday morning quarterbacks.

The National Guard unit had never been in a firefight before. This was their baptism. That was another issue. The most junior National Guard soldier was inside the South Side Observation Post (OP) while the firefight was happening. When the firefight reached a conclusion, I stayed on the rooftop. The soldier came out of the bunker with wide eyes and wasn't even able to speak at first. Then he said, "Holy… What the fuck…that was crazy." I said, "Bro, you'll' all right. You'll get used to it." But the truth was I wasn't used to it. The madness and lack of mission and cohesion never ended. I was barely hanging on. But I always try to inspire someone behind me regardless of what I am going through. The worst thought ever is dragging someone down. That soldier reminded me of just how young we were. His reaction was what it should've been after that madness. It highlights the complexity of the engagement and polarization. I hope that soldier survived the eventual suicide dump truck that came howling up the exact avenue of approach I was suppressing and annihilated the IP Station. He was a great guy who was put in a horrible situation. I'll never forget his reaction and facial expression. It was like someone had just seen the most beautiful but lethal fireworks display, and his brain couldn't discern whether to marvel or seek cover. Plus, the sky. It was beautiful.

> "I never had a problem with you. You didn't cause me any issues. Did we all hear that said to the doctors that you told them what they wanted to hear, yes, but I never heard it of your mouth. When The Iraqi Police firefight happened, I was out on vehicle patrol and was coming back that way. I didn't know any Iraqi Policeman had gotten hit until afterwards. From the angles, the darkness and confusion, one might say they should've stayed in place when fire was taken instead of dismounting and running around or called it in over the radio to be relayed as friendlies in the wire. Too many what ifs, but you never did me any wrong. A lot of people wanted to get with my squad. People use to stay 1st squad always gets into shit but always comes back."
>
> SGT Trent Nichols

Post Firefight: Lower-Level Courtyard

Downstairs, the IPs busted into the Iraqi Police Station like the disorganized, corrupt contingent they were, angry that they had to even fire their rifles and earn their paycheck for the first time, and that was only because they left the wire for nefarious purposes only to B-line two minutes later and jeopardize Marines as an operational liability.

They came into the Iraqi Police Station and declared they were all present and accounted for, which is basic arithmetic. *Then* they realized they were wrong and looked like incompetent, scared fools when

Chapter 12: Kill Zone

they said wait a minute, we left a guy somewhere…and don't even know where he is. They refused to retrieve him and started engaging in a shouting match with SGT Reagan and a soldier, accusing Marines of shooting at them from the rooftop. They played the victims as always, and the Golf Company Commander chasing promotion would play it up to avoid controversy. The fact that they wouldn't go retrieve the MIA just like they had refused to reinforce SGT Nichols's 1st squad five months earlier when a Marine was wounded 30 yards away shows the level of systemic corruption. Lack of bravery is no excuse. The Iraqi Police had no loyalty, and if they had, they wouldn't have left a man isolated and unaccounted for. If it was a hundred-dollar bill, they would've known its exact location in a heartbeat.

As the Iraqi Policemen started to become emboldened due to hurt pride, SGT Reagan justifiably pulled his pistol and said, "Shut the fuck up, MUJ," which was one of the most honest things I ever heard him say. The Iraqi Policemen refused to go find the MIA body, just as they'd refused to leave the compound for seven months when 1st squad was pinned down with wounded and needed a pickup truck to evacuate. A marine went out and couldn't find the body, which was not where they had claimed it was, further reinforcing my target acquisition and engagement. He eventually found the body and dragged him back with another Marine. There was still enemy fire at this time, showing how long the engagement lasted.

The initial location that they declared was also incorrect, reinforcing my decisive decision to engage the lone target in the ski mask with a weapon. They were isolated from the fleeing contingent in multiple directions towards the back of the vehicle patrol. SGT Reagan also omitted that he and the senior ranking National Guard soldier gave the Iraqi Police patrol radio commands to NOT dismount and to stay in vehicles and drive away to free up the field of fire. They refused to obey those decrees, opting to instead dismount and run in opposite directions, leaving one guy isolated far from where he should've been while wearing a ski mask with an AK 47 in the middle of a nighttime ambush while Army personnel were screaming over the radio, according to National Guard statements. You're damn right I took the shot. Not a moment of doubt. That's the industry I was in. The only doubt I had was the company command I was serving as the madness progressively escalated. But there seemed to be a ton of doubt down in the COC. Marine Infantry, Army National Guard, and Corrupt Iraqi Police Contingent, with no officers in sight, were all operating on independent and sovereign authority. I started to think I missed the memo about joining a leaderless fucked-up version of Joint Special Operations Command (JSOC).

LT Browne (USMC) said, "At the time, there was a lot of confusion about what had happened because the Iraqi Police contingent had said they had full accountability of their force. After they made that declaration, they realized they were missing one. So, there was confusion as to how he was killed, if this guy was even, in fact, an insurgent, because as SGT Nichols had said over the radio, this guy has a mask and rifle. He's got a bulletproof vest. We kind of thought for a second that this might be a bad guy until the Iraqi Police contingent said, wait, we're missing one. We realized, okay, this is an Iraqi Policeman. So, there was some confusion about what happened. We were all very careful about jumping to conclusions prior to having any real evidence."

Sometime later, another Marine asked me what I saw when engaging, and I was still processing myself, having just been on an adrenaline high. They'd told us the Iraqi Police truck had been strafed.

Chapter 12: Kill Zone

Within minutes, the Company Commander rushed to the scene and started playing CSI Investigator. Not once did the Company Commander inquire if all the Marines or National Guard were ok. No one was concerned about my viability, though I was hyped up from the adrenaline and sleep deprivation because SGT Reagan assigned me to head up to the rooftop and assume control of the machine gun.

The Company Commander, unlike LT Browne, wanted to rush to judgment and find a scapegoat to ensure his career mobility wasn't affected. He'd deferred all management and mitigation of the escalating chaos at the Iraqi Police Station compound and now went into instant cover-up mode.

I found the outcry for the Iraqi Police force to be inappropriate, disingenuous, and commensurate with seven months of twilight zone absurdity marked by corruption and incompetence. If it weren't for a paycheck, the command wouldn't have been able to even get them to show up. That was the universal language encapsulating the Iraq War from Washington down: Money. Lots of it. Taxpayer-funded. You can't fight for a cause the locales don't even stand behind. All the American loss of life up to that point had barely been fussed about. Never had I seen such an outcry each time a Marine in Golf Company was tortured, killed, or dismembered. But the moment an IP was killed because he was in the wrong zone, it was nuclear. Radioactive. Didn't matter what the facts were. Politics above all else. We couldn't even sleep because the IPs didn't want to work. I can tell you this much: not only were there no Marines by this point willing to die for a corrupt local militia, but each Marine and even Company Gunny were counting down every waking hour until we'd be egressing from that shady and corrupt war.

SGT Trent Nichols (USMC) said, "I never had a problem with you. You didn't cause me any issues. Did we all hear that you told them what they wanted to hear, yes. But I never heard it out of your mouth. When the IP Firefight happened, I was on vehicle patrol when the Iraqi Police had dismounted and scrambled, and I was coming back that way. From the angles, the darkness and confusion, one might say they should've stayed in place when fire was taken instead of running back or calling it in for it to be relayed as friendlies in the wire. We rolled up and Iraqi Polices were running up against the wall of the station as we blocked incoming so they could get in. We rolled had a vehicle convoy and rolled into a shitstorm with no good sitrep. Too many what-ifs. You never did me wrong. A lot of people wanted to get with my squad. We were always told 1st Squad always gets into shit but always comes back."

An Army National Guard NCO said, "There were at least three Iraqi Policemen we didn't trust. We called them the Three Stooges because they were too shady. They were always gone whenever there was an attack on the station."

In hindsight, I would've paid the IPs out of my own pocket so as not to jeopardize us for that final week of deployment since it was my job to be LCPL, squad leader, and Company Commander. It wasn't even Varsity Squad dealing with Freshman Squad. It was Varsity babysitting Pop Warner, who were only there to get their coach-funded slush after practice. In retrospect, that's the course of action I would've taken upon myself under the burden of commands of incompetent and indecisive company leadership.

The Company Commander, minutes after the firefight, went into career mitigation mode and demanded someone be held responsible for the dead Iraqi Policeman. He acutely accosted LT Browne, ex-

Chapter 12: Kill Zone

claiming, "Phillips has bad PTSD… We got to get him back to Base Camp now!" An Iraqi Policeman had been inadvertently killed in the chaos, and I took the shot. The Company Commander wanted a scapegoat, so he dispatched a 19-year-old to be interrogated by federal agents back at Base Camp in a deferential attempt to take the blame and spotlight off the commanding officer for months of negligent behavior.

Company Commander steered the investigation from the moment he said those words to LT Browne. PTSD had nothing to do with the shot I took. It certainly didn't help, but I followed orders that Gunny Rowe had given us with a week left in the bloody campaign. Meanwhile, LT Browne remained calm and collected, according to his nature and leadership, and advocated not rushing to judgment. But the Company Commander saw the writing on the wall. He was staring down the barrel of a gun for seven months of negligence throughout the company. Superiors would want answers. Answers he wouldn't want to give. Not once did I hear or see the Company Commander ask if the Marines in the firefight were ok. Not *once*. So, he had the NCIS vultures move in and briefed them, and they cherry-picked the pieces that fit their puzzle and obscured any that didn't conform to the narrative. It was like what they were doing in the Command Operations Center (COC) during the firefight while they were in contact with the Iraqi Lieutenant, according to an Iraqi Policeman statement.

My heart was still pounding. Already, the Company Commander had ensured I was going to be the scapegoat for the death of the Iraqi policeman who wasn't where he was supposed to be. I was in shock from both the complex firefight with Iraqi Policemen and insurgents intertwined like fireflies and the realization that the treasonous and murderous Company Commander was throwing me under the bus like trash once again.

As ordered, I subordinately relinquished my primary weapon, K-Bar, night-vision goggles, and two frag grenades without so much as a protest or ounce of belligerence. As always, I followed commands at every juncture throughout deployment while honoring The Fifth General Order during each evolutionary crucible thrown my way.

I was ordered back to Base Camp immediately and passed off to 1st SGT Watkins at H&S Company up at Battalion. I laid down in a corner up against a wall, still amped up and trying to dissect the firefight. In my book, the firefight was a complete victory. Not one Marine, Sailor, or Soldier had been killed or injured. Gunny Rowe's prudent decree had been executed with violent precision and zero hesitation. I had a shot and cleared my zone of fire where there wasn't supposed to be any Iraqi Policeman present. Retrospect is the industry of cowards. You win some, and you lose some, but if you act without hesitation, you will live to fight another day. If you dwell on what others who aren't in your boots think, you'll be a perpetual prisoner of thought and slave to paralysis. My blood sugar was starting to drop as the adrenaline began to attenuate.

I pulled my covers over my eyes and tried to calm down.

Back at FOB Rivera

As I was taken back and isolated at Base Camp, special agents from the Naval Criminal Investigative Service (NCIS) descended on FOB Riviera. Their job is to protect the Navy's blindside against any liability and to protect the Officer Corps. These agents are not Marines and don't understand Marines, who are a subset of society recruited and trained unlike any other and are not to be equivocated as their

Chapter 12: Kill Zone

job isn't the same. Marines are shock troops. NCIS has a rich history and legacy of deceit and aggressive entrapment as it relates to aggressive interrogative practices, especially homicide investigations. They've faced extensive criticism for the handling of investigations, particularly overseas. There have been reports of witness intimidation, mishandling of evidence, and deploying aggressive coercive.

According to statements, the Company Commander was the first person to meet with agents upon arrival at FOB Riviera the following day, along with the Battalion Assistant Medical Officer, who gave a statement that had been withheld since about all my health issues for months prior. They signed over my complete medical and psychological file into the custody of the investigative team days prior to my interrogation. This is where facts took a backseat, and the psychological motive of retributive intent was put front and center and made sure all witnesses conformed to it in any way possible. This is the point where Company and Battalion leadership decisively seized the high ground. Everything was going exactly according to plan. Vulnerable 19-year-old loyal LCPL. Pawn. Knocked off the table. No one the wiser. Flawless execution. How could such an LCPL put up any formidable defense?

The First General Order

20Jan07 at approximately ▓00, he received a radio call from the patrol asking for the HUMMVEE to be moved so they could enter the compound. ▓▓▓ asked the "Army" to move the HUMMVEE and he was told to tell the patrol to drive around the block and come back. A short while later, ▓▓▓ heard a loud explosion and he was informed it was an IED. ▓▓▓ said he received a radio call from the patrol telling him to tell the Marines to stop shooting at them (IP).
▓▓▓ said he was still in the central room when he told the Marines in the central room to have them stop shooting. ▓▓▓ said he heard laughing over the radio (Marines). ▓▓▓ then went to the roof and told the Marines to stop shooting at the IPs. ▓▓▓ then heard the IP Lieutenant call on the radio and say one of the IPs was injured.
When the shooting stopped, they found out one of the IPs was shot and killed.
Exhibit (5) provides details.

8. On 21Jan07, IP ▓▓▓▓▓▓▓▓▓▓ was interviewed; ▓▓▓ was the driver of the first vehicle in the IP patrol on 20Jan07. At approximately 1910, the patrol returned to the station ad noticed a HUMMVEE was blocking the entrance. The patrol was instructed to drive around the block until the HUMMVEE could be moved. The patrol drove to the mosque area then back in the direction of the IP station on ASR Lobster when an IED exploded between the first and second vehicles. The patrol began to receive fire from behind them so the IPs exited their vehicles and began shooting in that direction (towards the mosque). ▓▓▓ advised the Marines on the police station roof were firing in the direction of the mosque as well. After a few minutes, the shooting stopped and Lt ▓▓▓ instructed everyone to stop shooting. ▓▓▓ and Lt ▓▓▓ then began to retrieve their AK-47 magazines when the insurgents started shooting again. When the patrol began to shoot at the insurgents, they began to receive fire from the IP station rooftop. The patrol members were finally able to run inside the IP station. When the patrol members noticed ▓▓▓ was not with them, they went outside and found him lying in the road.
Exhibit (6) provides details.

9. On 21Jan07, IP ▓▓▓▓▓▓▓▓▓ was interviewed; ▓▓▓▓M was the driver of the third IP vehicle on 20Jan07. On 20Jan07, the patrol was returning to the IP station when they observed a HUMMVEE blocking the entrance to the compound. After circling the block, they returned to the IP station and noticed the HUMMVEE was still blocking the compound entrance. The patrol then drove west on ASR Lobster in the direction of the mosque. When returning to the IP station, an IED exploded near the second vehicle. ▓▓▓▓ made an immediate right turn. He stopped, exited he vehicle and began shooting in the direction of the mosque. When the shooting stopped, all three vehicles drove in the direction of the IP station. ▓▓▓ remembered seeing the occupants of the first vehicle walking toward where the IED exploded to pick up AK-47 magazines when the shooting started again. ▓▓▓ advised shots were coming from the IP Station in the direction of the IP vehicles at this time. Out of fear, ▓▓▓▓ went to the prone position. ▓▓▓ recalled someone in yelling in English, "ceasefire." As he headed into the IP

FOR OFFICIAL USE ONLY
PAGE 6

NCIS Statement extracted from Iraqi Police Lieutenant

Chapter 12: Kill Zone

> BROEKHUIZEN noted the se[con]d IP vehicle had heavy dama[ge] to include shattered windows, bullet holes, flat tires and engine damage.
> BROEKHUIZEN spoke with some of the Marines involved in the engagement who advised they returned fire to areas where muzzle flash was observed. Acting IP Station Chief, Lt ■■■■ told BROEKHUIZEN an IED detonated between the first and second patrol vehicle as they were returning to the IP Station. Subsequently, ■■■ and his men began receiving fire from locations north and south of their position; they returned fire. The IP patrol then began to move back toward the station when ■■■ observed an individual with a weapon behind him; the patrol stopped again and engaged this individual.
> ■■■ told BROEKHUIZEN he and his men were then fired upon by Coalition Forces

Partial statement by Golf Company Commander Mark Broekhuizen to NCIS Investigators about the intermingling of insurgents and Iraqi Policeman though he aggressively drove the psychological motive against LCPL Jonathan Phillips

The senior ranking National Guard NCO told investigators that they radioed the Iraqi Police patrol to not dismount from their vehicles and to push through the kill zone and vacate the area, and, true to form, they violated those commands, leaving an Iraqi Policeman isolated in a zone that should've been clear of friendlies. When the commands were disobeyed, they ordered the Iraqi Police patrol to run into the compound—putting my field of fire in jeopardy and not relaying those commands to the rooftop, even once the Army National Guard NCOs were up there with a radio and looking foolish, telling Marines to cease fire, thus endangering lives.

The Army National Guard NCO asserted from his Westward rooftop position that as I was engaging target, he had to reevaluate his prior opinion on the shifting fire due to my vantage point, the field of fire, and incoming rounds from FOB Riviera, who had an even better view of things and who I was coordinating with in rapid cerebral fashion.

The First General Order

STATEMENT

Place : FOB RIVIERA, IRAQ
Date : January 22, 2007

I, SGT STEPHEN THOMAS REAGAN, make the following free and voluntary statement to JEFF BRACKETT whom I know to be a Representative of the United States Naval Criminal Investigative Service. I make this statement of my own free will and without any threats made to me or promises extended. I fully understand that this statement is given concerning my knowledge of the shooting death of an Iraqi Policeman on 20Jan07.

I am currently assigned to 2/8 Golf Company, 2nd Platoon, 2nd Squad as a squad leader. I have been deployed to Iraq since Jul06. My social security number is ███████ and my date of birth is 06Sep82. I was born in ███████. I reside at ███████ NC. I have been in the U.S. Marine Corps since May03.

On 20Jan07, my squad was reinforcing the Iraqi Police station in Saqlawiyah, Iraq. We started this assignment on 18Jan07 (Thursday). We do two days of reinforcing the IP station, two days of mounted patrol (QRF- Quick Reaction Force) and two days of dismounted patrol (foot patrol). Our two days of reinforcing the IP station require us to be at the station.

On 20Jan07, I was in the COC (Combat Operations Center) with Cpl Neal and Cpl Copeland. Sometime after dark, I heard a loud explosion which was proceeded by gunfire. Cpl Neal and Cpl Copeland ran to their room to get their gear on. I got on the radio to advise COC Riviera that the IP station was in contact (engaged in fire). Once I let COC Riviera know, I ran to my room to get my gear on. I heard gunfire the whole time. I knew the post (roof) was returning fire as I could hear it. After I got my gear on, I ran back to the COC to try and find out what was exactly going on. I was told that an IP was wounded outside the gate of the IP station by a young IP (we call Hamid). I would say from the time I heard the first explosion until now was about 5-10 minutes.

I grabbed Cpl ███ and we went outside the gate and did not see any IPs. I saw the trucks (3 of them) which were about 70 meters from the front gate. I did not see an IP and was looking where they said (front gate area). I was still standing outside and I asked Cpl ███ to go get me a radio so I could run down to the trucks. The gunfire was still occurring. Cpl ███ came back out and told me to get back inside as they (IPs) said all the IPs were accounted for.

I went back inside the COC and the gunfire had stopped. I got on the radio again and I called COC Riviera and gave them a contact report. I then walked outside the COC and I saw the IPs standing with an interpreter (terp) (named Charlie). I could tell the IPs were upset as they were talking loud and making strong (quick) hand gestures. I believe there were about six of the IPs standing there. I asked the terp what was going on and he told me the IPs were saying the Marines had shot the IP. I became upset at this accusation and I kept saying why would my Marines shoot at flashing red lights (meaning the IP trucks had emergency lights on) and that it did not make sense. An Army Cpl (we call Koko) told me to "chill" out as they (IPs) were armed. I was also yelling that I went out there to look for the IP and grab him but they (IP) had said they were good. I did not understand because I could not find the IP when I went outside.

Page 1 of 3

NCIS Statement extracted from SGT Stephen Reagan (page one)

Chapter 12: Kill Zone

I then went back to the COC and radioed Lcpl Reisman who was standing North post on the roof. I could not reach him so I ran up on the roof and saw him. Lcpl ▮▮▮▮ showed me where the IP station had taken fire. Lcpl ▮▮▮▮ indicated they took fire from the Northwest (area near the mosque) and from the East (area known as traffic circle). I stayed up there for a while and I could see the IP trucks and they still had their flashing lights on. I then heard that the mounted squad (QRF) had gotten the body of an IP from the area near the trucks. I went down to the COC and heard that the IPs had gotten ambushed and were taking fire. I was still upset that the IPs were going to blame the shooting of the IP on Marines. I had heard that the IP had been shot and was dead.

The CO (Capt Broerhuizen) came to the IP station and he began talking to the IPs. The CO then came over and talked to our squad (10 Marines and one corpsman). We told him who was on post. The CO told us how the IP was hit and where the wound came from. The CO said the trajectory was at a downward angle (took this to mean from high angle). The CO then went back to talk to the IPs and I went back inside the COC. I began talking to Army Sgt Collette when Cpl ▮▮▮▮ came in and told me I needed to hear something. He told me it was about Lcpl Phillips. I knew right when he said Phillips that he was going to tell me that he (Phillips) shot the IP.

I just knew it as he has not been right since Oct06. In Oct 06, my squad was on mounted security patrol and we got ambushed. An IED went off underneath the last vehicle and it was a catastrophic kill on the vehicle. We lost three of my Marines, one interpreter, and one Marine was severely burned. The humvee was mangled and burning. After the explosion, we turned around and went back to try and help them. Phillips began to lose it, he was yelling and "freaking out". I saw one of the Marines had been blown about 40 meters from the scene and Phillips was just standing there staring at him. Phillips was losing it and I told him to calm down or he would be no help. We were still taking small arms fire and we got the casualties out (except for one). The squad took the casualties back and they returned to Riviera. I stayed behind because one Marine was still missing from the explosion. I believe this ambush occurred around 1245 and I did not return to Riviera until after dark.

When I came back to Riviera, I was told by another squad leader (Cpl Rapavi) that Phillips was losing it and he was talking crazy stuff. I then told my chain of command. I cannot recall if I told my platoon commander (Lt Browne) or if I told my XO (Capt Taylor) but I know I told one of them. I told them that Phillips needed help and what he had done at the scene and back at Riviera.

Phillips was then sent to see a psychologist at Fallujah (maybe the following day). I am unsure of exact dates. I know we had a memorial service for the Marines who were killed in Fallujah and Phillips came back with us. Phillips told me and everyone that he told the doctors what they wanted to hear so he could come back to the squad. I told the CO what Phillips had said and he told me to try and help him and that maybe Phillips needed to be around his friends to mourn.

For a little while, Phillips appeared okay. The day after Thanksgiving we (my squad) were back at the IP station (reinforcing duty) when Cpl Rapavi got shot in the neck by a sniper. Cpl Rapavi was on mounted patrol and he had gotten out to open the gate to let the vehicles in and he was shot and killed. Phillips was on post on the roof. I was inside the COC when Rapavi was shot and I immediately radioed Phillips. Phillips came across the radio and he just kept saying something like he got hit by a sniper and he was shooting back. He was very frantic and I could hear his gunfire and he was definitely out of control. He was shooting way too many rounds.

On another occasion sometime before we went to re-set training at Camp Fallujah. This was sometime around middle of Dec06. Re-set training is like a three day refresher at Fallujah where we can shoot small arms fire, eat good chow, etc. I was told by some marines that they did not feel comfortable with Phillips, they said he was there but he was not there (I took this to mean he was unstable). I then got

NCIS Statement extracted from SGT Stephen Reagan (page two)

all the Marines that lived with him (~~███████████~~) and talked to them individually. They all basically told me the same thing, that they did not feel safe with Phillips.

I then told my platoon commander (Lt Browne) and SSgt Bestman of the concerns with Phillips. I talked to them separate. I think SSgt Bestman went and talked to the Marines. The CO talked to all of us (Platoon Sgt, Platoon Cdr, Lt Koch (doctor) and myself. It was decided that Phillips would go back to Camp Fallujah to see the doctors again. S T R

We then went to re-set training and I saw Phillips at re-set training and I asked him what had happened and he said he was good and I was like no serious what happened. Phillips said no the doctors said he was okay. I was surprised. I was then told by my team leaders (Cpl Neal, Cpl Sellers, and Cpl Copeland) that Phillips was bragging again and how he pulled a fast one on the doctors. I then told Lt Browne what Phillips was bragging about. S T R

Lt Browne told me that he talked to the chain of command and the doctors at Fallujah. This happened all while we were still at Camp Fallujah. He told me the doctors had given him a clean bill of health and we decided that we would do the best we could for Phillips. S T R

I remember one time while Phillips was standing post at the IP stations (roof), I caught him reading a magazine. I could not believe this and I relieved him immediately and made him do cleaning all day at the station. I knew he was mad so when I went to the bathroom I carried my pistol as I sort of scared of him being unstable. S T R

In my opinion, Phillips should not have been out here in this combat zone. S T R

This statement, consisting of this page and two others, was typed for me by Special Agent Brackett, at my request. This statement is true to the best of my knowledge and belief. I have been given the opportunity to make any changes or corrections and I have initialed any changes that were made. S T R

Subscribed and sworn to me, this 22nd day of January 2007, at FOB Riviera.

Stephen Thomas Reagan

Jeff Brackett, Witness
Representative, Naval Criminal Investigative Service
Auth: Derived from Article 136,
UCMJ (10 U.S.C. 936) and 5 U.S.C 303

NCIS Statement extracted from SGT Stephen Reagan (page three)

"Since I've known Jon, he has exemplified what it means to be a stand-up guy, both in and out of service. From the moment we met, it was clear that Jon possessed a rare blend of integrity, dedication, and camaraderie. His unwavering commitment to excellence was evident as we

Chapter 12: Kill Zone

navigated grueling challenges. Whether it was during intense training exercises or in the heat of deployment, Jon's calm demeanor and ability to lighten the mood were infectious.

But Jon's character extends far beyond the battlefield. Off duty, he has always been the first to lend a helping hand, whether it was supporting a fellow Marine through a tough time or volunteering in the community. His sense of duty and compassion have made a lasting impact on everyone fortunate enough to know him.

In every aspect of his life, Jon embodies the core values of honor, courage, and commitment. His steadfast loyalty and unwavering moral compass have made him not just a remarkable Marine but an extraordinary human being. For two decades, Jon has been a pillar of strength and integrity, and I am proud to call him a friend and brother-in-arms."

LCPL Mike Silva

SGT Reagan had ordered me up to the North Post machine gun bunker to relieve the Marine on post, indicating once again by actions that my fitness or emotional stability was completely secure and trusted. His statement completely omitted that he ordered me to post immediately after the firefight because that would contradict the inaccurate assertions he was making. When someone came up to him saying, "I have to talk to you about Phillips," he said, according to his statement, "I knew right away what he was about to tell me because Phillips hadn't been right since the bridge ambush" (five months earlier). If he knew right away that it was me, why then did he have a tough time believing when the IPs were lying about being all present and accounted for, or when the MIA Iraqi Policeman wasn't where they said he was when he went out searching? Why, then, had he recommended me for a recon indoctrination program after I declined Search Evasion and Resistance (S.E.A.R.) school weeks before? LT Browne and SSGT Bestman can attest to those recommendations.

SGT Reagan wasted no time discrediting me and alleviating pressure from his blindside. If he "knew right away," then why the fuck was I exploited to the fullest by him for seven months? He maliciously made a false statement a week before the deployment finale. Evidence that demands a verdict. The guy changed his mind faster than a mouse trap engaged. Federal Special Agents threatened everyone to get the preordained outcome they prophesied. SGT Reagan was wounded like the rest of us in our subjective ways and didn't stand a chance like me up against seasoned federal interrogators, especially medicated. Company Commander and Medical Officer sold us all out.

SGT Reagan had pulled his pistol on the belligerent Iraqi Police as their pride got hurt. It was intimated to me by someone close to him that investigators threatened him on this event and forced a malicious statement against me under duress, which is commensurate with their coercive tactics. Turning Marines against Marines. His statement certainly omitted all the sexual vitriol behind the scenes that several Marines had caught him inflicting, the reason he felt the need to carry his sidearm around an unarmed junior Marine who never once raised a fist to anyone regardless of provocation. We were all losing our minds, and Gunny Rowe knew it. He just didn't know we were being prescribed hypnotics by the dermatologist Medical Officer.

Chapter 12: Kill Zone

His statement included nothing about the Iraqi Police patrol Lieutenant, whose statement indicated he had been radioing COC and being ordered not to dismount vehicles and to vacate the kill zone to prevent endangering Marines and potential crossfire. The reason is because of how chaotic the ambush was, lending credence to my scope paradigm. When NCIS is called onto a scene of an event, someone always goes down. They never walk away empty-handed. These guys will find dirt in a hermetically sealed vacuum chamber. That's what they do. There is also no mention of his tantrum and once again pulling his sidearm. But there is reference to it in statements taken by the National Guard, and SGT Reagan was aggressively questioned by a military judge because of that omission, portraying me as a psychotic.

Special Agents were completely fine with omitting material parts that helped portray me as a madman, though officer after officer on and off the battlefield confirmed and eliminated any symptom or diagnosis of psychosis or mania, once again directing attention to SGT Reagan's ulterior agenda and judgment. Neither is there any other mention in any witness statement that any Marine or sailor ever felt unsafe around me in the least. Those are the lies that were always fueled by SGT Reagan and his fixation and emasculation, which is extremely evident by Marines catching him in his diatribes and by his own signed statement. If there was a Marine in Golf Company that other Marines felt unsafe around, he would've been removed from the unit effective immediately.

He omitted to special agents that military intelligence from the interrogation and execution of the enemy sniper had debunked his falsehood about my suppressive fire in the marketplace being inaccurate and out of control. If his official claim was to be believed and he was legitimately going to shoot me without provocation, he would've never put me on post again, let alone immediately after a firefight in question two months later. He never once told the Platoon Commander or Platoon Sergeant about this fictitious claim that he was going to shoot a junior Marine, which is extremely telling because he made it up to investigators in one of his episodes. He once again also deployed the malicious claim about the magazine on post, which Doc Solbach can readily attest to falsehood.

I don't know why SGT Reagan would write the categorically false things he did, but I can attest to my own interrogation. By that point, I simply didn't care. But I never said anything negative about a fellow Marine or sailor, let alone anything that was patently false, evidence that demands a verdict. I'd seen enough needless death with zero gain or upside and lost too many good friends. The agents threw me in a thousand different directions, which, after talking to fellow Marines months later, seemed to be the status quo.

The Company Commander and Battalion Medical Officer stood to be convicted of crimes ranging from negligent homicide, dereliction of duty, and a host of other offenses, including medicating frontline troops. Those are the same culprits NCIS met with before anyone else and collaborated with before the investigation commenced. From that point forward, facts took a backseat. I think that's the hardest pill to swallow for me. I was messed up for sure from seven months of hell, but the firefight was what it was regardless, and I made the exact same call I would've made if I had to do it all over again and had it happened months earlier. You operate with the intel you have at hand, and you make split-second decisions to the best of your ability and don't second guess. I wasn't the one who let those untrained, corrupt IPs leave the compound for a two-minute random

Chapter 12: Kill Zone

joyride. I wasn't the National Guard who changed TTPs and blocked the ECP with a Humvee. I wasn't the IPs running in multiple directions, including the deceased, who was doing God knows what, running towards the vehicle column. When the guys on the bridge burned alive, when March was killed, when Raavi was shot in the throat, and when CPL Santiago lost his legs and fingers, I didn't hear an ounce of commotion. It was considered a mundane day at the office. But a group of shady IPs being outside the wire for unspecified reasons, not taking TTPS seriously per usual, and running in multiple directions between us and insurgents…it was World War III to Golf Company Commanders.

CHAPTER 13:
INTERROGATION

About four to five days later, I was still unable to sleep and wired. By this point, I had been without sleep for about a month. Caffeine and adrenaline are magnificent short-term weapons to facilitate combat operations. The Allied drug of choice was caffeine, whereas the insurgency opted for shots of chemical adrenaline and opium.

For the next week, I slept at Base Camp and was fortunate, through the Grace of God, to be assigned to SSGT Alfred Rivers' squad along with Lance Corporal Jeremy Hirata as my team leader in H&S Company. Months earlier, SSGT Rivers had been relegated to Base Camp after company command accepted the biased accusation from a corrupt Iraqi Interpreter over one of the most respected enlisted staff NCO knights in our company about another engagement with the enemy and accused the Staff NCO of violating the rules of engagement. As a result, SSGT Rivers was relegated back to Base Camp, his career was destroyed in the process, and Golf Company enlisted were deprived of one more senior enlisted Staff NCO.

Base Camp: Interrogation Trailer

They interrogated several Marines back at FOB Riviera and exploited the complexity of the dynamic to the fullest with the sole objective of ascertaining a scapegoat. They coerced by taking advantage, intimidating, and manipulating war-weary Marines after seven months of intense combat operations and sleep deprivation, with numerous medicated with controversial hypnotics. They exploited the squad who sustained more killed in action than any other squad in the Battalion combined. I was still on Ambien hypnotic and told to "keep taking it, and it would keep me calm." When you're 19 and wounded, you trust the officers who're appointed over you to have your best interest at heart. And LT Pugliese was always polite and professional, so I always assumed this was true.

I was escorted to an interrogation trailer somewhere in the back of Camp Fallujah. It was about the size of a silver bullet camper. Little bigger. It was dark in the trailer, and there were two agents. By this time, I was the last witness to be interviewed, and they had spent days combing over my medical and psychological records for the purposes of developing motive based around premeditated retributive intent and to gather ammunition to mindfuck me with. The one agent kept drawing incessantly with markers on a whiteboard behind them towards which I was facing as if the Sharpies made them morally decent or something. Give someone a giant marker, and suddenly, they're Einstein solving equations.

Throughout the interrogation, the agents made comments about how tired I was because I kept drifting off. Then, one agent instructed the other agent to get a can of soda and a candy bar. I deferred when the items arrived. Investigators exploited my speech issues and delayed reaction time to type up a coerced statement and not record the interrogation.

Chapter 13: Interrogation

LCPL Jonathan Phillips battlefield interrogation by NCIS Special Agent Steven Dreiss and his senior partner. Graphic Recreation.

I could still sense something was off, just like in combat. I don't merely mean concerning the investigation. It was as if the borders of the puzzle had already been assembled and linked together. All they were interested in was me filling in the main body and convenient matrixes with the narrative they had already constructed as to intent and motive.

The First General Order

No matter how I tried to explain my recollection, they'd already made up their mind. Company Commander already got to dictate the framework and distance himself, playing the noble citizen and crime scene investigator, putting his criminal justice college degree to work like an eager Boy Scout seeking a merit badge. All they were interested in was filling the preordained puzzle pieces inwardly to isolate the firefight in question with what they had already accepted as gospel and without any consideration for the seven months of prior operations and injuries and the elephant in the room, which was complete company command failure at every juncture throughout deployment. They used the death of all my fellow comrades to pull the strings they wanted to, and I even teared up and felt like the agents were right and that I was responsible for all their deaths. I was concentrating through scope without peripheral vision. I told investigators that I saw someone running in front of the IP truck—running in the opposite direction and towards the lead Iraqi Police truck.

I engaged a military-aged individual with a ski mask running from a zone that was supposed to be clear and who appeared as a threat to the Entry Control Point and the IPs who had fled in the opposite direction. NCIS was investigating me because the Iraqi Police Vehicle was hit, and they drove the narrative that I maliciously engaged it, isolated the event, and omitted all surrounding combat complexity and volatility. I engaged and sawed leftward, and he was hit in the arm because he got up and ran into the market buildings. They then said, "With your aim and all the reports of firefights we've read about, there's no way your command is going to believe you missed him." They said they believed me and then made it like it was a psychosomatic thing where he was an insurgent and that it was completely understandable. Meanwhile, I'm 19, and my cognition

Chapter 13: Interrogation

is diminished, my anxiety is through the roof, and I haven't slept in months. Caffeine was the only thing keeping me alive. At the time, I couldn't articulate the feeling of dissociation overtaking me. It was like I was watching the conversation from an objective point of view, and I didn't care anymore. Seven months of Umbrella Corporation at work and some of the finest patriots had fallen, and no one could say why or to what end. And here I was, in a dusty interrogation trailer in the middle of Iraq. I truly didn't care anymore. I later realized the hypnotic Ambien combined with caffeine and combat had produced a warped paradigm.

The Iraqi Police came into the compound claiming they were engaged by insurgents in close-quarter combat and that, at the same time, they received fire from the Iraqi Police Station Rooftop while also taking fire from the <u>East</u>, which was my zone of coverage. As they got into the Iraqi Police Compound, they asserted everyone was present and accounted for, then renegedt. According to NCIS statements and translator, several Iraqi Policemen claimed the deceased never left the pickup truck and died where he sat in the truck …which begs the question of either how they came to that conclusion when fleeing or, more likely, that NCIS and their interpreter were misleading, because Marines retrieved the body, and it certainly wasn't in the truck. He was running towards the truck at the time of engagement, and FOB Riviera rooftop engaged to the North-East. If the Iraqi Policemen were that confused and undisciplined, scattering in various directions, it would certainly be no less chaotic for the Marines on the FOB Riviera rooftop and IP Station rooftop.

The deceased was shot through the heart and killed on impact, according to the Medical Officer. The version investigators aggressively drove made zero sense and is physically impossible, lending credence to my night vision scope paradigm that the individual "Got up and ran" as I was engaging him in running towards the Iraqi Police truck. Agents twisted my version with their version and assured me it was fact because they aggressively postulated that they had irrefutable drone footage. They wouldn't accept any other version and assured me I must be confused because of all the fallen comrades and all the injuries they'd seen notated in my medical records.

They kept walking it backward and talking about all the fallen comrades I'd lost earlier and that if they were in my shoes, they'd be pissed and motivated by justifiable retribution. They highlighted and homed in on the fact that I was first to gear up and make it to the rooftop. Now, I was accused of being too quick and reactive. They refused to understand or acknowledge that by being first, I took the brunt of gunfire from an elevated position, and my suppression paved the way for other Marines to get up the stairs and to the far side rooftop wall. I told them I'd been trained to simplify things and establish fire superiority at the start of any ambush to set the tone and dictate ferocity. It was psychological warfare and smart fire and maneuver tactics. They'd only engage in highly structured and isolated lines of inquiry. They'd say a line, then trail their voice off suggestively until I picked up and finished their sentence. I told them I saw a target that didn't appear to be friendly in the high-stakes situation, and they said they believed me and that it was an insurgent or, at the very least, appeared that way in all the confusion. They knew by official Iraqi Police statements that there were insurgents running up while I was engaging from the North-West and North-East. They said there was absolutely no reason I would need a lawyer and that it would only "complicate things."

Chapter 13: Interrogation

They deployed the ambush that killed CPL Rapavi to accuse me of being trigger-happy, unrestrained, and psychotic. They ran with the narrative that I was out of control for suppressing targets while 3rd Squad was pinned down and one Marine was pulling Nick behind cover—even though the sniper would've taken out that Marine as well because I was the one with the vantage point with direct line of sight to, in what witness statements confirmed, was the "most likely position of the enemy sniper" in a condensed marketplace. This all stemmed from SGT Reagan's Ambien-fueled statement saying that the day I suppressed the enemy sniper who killed CPL Rapavi, I was out of control even though everyone who was there contradicted him as he wasn't even involved in the firefight and was downstairs staffing the radio.

Every time I'd inject material context, they'd do a B-Line and say let's get back on track to the matter at hand to make my first-hand recollection and account of what I could remember feel insane and unwarranted. Then they would say, "No, that can't be true because we have footage of the firefight even though you may not be able to recollect everything. We can help piece it together and take care of the wording."

They would have me initial each structured segment they mandated and reminded me that the investigators were already aware of all the additional events surrounding deployment and the firefight complexity but that they needed to deal with procedures regarding the isolated firefight.

> During the interview, S/PHILLIPS never reported he perceived the IPs as a threat. Exhibit (34) is S/PHILLIPS' sworn statement.
>
> 34. On 31Jan07, NCIS met with S/PHILLIPS. During casual conversation, NCIS inquired if S/PHILLIPS was okay and how he was doing. When asked if he wanted to further discuss the 20Jan07 incident, S/PHILLIPS responded, "What else is there to say?"
> S/PHILLIPS was then asked if he wanted to change or add anything to the statement he provided on 20Jan07; he said he did not. S/PHILLIPS was fingerprinted, photographed and driven back to his command. Exhibit (35) provides details.
>
> 35. On 31Jan07, NCIS contacted SSgt Robin TOWNLEY, G2X, I MEF (FWD) and inquired if any unmanned aerial vehicle (UAV) footage existed for views of the Saqlawiyah, Iraq area on 20Jan07. TOWNLEY advised no
>
> FOR OFFICIAL USE ONLY
> PAGE   14
>
> 21JAN07-24IZ-0015-7HMA   14FEB07
>
> SUBJ: S/PHILLIPS, JONATHAN ANDREW/LCPL USMC
>
> UAV footage existed, exhibit (36) pertains.
>
> 36. NCIS received additional medical reports pertaining to S/PHILLIPS' 27Jan07 visit with Lt Evan ALTMAN, USN, MC, Psychiatrist, exhibit (37) pertains.
>
> 37. LtCol Kenneth M. DETREUX, CO, 2NDBN, 8THMAR, has been briefed on the aforementioned. 2ND, 8THMAR is expected to return to Marine Corps Base (MCB) Camp Lejeune, NC (CLNC) on 14Feb07. This investigation is pending contact with V/HOMADI'S family to discuss exhumation issues, re-contact with the IP witnesses and examination of items seized as evidence.
>
> DISTRIBUTION
> NCISHQ: 0023 (M)
> INFO: 24C/24IZ/ LtCol Kenneth M. DeTreux, CO, 2NDBN, 8THMAR, MCB
>   CLNC (M)

Naval Investigators lie about the existence of drone video footage.

I remember becoming physically exasperated. My blood sugar was crashing dramatically. I was starting to dry heave as I'd been doing for months from combat stress. In several instances, the investigators snapped their fingers to prevent me from dozing off, and the feeling of being subordinately jolted back to the lecture of what did and didn't happen in a firefight behind enemy lines by two investigators who were neither present in the relevant firefight nor personally experienced by any baptismal combat experience was surreal.

I told them that as a lance corporal gunfighter and Automatic Rifleman, I was trained brilliantly by Corporal Nicholas Rapavi to

Chapter 13: Interrogation

respond to enemy ambushes by immediately establishing fire superiority and deterring further enemy aggression by delivering overwhelming violence of action and deferring the rest to leadership. Otherwise, chaos would be multiplied many times over in an already precarious hierarchical and shifting combat dynamic. Corporal Rapavi would train us endlessly back in North Carolina to respond to enemy ambushes methodically so that when the time came, the instinct and protocol were abjectly cerebral and automatic. He would instruct us to break the enemy's spine and push through the kill zone by speed, communication, and overwhelming violence of action. But nothing you say matters when the narrative is preconceived and preordained.

They knew I was crashing from months of excessive caffeine intake and sleep deprivation. I was unable to formulate a statement of events coherently or legibly to their satisfaction. So, they seized the opportunity to draft up a statement on their desktop and said they'd drive me back to my section at South Camp so I could get some sleep once I signed and initialed the typed statement they'd printed off.

When you haven't slept in months, have seen so much unnecessary and inexplicable death, and you're thrown into a room with two seasoned Human Exploitation Team Memberse determined to reach a preordained outcome, it's mental torture and exasperation. Plus, in your head, you're not thinking that any American would ever operate like that. In the end, I remember mentally just throwing my hands up and saying, "What else is there to say?" I meant it.

They acted as if emergency flashing lights were the smoking gun, and they just solved the JFK Conspiracy. No shit, I was there, and it added one more beautiful distraction.

The First General Order

STATEMENT

Place : NCISRA Camp Fallujah, Iraq
Date : January 25, 2007

I, LCpl Jonathan Andrew Phillips, ▓▓▓▓, make the following free and voluntary statement to Special Agent Steven J. Dreiss whom I know to be a Representative of the United States Naval Criminal Investigative Service. I make this statement of my own free will and without any threats made to me or promises extended. I fully understand that this statement is given concerning my knowledge of the death of the Iraqi policeman on 20Jan07.

For identification purposes, I am a white male being 5' 11" in height and weighing approximately 185 lbs. I have black hair and hazel eyes. I was born in Fairfax County, VA on 21Mar87. I enlisted in the USMC on 18Jul05 and went to MCRD Parris Island, SC for training. I subsequently went to Camp Geiger, NC for my infantry training. After Camp Geiger, I was assigned to Golf Company (G CO) Second Battalion (2NDBN), Eighth Marines (8THMAR). I was subsequently deployed with my company to FOB Riviera in Saqlawiyah, Iraq. My duties include QRF, protecting the IP Station and conducting dismounted patrols in the area.

Special Agent Steven Dreiss advised me of my Article 31b rights indicating I was suspected of causing the death of an Iraqi Policeman on 20Jan07. I waived my rights and agreed to be interviewed.

On 20Jan07, I was assigned to the IP Station that sits on ASR Lobster near the intersection of ASR Salmon in Saqlawiyah, Iraq. I just completed my shift that included providing security from the roof area of the IP Station. I'm not sure what time I completed my shift. I went downstairs and to hang out. I think I cleaned my weapon, a M249 SAW, and listened to music. At one point I was in the pantry on the USMC side of the compound; ▓▓▓ was in the pantry with me. At this time we heard an explosion. I'm not sure what time the explosion happened. Soon after the explosion, I heard gunfire and small arms fire (SAF). ▓▓▓ and I immediately ran to our room and grabbed our gear. There were probably other people in the room but I'm not sure who else was in there. ▓▓▓ and I then proceeded to the rooftop of the IP Station. As I was proceeding to the rooftop, I heard a lot of incoming and out going gunfire.

When the whole engagement started all I could think about is my safety and the safety of my Marines. I believe my mindset has been influenced by three traumatic incidents that have affected me deeply. One incident was the deaths of LCpl Johnson, LCpl Hale and Cpl Payne and the injuries of other Marines during a convoy movement on 06Oct06. I was in the HUMMVEE in front of them when an IED blast hit their HUMMVEE. I attempted to assist them and provide first aid. It was one of the most horrific incidents I have ever been a part of. The second incident happened on 18Oct06 when my friend, LCpl Brent Mhuele, was by sniper fire during security halt near the IP Station. I was standing five meters away from Mhuele when he was hit in the right shoulder. I returned fire in the direction of where the sniper fire originated. Mhuele was medically evacuated to the U.S. where he is recuperating. The third incident was the death of my squad leader Cpl Rapavi on Thanksgiving Day 2006. Rapavi was killed by a sniper at the IP Station; I was on post looking right at him when it happened. And most recently, about a week prior to this incident, the IP Station was hit by RPG and gunfire. I was there at the IP Station when it happened and responded to that incident as well. There is also a lot of

Page 1 of 3

NCIS 5580/26 (1/2001)   (Formerly NCISFORM 016/04-81)

NCIS Statement extracted from LCPL Jonathan Phillips (Page 1)

Chapter 13: Interrogation

Continuation of voluntary sworn statement of
LCpl Jonathan Andrew Phillips, ▆▆▆▆▆
on January 25, 2007

talk around the IP Station that some of the IPs cannot be trusted. Because of the events I experienced, I believe I have developed distrust of the Iraqis.

Upon reaching the rooftop, I proceeded to the north post that overlooks ASR Lobster. We were receiving fire from the Mosque area and from some rooftops and tree lines northwest of the IP Station. I could also see gunfire coming from FOB Riviera going towards the tree line area. I later heard that we received fire from a position east of us. ▆▆▆▆▆ was on my right and either ▆▆▆▆▆ was on my left. I think there were eight of us on the roof. I began shooting towards the rooftop and tree line area northwest of my position. I had a night vision scope on my SAW. I had 5.56 rounds. I expended an entire chain of 5.56 rounds during this engagement. After expending all my rounds I reloaded my SAW. I think I fired a couple of more rounds after I reloaded my SAW. I think one out of every five rounds is a tracer round. I'm not sure how long the first engagement lasted. After a short while it stopped.

Shortly after the first engagement, I saw at least two Iraqi police vehicles pull up in front of the IP Station on ASR Lobster. I was able to see that the Iraqi police vehicles had their emergency lights on. Soon after they stopped in front of the IP Station, there was additional gunfire. I was able to see tracer rounds coming from the FOB. The other Marines and soldiers on the rooftop began shooting.

It was at this point something in my mind just snapped. I can't explain the feelings I was experiencing. I felt enraged and wanted revenge for what happened to my fallen comrades. In my mind the IPs were no different than the insurgents. At this point, I aimed my SAW in the direction of the Iraqi Police vehicles and fired some rounds. I think the distance between my position and the Iraqi police vehicles was approximately 30 meters. I don't know how many rounds I fired at the Iraqi Police vehicles. I saw an Iraqi Policeman outside one of the vehicles, aimed at him, and I shot him and he fell. I think I shot him in the arm. I noticed the left side of his body jerked a little bit. I saw him fall and he got back up which surprised me. I believe he was standing near the front of the first vehicle when I shot him. At some point I heard ▆▆▆▆▆ yelling at me to ceasefire because I was firing in the direction of Iraqi Police. I don't recall continuing to fire at the Iraqi police cars after I was told to ceasefire. I made a comment to Parcells like, "They're all Muj," meaning mujadeen. I also made the comments like, "I guess Marines aren't the only ones dying around here," and something about I couldn't help where my red dot goes. I also remember telling ▆▆▆▆▆ that I shot the Iraqi policeman and I believed I hit him in the arm.

After the shooting stopped an IP came upstairs to the roof. I'm not sure what he was saying but it was something about one of the IPs were killed. I remained on the roof until we were told to go down. I'm not sure how long I was on the roof for.

After the engagement, I realized I fucked up and felt terrible about what happened. I approached ▆▆▆▆▆ and asked them not to say anything. I approached him either in the courtyard or in our room. Our rotation was eventually up and I went back to FOB Riviera. Lt BROWNE pulled me aside and he took my weapon away. I was brought to the batalion aboard Camp Fallujah this same night. I am deeply sorry for what I did.

Page 2 of 3

NCIS Statement Extracted from LCPL Jonathan Phillips (Page 2)

The First General Order

MILITARY SUSPECT'S ACKNOWLEDGEMENT AND WAIVER OF RIGHTS

Place: NCISRA Camp Fallujah, Iraq
Date: January 25, 2007 0828

I, LCpl Jonathan Andrew PHILLIPS ███████ ave been advised by Special Agent Steven J. DREISS that I am suspected of causing the ████ of an Iraqi policeman on 20Jan07.

I have also been advised that:

☒ (1) I have the right to remain silent and make no statement at all;
☒ (2) Any statement I make can be used against me in a trial by court-martial or other judicial or administrative proceeding;
☒ (3) I have the right to consult with a lawyer prior to any questioning. This lawyer may be a civilian lawyer retained by me at no cost to the United States, a military lawyer appointed to act as my counsel at no cost to me, or both;
☒ (4) I have the right to have my retained lawyer and/or appointed military lawyer present during this interview; and
☒ (5) I may terminate this interview at any time, for any reason.

☒ I understand my rights as related to me and as set forth above. With that understanding, I have decided that I do not desire to remain silent, consult with a retained or appointed lawyer, or have a lawyer present at this time. I make this decision freely and voluntarily. No threats or promises have been made to me. JAP

Signature: _[signed]_
Date & Time: 0125 0830

Witnessed: _Steven J Dreiss_
Jeff Brockett

NCIS Statement extracted from LCPL Jonathan Phillips (Page 3)

Chapter 13: Interrogation

```
-----Original Message-----
From: Schrantz Capt William J
To: Ralston LtCol Minter B
Sent: Fri Feb 23 07:02:42 2007
Subject: FW: [U] FW: 70402016MI.doc - S/PHILLIPS, JONATHAN ANDREW/LCPL USMC

Sir,

Are you and Col Berger aware of the below NCIS case from Iraq that has been
brought back for adjudication? I am sure you are. COS is informed.

Below is all that I have and I wanted to check with you to see if you could
provide some specifics as RFIs are trickling in: Do you know where the Marine is,
is he headed to PTC, does 2/8 have a hard copy of the investigation from NCIS
yet, etc.

I was about to call 2/8 to ask but wanted to keep you informed. If you are not
familiar with the case and don't know the above do you mind if I call Maj Riordan
directly? I am confident we are going to have to have several conversations over
the next few weeks.

Thanks, Sir.

V/r,
Joe


Subject: 70402016MI.doc - S/PHILLIPS, JONATHAN ANDREW/LCPL USMC

632020  11:56  20070214  IN:SSDEMAIL #38475  OUT:CRFO-IZ-SSD #350



                                                              14FEB07
REPORT OF INVESTIGATION (INTERIM)
                         CONTROL:  21JAN07-24IZ-0015-7HMA
DEATH (II)

S/PHILLIPS, J█████▓REW/LCPL USMC
  M/W/MEE3/S█         /21MAR87/FAIRFAX, VA
  DUSTA: GOLF CO, 2NDBN, 8THMAR
V/█████████████████      IRAQI POLICE
  M/W/FNIZ/N//03MA▓77

COMMAND/SECOND BATTALION, EIGHTH MARINES/12170

MADE AT/24IZ/CAMP FALLUJAH IRAQ/STEVEN J. DREISS, SPECIAL AGENT

EXHIBIT(S)
(1) Statement of Capt Mark BROEKHUIZEN, USMC/21Jan07...(Copy 0023 and
    Command)
(2) IA: Results of interview of IP Mohamed█████████1Jan07...(Copy
    0023 and Command)
(3) IA: Results of interview of IP Namir██████/21Jan07...(Copy
    0023 and Command)
(4) ██ Results of interview of IP Lt Mohama█
    █████/21Jan07...(Copy 0023 and Comm██████
(5) IA: Results of interview of IP Oma█████1Jan07...(Copy
    0023 and Command)

                                  2
```

Remnants of hierarchical collusion including
future Marine Commandant General David Berger

The First General Order

```
-----Original Message-----
From: Schrantz Capt William J
To: Ralston LtCol Minter B
Sent: Fri Feb 23 07:02:42 2007
Subject: FW: [U] FW: 70402016MI.doc - S/PHILLIPS, JONATHAN ANDREW/LCPL USMC

Sir,

Are you and Col Berger aware of the below NCIS case from Iraq that has been
brought back for adjudication? I am sure you are. COS is informed.

Below is all that I have and I wanted to check with you to see if you could
provide some specifics as RPIs are trickling in: Do you know where the Marine is,
is he headed to PTC, does 2/8 have a hard copy of the investigation from NCIS
yet, etc.

I was about to call 2/8 to ask but wanted to keep you informed. If you are not
familiar with the case and don't know the above do you mind if I call Maj Riordan
directly? I am confident we are going to have to have several conversations over
the next few weeks.

Thanks, Sir.

V/r,
Joe


Subject: 70402016MI.doc - S/PHILLIPS, JONATHAN ANDREW/LCPL USMC

632020 11:56 20070214 IN:SSDEMAIL #38475 OUT:CRFO-IZ-SSD #350



REPORT OF INVESTIGATION (INTERIM)                              14FEB07

DEATH (II)                    CONTROL: 21JAN07-24IZ-0015-7HMA

S/PHILLIPS, J█████ ███REW/LCPL USMC
M/W/MEE3/S█████████/21MAR87/FAIRFAX, VA
DUSTA: GOLF CO. 2NDBN. 8THMAR
V/██████████████████████████     IRAQI POLICE
M/W/FNIZ/N//03MAY77

COMMAND/SECOND BATTALION, EIGHTH MARINES/12170

MADE AT/24IZ/CAMP FALLUJAH IRAQ/STEVEN J. DREISS, SPECIAL AGENT

EXHIBIT(S)
(1) Statement of Capt Mark BROEKHUIZEN, USMC/21Jan07...(Copy 0023 and
    Command)
(2) IA: Results of interview of IP Mohamed████████1Jan07...(Copy
    0023 and Command)
(3) IA: Results of interview of IP Namir█████████/21Jan07...(Copy
    0023 and Command)
(4) IA: Results of interview of IP Lt Mohama█████
    █████/21Jan07...(Copy 0023 and Comm████)
(5) IA: Results of interview of IP Oma████████1Jan07...(Copy
    0023 and Command)
```

Remnants of email chain between General Berger and his staff inadvertently turned over on discovery pertaining to the controversial January 20th firefight and as they collude and design LCPL Jonathan Phillips as a fall guy for the trail of negligence and command failure by 2/8 leadership.

Chapter 13: Interrogation

```
Berger Col David H
Subject:            FW: [U] FW: 70402016MI.doc - S/PHILLIPS, JONATHAN ANDREW/LCPL USMC


Colonel Dave Berger
Commanding Officer, 8th Marine Regiment
Cml: ▓▓▓▓▓▓▓▓
DSN: ▓▓▓▓▓▓

This communication may contain individually identifiable information the
disclosure of which, to any person or agency not entitled to receive it, is or
may be prohibited by the Privacy Act, 5 U.S.C. §552a. Improper disclosure of
protected information could result in civil action or criminal prosecution.

-----Original Message-----
From: Schrantz Capt William J
Sent: Friday, February 23, 2007 7:59
To: Berger Col David H
Cc: Jennings Capt Charles D
Subject: FW: [U] FW: 70402016MI.doc - S/PHILLIPS, JONATHAN ANDREW/LCPL USMC

Sir,

I sent the below to LtCol Ralston to just gather a few quick answers to where the
Marine was located and whether a hard copy of NCIS investigation had been
delivered to them. I did email Maj Riordan already and will call later to discuss
with him. Just trying to help navigate this through the early stages. The Senior
Trial Counsel, Maj Cadwalader, is ready to receive the RLS form the CO at any
time. Col Starnes is aware as is MEF SJA. The below information all came from II
MEF (Fwd) via email.

Please let me know if you would like any additional information on this.

V/r,
Capt S

-----Original Message-----
From: Ralston LtCol Minter B
Sent: Friday, February 23, 2007 7:52
To: Schrantz Capt William J
Subject: Re: [U] FW: 70402016MI.doc - S/PHILLIPS, JONATHAN ANDREW/LCPL USMC

Joe,

Request you read Chuck and CO in, then get in touch with Sean.

I'm in Quantico and not much help.

Thanks,
Mint
```

Continued Email chain between General Berger, 2/8 Battalion Executive Officer (Major Riordan) and other officers pertaining to controversial January 20th Firefight as they collude to design LCPL Jonathan Phillips as a fall guy for trail of command failures 2/8 Leadership.

All the statements supported and corroborated that I verbally didn't even know if I was able to get the guy deemed hostile when I engaged because he left my field of fire around the time, I ceased fire. I told NCIS, and they said, "With your aim, no one in your command is going to believe that you missed that guy." These are guys who have absolutely no understanding of warfare, weapon systems, or combat action. We were both speaking foreign languages with no interpreter or translator present. They cherry-picked the words that matched their language, preference, and narrative. These are guys who show up after firefights to dissect, intimidate, and judge those in the firefights with a non-military mind.

Meanwhile . . .

Back at FOB Riviera:

Gunny Rowe once again called a meeting on the lower deck, away from company command, in the same makeshift galley of his infamous "take the shot" decree weeks earlier with all the enlisted after the firefight at the Iraqi Police Compound 70 meters away. Below is a paraphrased excerpt from one of the Marines present:

> "Gunny Rowe called all the enlisted Marines to the lower-level galley. He informed us an Iraqi Policeman had been killed in a recent firefight and that they were blaming the Marines as always. Gunny made it clear that the dynamic had spiraled out of control and been deferred by the Company Commander for the past seven-month deployment. With merely a week remaining, he urged us once again plainly to not hesitate to eliminate the threat should any of the Iraqi Police Force become aggressive and hostile. Gunny, like everyone else, was fully aware of the systemic corruption in the Iraqi Police Force ranks by this point and the complete deference by the Company Commander to deal with the threat and chaos, living up to his reputation as a lazy and incompetent leader."

Chapter 13: Interrogation

Lance Corporal Mathew Frederick

As all this was unfolding, LCL Hirata was the 2/8 Security Commander for the HET Team. They had just gotten back from a mission escorting the newly arrived HET SSGTs to FOB Riviera. He told me that PSD executed the escort mission flawlessly. They left the HET Team and LT Anthony Friel at the IP Station with explicit orders to radio for convoy extraction at FOB Rivera, where HET PSD, along with 2nd Squad, were on QRF because of how valuable HET is to preserving American and Coalition life and how lethal the environment was during the Civil War that was raging as 2/7 unit arrived in the country.

LCPL Jeremy Hirata and his PSD never got the radio call while waiting and standing by geared up in the vehicles from The IP Station awaiting deployment. But 2nd Squad QRF certainly got the radio call.

LT Anthony Friel at IP Station circumvented LCPL Hirata's PSD in typical arrogance since he was the Company Commander's only loyal subordinate. LT Friel radioed the Company Commander at FOB Riviera COC and was cleared to violate Golf Company's established and non-negotiable protocol and walk the HET team back to FOB Riviera on foot through the open marketplace and down Sniper Alley.

They barely even made it outside the IP Station parking lot gate. The HET SSGT was struck once in the vest. No one opened and suppressed the sniper. Everyone was even more terrified after how they treated me on top of seven months of terror campaign by the Golf Company Commander. The sniper instantly reloaded and gunned down the fresh SSGT, ending his life before his war even started. That's why I operated the way I did, just like CPL Rapavi trained me to. The same marketplace CPL Rapavi was gunned down at, and

Nighttime IP Complex Firefight happened, and the spot I'd been engaging thrilled with potential sniper positions.

When you suppress a sniper, it deploys an instantaneous psychological statement and corresponding question: How badly do you want this target that you thought was soft? Bad enough to let a saw gunner take you out? Or do you want to live another day? I was perpetually ready to die right there and then and take the assassin with me. Golf Company Commander had marvelously gotten his wish: a sniper operating in the AO who truly felt confident and impervious to retaliation. Well done, Sir. Now you can explain that to the family of that newly arrived HET SSGT. You're a case study on OCS candidate vetting.

Naval investigators were on site dissecting the firefight from the IP Station. These were the typical events that NCIS was uninterested in since they involved officers. They had more urgent matters, such as putting battle-hardened front-line enlisted Marines in the hot seat, dissecting every split-second decision they made or didn't make under fire, with their only legitimate guilt being they lacked college degrees and the corresponding protection of the collective officer corps. Once again, the incompetent and negligent officer knocked off an SSGT HET operator for no reasonable gain whatsoever, then covered it up, and the Marine Corps told a nice story to his family as they received his flag-draped casket. That SSGT trusted 2/8 and Golf Company leadership to teach him and not lead him into a needless trap. What happened that day was premeditated murder at worst and negligent homicide at best. Clear and simple.

Deployment Ends:

Chapter 13: Interrogation

Memorial Tribute to 2/8 Golf Company Marines
Left To Right:Top To Botoom
CPL Nicholas Rapavi, CPL Bradford Payne, LCPL John Hale,
LCPL Stephen Johnson, LCPL Howard March

CHAPTER 14:
NEW BATTLEFIELD

I arrived home stateside on February 17th, 2007. My parents were waiting for me when I got off the bus. I was scared to see them. I wasn't the same person that looked back over my shoulder when leaving them at the airport seven months prior, nor could I hide the emotion. I spent three days with my parents. I was broken and didn't know what to do. As was the case in Golf Company, it was on me to figure it out and perform. We went to a restaurant to have dinner like many times before, and I kept begging for a shot of alcohol even though the Marines who knew the old me would tell you I was in the minority of people who didn't drink. I'd never known what a panic attack was and didn't even know that's what I was experiencing. At the hotel, I woke up the next morning in the bathtub with a blanket—my brain had needed the border of a wall for security that we were used to sleeping with or being on a machine gun on the rooftop with a bunker bucket seat. Being back home now didn't make sense. And after that interrogation, I honestly didn't know what to think about anything or what I even believed. Having operated as a squad and platoon for seven months, I was now cut off, and my perimeter was compromised.

My parents departed back to Massachusetts. They said they were going to buy me a plane ticket so I could fly home on leave the following week. I was subsequently placed on restriction by Company Commander, who told me that no matter what the investigation yielded, I would be allowed to go home on leave and that my distinction more than warranted it. His words of affirmation were neither needed nor embraced. SSGT Rivers knew all too well what a dirtbag the commander was and shot him a look that conveyed how close the commander was to death. His antics had gone too far.

Later That Night

I rested on my barracks with my feet up against the wall, trying to process the past seven months. There was an unforgiving and ominous pounding on the metal door that sounded like thunder because of the flimsy metal. I was summoned to Battalion Headquarters by three enlisted Marine escorts on orders from the Battalion Commander late at night under the cover of darkness. All that was missing were night vision goggles. Just when I thought that war couldn't get more ludicrous and questionable, he called me in and closed the door. He told me that the ground commander had put everyone in a terrible position and that it wasn't my fault. He said it was out of his hands and that he'd "do whatever he could from his end and that he was behind me," but I was being charged with Article 118 (Murder) for the incident in question, and it was "out of my hands and determined many levels above my head." I was being portrayed as a flight risk and maniac after walking free in full compliance for the past three weeks.

I was ordered into pre-trial confinement, though empirically annotated by several officers that I was neither a flight risk nor danger to myself or anyone, according to the Platoon Commander and

Chapter 14: New Battlefield

Medical Officer's attestation. I'd walked freely for the past three weeks at Base Camp overseas and the past three days stateside. The command wanted me roaming free overseas so that the investigative agents could try and dig dirt up on me or hope I'd do something out of character to make them look less guilty. General Berger's own email correspondence indicates they were having "several discussions in the coming weeks." After three days stateside, they isolated me so I couldn't participate in proceedings once the shady, expedited battlefield investigation was concluded. They wanted my mental health to rapidly decline in mandatory solitary confinement and deprived me of mental health care and fresh air so that any resistance or rebuttal would be nothing more than incoherent and optical insubordination. But once again, their hopes failed.

The deployment concluded, and with it, 2/8 Company and Battalion Command Leadership looked up, noticed the rain had stopped, and that there was no need for their umbrella of fire superiority. The asset was now a liability. PTSD, they instantly called it. They had seven months to do so. They got seven months, fast-tracked for promotion, and their choice of luxury duty stations. I got a prison cell with no light and cockroaches. I guess a prison cell was an upgrade. I did a quick inventory: my balls were still attached, which is more than the leadership can claim. I didn't say one word to the Battalion Commander. I did an about-face. It's bad enough being a traitor, but any legitimate leader would've walked the asset he used for seven months to the Brig personally. Instead, he chose to do what 2/8 commanders were well known for by that point: pawning off the dirty work to 19-year-old subordinates so he'd be back home in time for dinner.

Little did they know I come from a pedigree that is well-versed in confronting evil head-on. The confinement order signed by the 2/8 Battalion Commander was clearly written by someone significantly higher in rank and billet per the national security language. Fall guy.

LT Browne and SSGT Rivers ran to Battalion that night and met me as I was leaving the Battalion Commander's office. I gave my flip phone to SSGT and LT and told them to call my mom only if things got bad enough, as she was in remission from cancer at that point and, after a deployment of worrying about me, didn't need any further anxiety.

I never fled from charges, no matter how absurd and disingenuous. No matter how humiliating and anxiety-ridden the campaign waged against me was. The 2/8 Marine escorts tasked with delivering me to Battalion headquarters were abjectly appalled at their assigned task and even offered to look the other way for five minutes should I want to flee to some off-base backwoods haven until the command regained some sense of logic and honor. That's what Marines do. They stick together. They back each other up. They fiercely rush into battle to reinforce their Spartan brethren regardless of the consequences, whether on foreign battlefields or in the halls of the Department of Veterans Affairs, where they're relegated once they're no longer deemed an asset capable of one thing: violent deployment. It's a breed unlike any other. A specific personality profile subset to be recruited, harnessed, and channeled. I had no intention of running like the Company Commander from the matter at hand, no matter how frightened, cut off, and abandoned I felt in that moment.

Chapter 14: New Battlefield

UNITED STATES MARINE CORPS
2D BATTALION, 8TH MARINES
2D MARINE DIVISION
PSC BOX 20104
CAMP LEJEUNE NC 28542-0104

IN REPLY REFER TO:
5811
CO
26 Feb 07

From: Commanding Officer
To: Initial Review Officer, Marine Corps Base, Camp Lejeune, NC

Subj: PRETRIAL CONFINEMENT

Ref: (a) BO 1640.10D
(b) MCM 2005, R.C.M. 305

Encl: (1) NCIS Investigation
(2)
(3)
(4)
(5)
(6) ▒▒▒▒gement of Article 31 Rights by Lance Corporal Jonathan A Phillips
(7) Statement of Lance Corporal Jonathan A Phillips

1. In accordance with references (a) and (b), the following information is furnished in support of my decision to continue pretrial confinement of:

NAME: PHILLIPS, JONATHAN A   SSN: ▒▒▒▒▒   GRADE: E-3
UNIT: COMPANY G, 2D BATTALION, 8TH MARINES   AGE: 19
AVERAGE PRO/CON MARKS: 4.3/4.3   EDUCATION: HS DIPLOMA
AFQT: 31
TIME AND DATE CONFINED: 1850   ON 20070223
MARITAL STATUS: SINGLE   WIFE/CHILDREN IN LOCAL AREA: NO
NUMBER OF CHILDREN: ▒   OFF-DUTY EMPLOYMENT: NONE

2. The named detainee is alleged to have committed the following offense(s):

Charge I.

Viol of Art 118 of the UCMJ (Murder): Lance Corporal Phillips intentionally shot and killed an Iraqi Policeman without proper justification on 20 January 2007 during a firefight with insurgents in Saqlawiyah, Iraq.

Charge II.

Viol of Art 134 of the UCMJ (Reckless Endangerment): Lance Corporal Phillips willfully discharged his M249 with intent to endanger Iraqi Policemen on 20 January 2007 during a firefight with insurgents in Saqlawiyah, Iraq.

3. Basis upon which the named detainee is suspected of having committed the above alleged offense(s): The detainee was confined because of the

National Security Pretrial Confinement Order issued against LCPL Jonathan Phillips (Page One)

The First General Order

Subj: PRETRIAL CONFINEMENT

significant evidence gathered which links him directly to the murder of an Iraqi Policeman. The evidence denotes a willful and gross violation of the standards of conduct expected of any Marine and the evidence also points to the fact that the detainee fully admits to this offense and is a potential danger to society. The evidence considered includes: an investigation conducted by the Naval Criminal Investigative Service (NCIS) regarding the ~~incident in question~~ ▓▓▓▓▓▓▓▓▓▓▓▓▓▓▓▓▓▓▓▓▓▓▓▓▓▓▓▓▓▓▓▓ Lance Corporal Phillips.

    a. The detainee represents a significant risk to all personnel residing in the barracks. The detainee clearly displayed cruel and malicious intent in intentionally murdering an Iraqi Policeman that had not demonstrated any form of hostile action or intent. The detainee cannot be permitted to reside in the barracks because he is a serious threat to the good order, discipline, and safety of the entire Battalion. Lesser forms of restraint are inadequate due to the violent nature of the offenses of which he is accused. The seriousness of the crime the detainee is accused of committing elevates the risk of him fleeing to avoid trial and punishment. This incident has the potential to affect United States foreign relations and the reputation of the Marine Corps and nation as a whole. It is in the best interest of the government to retain the named detainee in pre-trial confinement in order to ensure his appearance at trial.

    b. The detainee made a written statement to NCIS and admitted to shooting the Iraqi Policeman. He has made no attempt to deny these allegations in his statement and has exhibited signs of instability. His loss of control makes him a potential danger to those around him and proves lesser forms of restraint inadequate to ensure his appearance in court.

    c. The detainee is accused of crimes for which he could be confined for a great time. There is limited risk that his pre-trial confinement will exceed the potential sentence he could be adjudicated at a General or Special Court Martial.

4. In making my decision, I also considered the following matters in extenuation and mitigation. It is my opinion that a lesser form of pretrial restraint is inadequate and continued pretrial confinement is necessary:

    a. To ensure the presence of the accused at trial because:

        i. The detainee is accused of a violent crime of an extremely sensitive nature and it is in the best interest of the Government to ensure he stands trial.

        ii. To prevent the detainee from committing serious criminal misconduct because of the detainee's previous alleged violent actions and tendency to act on impulse. For these reasons the detainee poses a serious risk to the safety of himself and others.

6. The point of contact at this command is Major Riordan at 451-7831.

K. M. DETREUX

National Security Pretrial Confinement Order issued against LCPL Jonathan Phillips (Page Two)

Chapter 14: New Battlefield

LCPL Jonathan Phillips being processed in cage after being escorted to pretrial confinement under National Security

I was escorted by the three Marines to the Brig on base. I spent an hour standing in the external intake dog cage, looking out into the darkness, shivering, and holding the fence because I refused to strip down naked and be stripped of my remaining dignity. It was about to be a one-sided fight. The junior guard realized I wasn't fucking around, and the more he yelled, the more I gazed into the dark forest contemplating if he was worth a second murder charge, this one legitimate. Soon after, Duty Brig Supervisor (DBS) Staff SGT Sullivan broke up what was rapidly devolving into a hand-to-hand situation and deduced I didn't meet the typical prisoner personality profile. I would've killed anyone trying to strip me naked in a dog cage. Some things are just worth fighting for.

Staff SGT Sullivan is a great man. Later in my sentence, he compassionately confided in me that with every fiber of his being, he just knew it made no sense that I was sent to the big that night. Energy doesn't lie.

Chapter 14: New Battlefield

For My Attorney [NCIS Interview]

When verbally going through what happened with NCIS prior to the agents typing their version up and having me sign it I repeatedly stated that I did not intentionally shoot that man, but they refused to accept that as my statement. They said that based on the other statements previously made ~~scribbled~~ and throughouly reviewing my medical records, as well as video footage that they knew what really happened even if I was confused. I remember them saying that my command would never believe me because I was such a good shot. The kept sympathysing with me because of what they read in my medical records, and ~~scribbled~~ that I didnt deserve to be put through any more pain. They kept saying if in my shoes they would have reacted the same exact way and that I was a good marine doing my duty. They said in order for me to help myself I needed to cooperate, one of the first things they said while urging me to waive my right to an attorney being present during the interview it would just make things more complicated and messy.

Handwritten notes by LCPL Jonathan Phillips pertaining to battlefield interrogation trailer.

② They kept saying "Jon we believe the man you shot was ⊗ in your mind an insurgent, a mousie not a police officer" and constantly reminded me of comments that I had reportedly made to prove that theory and that I felt like I was protecting my fellow marines. Those two men bullied me into that statement by messing with my mind and emotions. Even though I knew I did not mean to shoot that man I was terrified and in a vulnerable/paranoid state which proved perfect for the two Special Agents. At the time I did not realize how much they took advantage of me and exactly how they worded the statement I signed. Those two agents did not have the right to bully me. They kept saying I was a good marine and would have done the same thing brainwashing me into their mindset. The Agents did not allow me to write my version of what happened but pick and choosed from my confused word and then typed it up. They kept saying not to worry about it that it was "just a tiny bump in the road for my life" and that I would finally be able to move on and go home. I remember them constantly offering me food,

Handwritten Notes by LCPL Jonathan Phillips pertaining to NCIS Battlefield Interrogation and coercive tactics.

Chapter 14: New Battlefield

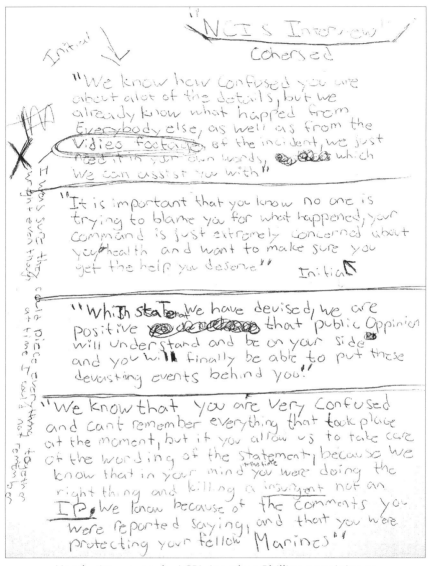

Handwritten notes by LCPL Jonathan Phillips pertaining to NCIS Battlefield Interrogation and NCIS Coercive tactics

Experienced Brig guards know who fits the criminal profile and who doesn't. Even in chains and mentally and physically wounded, I was professionally subordinate. But there were certain things no one was ever going to do to me and get away with. It was the same battle-

The First General Order

field mindset that was applicable a week earlier. I was then processed by the Brig Medical Officer.

CHRONOLOGICAL RECORD OF MEDICAL CARE

Division Psychiatry, 2d MARDIV, II MEF

Date: 02 MAR 07

This 19 y.o. Stude / Marine with 1 yrs. and 8 mos. of active duty stationed at Camp Lejeune. He was seen for a psychiatric evaluation on 27 JAN 07. He was referred by Battalion Aid Station Medical Officer for further evaluation of PTSD

On interview (done on a voluntary basis), the patient verbalized his understanding that he was referred for mental health evaluation because At brig for 7 days, 2° to Alligations of manslaughter for when a Iraqi Police officer was shot. Pt very depressed, nightmares (3 Fellow Marines died in IED blast in front of pt) — other deaths also. Hypervigilant, Jumpy, irritable, Avoidance, Ø Psychosis, Ø Manic sx, Ø Genl worries, Ø Obsessive qualities.

Side notes:
- Tob: Ø
- S: ⊕ 3-5 hrs
- I: ⊕ ↓
- C: ⊕ Hopeless/Helpless
- E: ⊕ ↓ depressed
- C: ⊕ ↓
- A: 2-3 meals
- PC: Ø
- SQ/SI/HI: Ø
- A/VH: Ø

Prior tmpt those Depakote Risperdal &

MEDICAL HX: Ø
MEDICATION ALLERGIES: PCN
MEDS/SUPPLEMENTS: Ø

ALC/DRUGS: The patient denied a history of drug or alcohol abuse. There is/is not a family history of alcoholism/addiction. (1) Pattern of substance use resulted in failure to fulfill work/school/home roles? Yes/No (2) Patterns of substance use in physically hazardous situation? Yes/No (3) Pattern of recurrent alcohol-related legal problems? Yes/No (4) Pattern of substance use despite its causing worsening interpersonal relationships? Yes/No [Substance Abuse: one or more criteria in past 12 months-------- (1) Tolerance? Yes/No (2) Withdrawal symptoms? Yes/No (3) Tried to cut down but couldn't? Yes/No (4) Preoccupied with finding next drink? Yes/No [Substance Dependence: three or more criteria met in past 12 months]. -------- Prior treatment for substance use? Yes/No
He has/has not used illicit drugs. Ø

Motor Tic — Eye blink blinking & Mouth

PAST PSYCH. HX: The patient grew up in the setting in a/an intact/single parent/disrupted by divorce family. He was reared mostly by his Mother. Family history of mental illness was denied/included N/A marks. He related with his teachers without/with some/with considerable difficulty. He never ran away/ran away from home Ø times. He was/was never expelled/suspended from school for various reasons. He admitted to/denied a history of (please circle): nail biting, frequent fighting, stealing, reckless driving, fire setting. Police record is denied/included charges for school problems / domestic problems. The patient is not/is married and has Ø children. Marital adjustment was described as N/A
He enlisted in the Marines/Navy because I wanted to serve my country.

PATIENT'S NAME: Phillips, Jonathan A.
RELATIONSHIP TO SPONSOR: SELF
SPONSOR'S NAME: SELF
DEPART./SERVICE: DOD/USMC
SSN/IDENTIFICATION NO: 20/031-94-2666
SEX: MALE
STATUS: AD
RANK/GRADE: LCPL
ORGANIZATION: 2/8
DATE OF BIRTH: 21 MAR 87

Pre-Trial Confinement Medical Evaluation
after being processed in external cage.

Chapter 14: New Battlefield

I was in shock at what was happening. After everything on deployment, I was being hung out to dry, and even the Brig intake officers were suspicious. The Brig Medical Officer notated all my health issues, including hypervigilance, depression, tics, and insomnia, and highlighted zero presence of psychosis or mania, which was once again evidence that I was telling the truth. My mind started to shut down, like a safety mechanism or surge protector. It was like after the bridge ambush, trying its best to biologically protect itself from a system that was dishonoring the sacred nature of the Fifth General Order. There was no honor in what they were doing. It's important to emphasize that the Brig intake medical evaluation below is like the physical condition I was in during battlefield interrogation by federal agents, which was why they intentionally chose not to record the interrogation with even a tape recorder.

It was pure humiliation. I thought about my sick mom who waited seven months, not sleeping, waiting to know if I'd be killed, wounded, or make it back home to her as she watched the news of the all-out Civil War that initiated during our deployment. Now, I was being strip-searched, denigrated, and placed in a 5 by 8 cell alone with all the demons from deployment. It was tragic for the Fifth General Order. Because I was still experiencing insomnia, the first thing I did, being confined to my cell, was notate everything methodically that I could recall from the interrogation so that it was fresh.

The First General Order

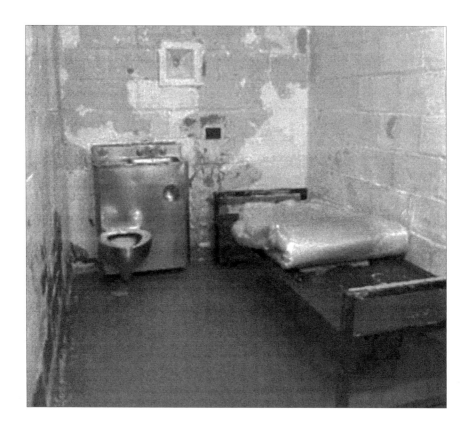

Chapter 14: New Battlefield

Pre Trial-Confinement Cell Recreation

I was now the enemy. I was placed on Maximum Security status. This meant C Row with no light. I'll never forget the sound and sight of the cell door in solitary confinement clinking shutt. There was nothing to separate time or space. No fresh air, ventilation, or heat. Backed up raw sewage from rows and rows of solitary confinement.

The First General Order

To shower, I had to be handcuffed like a serial killer and placed in a 3-foot by 6-foot dog cage with a pressure washer nozzle akin to a firehose. Water would go from burning hot to freezing cold. Anytime they escorted me from my cell, I was chained up in full shackles from head to toe and forced to waddle like a penguin. They wanted me to suffer and deteriorate. Chaplain Burns came to visit from the unit and was appalled at the treatment by the Navy and Marine Corps.

Mice would crawl over me. Cockroaches were everywhere because of how old and decrepit the Brig was, just like the infamous Camp Lejeune contaminated water system on base. My T-shirt would fall to the ground inadvertently as I turned over, tossing and turning. As it hit the floor, the ground would shift from the scattering army of cockroaches. I would wake up with a mouse on my chest, and after calming myself after days of this shock, I realized we were comrades on a battlefield. We were both considered vermin. I would save pieces of a PB&J Sandwich and feed them. I figured it would keep them from biting my chest while I was asleep, as was the case a couple of times. In my mind, I thought they and their rat counterparts would combat the cockroaches. It was time to pick a side and win at all costs. I saw more victory in that cell than in seven months of the bloodiest campaigns of the Iraq war.

Two to three days after arriving in solitary and experiencing a new level of shock, I was in delirium and dissociation, and my brain began to go offline from medication and lack of fresh air and sunlight. At this point, I was taken and given an official 706 Legal Competency evaluation by Naval Doctors. I didn't know what that even was. The Brig Medical Officer notated the severity of my cognitive health, and that was the condition I was in when sent before the 706 Board without representation. My statement to them made even less sense than the original investigative statement except for the migraine and vision deficit admissions during the firefight from all the Bright lights, interference, and complexity of the nighttime ambush. LT Commander Langensfeld was an exceptional leader and psychologist who administered the 706 board. He could instantly tell something was off as he tried to talk to me and look at the file and charges 2/8 and JAG had forwarded to him. I remember him asking me if I knew what was happening, and I said no, that I was simply escorted to his office without any explanation.

He got visibly upset and went a short distance across the hall to his boss's office, a civilian defense contractor with white hair. I believe his name may've been Dr. Coffey. I could hear the argument from across the hall no more than ten yards away. He was yelling at his superior, saying, "This isn't right, Sir! This kid has rights! He barely even knows where he is!" I hadn't even been assigned a military lawyer even though the command all along knew how incapacitated I was, nor did anyone tell me anything, which, in the minds of the guilty commanders, seemed to be working flawlessly. Dr. Lengensfield would not be the last Navy doctor who would be disgusted and outraged at how I was being treated.

Days later, I was languishing in a cell mid-way down C-Row, which had no ambient light and was cut off from the outside world. The words echoed down the corridor emanating from the guard at the end: Attention on Deck! I stood there in my Brig-issued boxers for about a minute, not knowing who was en route or which cell they were en route to. Fortunately for me, I had the luxury of a visitor from the outside world. Unfortunately, it was Golf Company Commander Mark Broekhuizen, wasting no time to be the first weasel, as always, to control the flow of information.

The First General Order

With his voice lowered towards the bars, he tried to convince me not to publicize sensitive matters from deployment or open my mouth during the legal process, claiming it would put Marines deployed at risk and there were sensitive matters involving national security at stake but wouldn't expound. I thought to myself: Your command leadership is a national security issue. He said he'd consulted with 2/8 JAG Rep and they both agreed that the battlefield-coerced confession was laughable. He said they'd also agreed that nothing beyond the rooftop in question had any material relevance to the current matter at hand. I stood subordinately at attention, mentally in shock at the arrogance. He said, "I know I told you, no matter what happened with the investigation, you would be given full leave to go home and visit your family. It was out of my hands…that's my bad," like he had inadvertently cut me in the chow line. He came close to the cell bars so no one else could hear, and I smelled the same alcoholic stench as I had on the smoke deck at FOB Riviera. This guy is a class act. His face was also droopy, as if his spirit had been leaving him for months, and the only thing standing in the way was a pulse.

I soon realized he'd made that disingenuous promise so that I would be off-guard. He knew if I went home on leave and got some rest, I'd be able to mount a viable defense. He told me I was a great Marine, and after talking to the Battalion JAG rep, they needed me to "take one for the team," but that he'd be defending me with the truth behind the scenes on his end and to let him deal with setting the record straight. That was the last time I ever saw the jackal again. He was an absolute drunk and a coward.

The General's internal emails from overseas as Regimental Combat Team Commander show that he and the prosecutor and Battalion Executive Commander all knew about their plan to charge me and

Chapter 14: New Battlefield

were colluding, yet it took weeks after being thrown in solitary confinement to even get a JAG lawyer assigned to my case. They had me isolated as a soft target.

LT Browne came to see me every night. Gunny Rowe came and told me not to lower my head for the disgusting command. And VPL Sellers came once with Gunny Rowe and made the Battalion command allow him to be there for van escort when they took me to 706 Naval Board in full shackles, along with Matt and two other top-tier NCOs. My parents came, along with Aunt Sheila and Uncle Charles. SGT Reagan never once showed up, even though he lived in NC.

> "He didn't have a pillow. He was being given two meals a day, tops. He was on medication. He looked exhausted. He wasn't being taken care of. The accommodations were horrendous. When I went to see him, he had to stick his hands through the bars so they could handcuff him, bring his hands back into the bars, clip himself, and be handcuffed to his belt, like this guy is Jeffrey Dahmer of something. They would open the cell and put me in a little locked room to meet with him. He looked down, just drained, broken. Restrained, broken. Completely broken. I had a lot of different emotions. I was incredibly pissed off. Here is a Marine who just spent seven months in the most austere conditions imaginable, and he's greeted by being handcuffed and taken to military prison. That is not how you treat heroes."
>
> Marine LT Cameron Browne

Weeks later, my mother called my barracks roommate and said they hadn't heard from me in days since departing base when they came to visit to see me get off the bus. I wasn't even allowed to use the phone in the Brig or afforded one phone call at the time. It was national security language. I was abjectly isolated and cut off from the world. Flawless execution. If not for LT Browne and Gunny Rowe threatening to raise alarm bells, I'd have had zero visitors and not even a JAG rep until he eventually showed up, even though the emails blatantly indicate that the General, prosecutor, and Judge Advocate General had the case for three weeks by this point. Three weeks to plot their escape and abdication. I'd previously told her I'd be coming home on leave a week after they headed back home from the homecoming ceremony.

My barracks roommate in H&S Company told my mom, "You didn't hear…something happened…some men came to take him late one night under orders to escort him, and he's in the Brig. I haven't seen him since, and I've asked around. No one knows what to say. They won't tell anyone anything. Phillips saw more combat than anyone in the Battalion, and now they're doing this to him after he stayed in the fight for the entire deployment. When they took him away, he was exhausted in every way from dealing with these people. The entire Battalion knew the rumors about how horrendous Golf Company's command leadership was."

My dad called the unit after my terminally ill mother heard that news. My dad got on the phone immediately after being told I was charged with murder and retained civilian legal defense to figure out what was going on. My mom, dad, Aunt Sheila, and Uncle Charles were on the next plane to base. My mother and father's first stop was the office of the 2/8 Battalion Commander.

Stellar gunfighter SSGT Rivers had been in contact with my extraordinary Platoon Commander. SSGT Rivers had my old school

Chapter 14: New Battlefield

flip phone that my roommate gave him when I was taken. He knew something was up because months earlier, the Company Commander had ruined his career and deprived Gold Company Enlisted Marines and Sailors of one more of our finest senior Staff NCOs.

My barracks roommate went and grabbed SSGT Rivers, who at once called LT Browne. They immediately called my parents. They and LT Browne immediately made plans to meet, along with my Aunt Sheila and Uncle Charles, outside the base's seven-day convenience store exchange. When they met up, my parents told me LT Browne was in tears. He tried his best to give them a synopsis of deployment and what he currently knew, which was very little because he was realizing the Company and Battalion Commanders had intentionally kept him out of the loop and flow-of-information pipeline so that he couldn't set the factual record straight at any point.

The Company Commander knew exactly what he was doing. They were trying to figure out how to isolate the one honorable and masculine wrench wedged in their socket of depravity. But he wouldn't budge.

Combat was arduous enough, but I was liquidated when vulnerable and malleable and mentally called it quits in solitary at that point. I just sat there looking out at the bars. Then, two variables stood in the command's path that they could've never seen coming—two steadfast and capable parents, my Aunt Sheila and Uncle Charles, along with an honorable officer, showed up and took my hand. It's not flattering for me to admit, but it's God's Honest truth. The Department of Defense went into full-fledged panic mode. There's one thing the Department of Defense and I agree on unequivocally: this was the height of friendly fire for sure. Because of that, we were on the same page.

I never talked about my family. I barely ever called home to my family. No one even knew my mom had cancer. I never sought sympathy. CPL Rapavi was the only one who knew anything about my parents. That's why the command had no idea that my family would come to reinforce the perimeter. None of the other Marines in Golf Company's parents would have afforded a $200,000 price tag to protect their child.

That's what Golf Company Leadership were banking on to cover their tracks. They thought they were setting up a hasty ambush. One of the reasons I didn't call home on deployment was because my mom was in remission from cancer, and I wasn't going to put added stress on her. Especially if I didn't think I could be strong during the call, which became impossible. The other reason was I found it increasingly arduous to compartmentalize what was going on in Golf Company while thinking about who the next memorial service would be and what was going on back home stateside. There was no margin for error. Every Marine had to balance two jobs by this point: theirs and that of the Company Commander.

My parents' next stop was 2/8 Battalion Commander Kenneth Detreux's office. Up until this point, the 2/8 leadership or convening authority had no idea that my father was the current Director of Global Security for the Bose Corporation, a former Major in the Judge Advocate General, a former FBI Agent, and a former Department of Defense employee. That's when the Department of the Navy and Marine Corps went into panic mode because they knew the facts from the start, but suddenly, I wasn't the soft target and easy meal they'd factored in. My father and mother went to the Battalion Commander's office. They inquired and professionally demanded answers following their intimate conversations with LT Browne. The

Chapter 14: New Battlefield

Battalion Commander went on to say, "I feel terrible…it's like one of my children is in prison."

He then went on to say, "We've learned much about this situation for future purposes." My father wasn't an idiot. He held the commander's feet to the fire and asked him what he was going to do to reconcile the record. When my dad wouldn't back down, the commander said, "You got to drop this, Mr. Phillips…I mean, how far are you willing to take this?" My father responded, "I'll take this all the way to Washington, D.C."

My father then informed the sheepish officer that he had just retained one of the best private defense attorneys infamous for defending a litany of other service members who the military had tried to railroad, including Marine Officers and Green Berets, and informed him that he was already in contact with LT Browne my Platoon Commander. That changed the commander's demeanor and tone right away. Before leaving, the commander had the audacity to turn and say, "We've learned a lot from this for the future," as if that was going to quell my dad. My dad wasn't some wounded, vulnerable lance corporal. The Commander was accustomed to manipulating and railroading teenagers with absurd lines of feigned sympathy. Translation: "We've learned how to avoid responsibility even further in the future and use young men without anyone the wiser." A conciliatory statement posed like only a coward accustomed to deploying and discarding pawns would propose.

After leaving that office, the Department of the Navy depressed the clutch and shifted into higher gear of panic mode, trying to put as much distance between them and the facts while looking anxiously in the rear-view mirror. But not even a Ferrari was fast enough to cover up their empirical guilt and trail of lies, omissions, and contradictions.

That was the meeting that sent the United States Marine Corps into a frenzy. The Battalion Commander's Office Commander had used an asset and now thought he was going to discard me with no one the wiser. These are the lies these types of people tell behind the scenes. They abdicate moral and ethical responsibility in secret, turn around in front of the scenes, and lecture everyone on espoused virtues like honor, integrity, and accepting responsibility for one's actions. They're the type of people who pray in the pews only to run over grandma speeding out of the church parking lot to beat the melee.

Each night after heading home from duties at Division, LT Browne would come and sit at my dark cell for an hour on top of his hectic position at division as adjutant and in addition to what he was dealing with mentally and physically from the battlefield. After about two weeks of solitary degradation, one night, he reached his tolerance threshold. He confided in me his utter contempt: "You're not going to want to hear this, but from what I'm seeing and hearing, I think they're legitimately hoping you'll do something really stupid and make their job really easy." He was referring to physically falling on my sword. But this wasn't combat, and I didn't have a frag grenade. Even if I did, I would've tossed it in the distance. In fact, the decision to absolve Company Commander Mark B had already been made all the way to the Pentagon. They were never going to let me leave the Brig alive. Dead men tell no secrets. The devil hides in the details, and these people are evil. Below is the official pretrial confinement order. You'll notice the language towards the bottom and the fact that they had already made up their minds about who was to fall involuntarily on their sword.

CHAPTER 15:
BEST LAID PLANS

Things were rapidly indicating the convening authority was in a frenzy because not only were my parents not who they thought they were, but LT Browne wasn't backing down in his honor, integrity, and fortitude. No other Golf Company's family could afford to retain top-tier civilian counsel or even know where to start when confronted with such treatment. Command was baking in that.

Along with my mother and father, LT Browne went to war with the Pentagon. LT Browne is a consummate guardian angel. He was the only reason the 2nd Platoon survived the Civil War in the Sunni Triangle. Suddenly, things got increasingly bizarre in the military hierarchy. JAG Major said he'd never seen this type of expedited deal and then asked me, "What the fuck went on over there?" He was referring to the Pre Trial-Agreement (PTA) proposal that had just been sent down the ladder all the way from the top, pre-signed with the division commander and future Marine Corps Commandant, General David Berger. No negotiation. No chance to look it over. No other signatures. The moment they realized who my family was, on top of LT Browne being my Platoon Commander personally briefing the General on what did and didn't happen, the General downgraded the defamatory charges from murder to voluntary manslaughter, already declaring the battlefield investigation was prejudicial and repulsive and invalidating the malicious statement by SGT Reagan. The statement made no sense because he retained me in his squad, deployed me at every juncture, and refused to drop me or reassign me. He falsely labeled me as psychotic, though no other officer or Staff NCO ever reported anything less than complete subordination, even through numerous psychological evaluations.

I was ordered into pre-trial solitary confinement under the signature of the Battalion Commander because they thought I was a soft target. I'd never once talked about my family to anyone. I put my time in and sought and absorbed mentorship. I never gave the impression of white-collar pedigree, always went where I was told, and performed whatever duty was asked of me as I had been raised. We had a job to do regardless of how murky and chummed the waters were. The Pentagon thought they'd hatched the perfect scapegoat to cover up 2/8 Battalion and Golf Company Command Leadership, which had exposed the Pentagon and the Bush Administration to liability amid political discomfort with the losing war.

Considering the "extenuating" circumstances, the General proposed that I serve a 24-month sentence (at the max), allowing them to cover up the scandal. I would receive a full, honorable discharge and medical retirement. He made it clear—unnecessarily so—that it related to the deeper scandal at the heart of command-level failure. He also gave the JAG defense team and prosecutor the impression that there was considerable room to further reduce the sentence. By this juncture, the facts were rapidly being investigated and trickling in as too many events under the leadership of Golf Company Commander Mark Broekhuizen.

The shark frenzy was only getting started since Golf Company Commander and Battalion Commander had chummed the water,

Chapter 15: Best Laid Plans

forcing a feeding frenzy for everyone upstream. Suddenly, General Berger chose a young officer from thousands of potential candidates to be his personal adjutant and aide de camp. That man was LT Cameron Ross Browne. My Platoon Commander. I should've realized that it wasn't a coincidence, but at the time, solitary confinement and JAG persecution had taken a toll on top of battlefield and psychological interrogation overseas. The message was clear: LT Browne was off limits to anyone in the Department of Navy and Marine Corps. They knew that LT Browne would testify to everything and go head-to-head with anyone trying to scapegoat in a campaign to absolve 2/8 Battalion leadership and Golf Company Commander. They now realized there was no way to act like the coerced confession was in any way legitimate.

Even Saddam Hussein's interrogation was recorded every step of the way. Substantiation. Credibility. LT Browne made it clear that the division was taking decree from the Pentagon and the Department of the Navy. I was treated lower than Saddam in interrogation. But we were about to share the same fate if evil had its way.

General David Berger would go on to climb the hierarchical ladder and became the 38th Marine Corps Commandant. He was intimately briefed on everything that happened and didn't happen on that deployment relative to commanders and me because the General made LT Browne his personal adjutant, and he relayed everything tactfully. There was a zero plausible deniability factor. My Platoon Commander is one of the most honorable men I know and a blood brother. General Berger also stood by, actively or passively, as the 2/8 Battalion Commander was fast-tracked for full-bird colonel and didn't so much as reprimand Company Commander or Battalion Executive Officer.

The First General Order

General Berger had allowed the narrative that I was a cold-blooded murderer, a danger to society, and a flight risk who intended to crush my mental health to be signed off before fully investigating the situation. The General and prosecutor behind the scenes would acknowledge how salacious the accusatory campaign was against me, inconsistent with the facts. Thirty-eight days after sending me to solitary, in the words of my Platoon Commander, "like I was Jeffrey Dahmer or something," and labeling me a danger to fellow Marines and a flight risk, he released me from confinement to roam free just like I'd been doing for the entire investigation and deployment.

While in pre-trial confinement, the command made it all but impossible for comrades to communicate with me, except for three great Marines who didn't take no for an answer. The Golf Company Commander and Battalion Leadership were doing their best to isolate me from everyone and portray me as a cold-blooded murderer to cover for their crimes of treason and endless dereliction of duty. CPL Sellers was one of my team leaders overseas and an absolute lion in every sense of the word. Being a turret gunner in his gun truck team was an absolute honor. He was a true leader and gunfighter. If Gunny Rowe hadn't agreed to sneak him in the Brig, he would've attached a claymore to the front gate, tossed grenades and smoke canisters, and cleared the structure within minutes before finding my cell. A violent man in the best sense of the word.

Open Bird Cage: Released from Pre-Trial Confinement

The 2nd Marine Division wanted to court martial the Company Commander for the fiasco he set in motion. General Berger completely invalidated SGT Reagan's malicious drug-induced and sleep-deprived statement when releasing me from pre-trial confinement, dispelling all defamatory accusations and false narratives that I was psychotic at any point or in any way. Injured, sure. Psychotic, absolutely not. But psychosis served as a great pretext to offload negligence and many events that happened on deployment.

After being thrown in the Brig and then released, I was unable to cope with reality. It wasn't just the physical torment of solitary confinement straight from the battlefield after being exploited for seven months. It was the incongruence and betrayal through the lies that were being told to offset the official record. Nothing made sense after giving everything I had for seven months of deployment and being humiliated in front of my family. I was in such bad shape after solitary confinement that the 2/8 Battalion Medical Officer admitted me to the Naval Psych Ward for the next 90. While there, I was under the protection of an extraordinary Navy doctor, Commander Janet Carlton. Commander Carlton was extremely protective of me and was repulsed by what the Navy and Marine Corps were doing. It was the weight of the world. The Pentagon came down on one person, no matter the facts.

The First General Order

Phillips, Michael

From: Cgittins@▮
Sent: Tuesday, July 03, 2007 9:59 AM
To: george.cadwalader@▮
Cc: Cgittins@▮
Subject: Re: Phillips PTA

George:

Mr. Phillips is not acting for the defense, but he raises interesting issues which you and I have discussed and you supported in terms of the plea offer I submitted.

My client is going to sign the PTA on the table, however, I have no certainty that he is provident.

"Heat of Passion"? That is problematic since my client was not necessarily "angry" and the fear he apprehended was the same fear everyone else fears in a firefight. Wrongful? His position had taken fire in the general direction from which the IPs had come. The guy he shot was wearing a mask covering his face, like many insurgents do and it was at night and a relatively long distance shot.

The difference in theory for the PTA we proposed was that he negligently failed to confirm the target he engaged was hostile resulting in the death of the Iraqi, which eliminates the problems identified above, which are difficult issues for providency. Moreover, even if he makes it through providency, there is no guarantee that the appeals court will buy it given the fact that they had taken fire and were engaged in active combat. I agree that the split second nature of the act has significant meaning, but we interpret it differently.

As for Mr. Phillips, I think the USMC will be hearing a lot from him in the future depending on how his son is treated. I have tried to keep him calm, but he obviously feels strongly enough to write the general without telling me about it. He is a lawyer and a former FBI agent and now corporate lawyer for Bose, so when he speaks, people will listen and if he has issues with how his son was treated by the USMC commanders and doctors in the field, people will listen too. He is not a crack-pot; he is a competent former JAG, attorney and FBI agent knowledgeable in issues of the law.

He has also decided to have an independent review out of his own pocket of the conduct of the doctors decisions to return his son to duty with the clear contra indications that were documented and referenced in both the 706 board and the medical records. But for the Feres doctrine, the docs would likely be on the wrong end of a million dollar lawsuit. This independent review is occurring as we speak. We will present this in E & M and I am sure he'll make use of it in other fora if he thinks his son got a raw deal at the end of the case. Obviously, this was an unfortunate case for LCPL Phillips, but the evidence shows that it was completely avoidable with competent, real, medical evaluation and diagnosis, in theater, not after the fact.

I'll have the signed PTA to you first of next week and we'll see how he does in providency. I agree that the deal is too good to pass up given the discharge protection, but I am not sure I can fit a square peg into a round hole, but will nonetheless try to make it happen.

Charlie Gittins

Attorney & Counselor at Law

Law Offices of Charles W. Gittins, P.C.
P.O. Box 144
Middletown, VA 22645

Remnant of Internal Email between defense and prosector detailing prosecutorial misconduct admitting to lack of providence and colluding to push plea agreement through despite facts and evidence due to scandal.

Chapter 15: Best Laid Plans

> **Phillips, Michael**
>
> **Subject:** FW: Request for Reconsideration
>
> **From:** Phillips, Michael
> **Sent:** Monday, July 02, 2007 10:55 AM
> **To:** 'David.H.Berger@USMC.MIL'
> **Subject:** FW: Request for Reconsideration
>
> Brigadier General Berger,
>
> My wife and I respectfully write this letter to you concerning our son LCpl Jonathan Phillips, a member of the 2/8 who is facing charges of Voluntary Manslaughter while deployed in Iraq on January 20, 2007. You recently rejected a request by Jonathan's defense counsel and supported by the military prosecutor, as part of a plea agreement, to reduce the charges to Negligent Homicide.
>
> We believe that rejection may be partially based upon statements given after the incident by Jonathan to NCIS investigators. We suggest that the statements are inaccurate, do not reflect Jonathan's character and were the result of overaggressive NCIS agents planting their version of facts into a Marine who was mentally unstable at the time and had just experienced a horrible situation. Specifically, the NCIS statements can be interpreted to show that Jonathan intentionally shot the Iraqi Policeman to avenge the death of several of his friends over the previous months. As a former FBI agent, I can well understand NCIS agents aggressively interviewing Jonathan after such an incident. However, this is not the truth; Jonathan did not intend to kill the Iraqi Policeman. It was a tragic accident in battle, significantly amplified by Jonathan's impaired mental condition at the time, as we have outlined below.

Email from Michael Phillips (Father) to Future Marine Commandant General Berger pertaining to vetoing the prosecutor's recommendation first Paragraph] Marine Times Article Continued (Page 3)

During the first week in the hospital, after being released from the Brig and isolated from 2nd Platoon, I was overcome with tears. Under the leadership of Steve Jackson, one of the best NCOS and leaders I've ever known, the 1st Squad came to support and embrace me and make sure I knew that no matter what lies the commander was telling, they were behind from the start and until the end. I was reunited with my former teammates Timothy Derrick and White, one of the sharpest junior Marines in our group. I trusted his character and integrity so much that he was the one I'd leave my death letter with when leaving on operations overseas. The 1st Squad is one of the best squads ever known in a platoon, with complete talent and courage up and down the ranks. The next day, SSGT came to see me with his wife. He was still in absolute outrage and disbelief at what the command was doing, especially after all the carnage we knew the

The First General Order

Company Commander had left in his wake overseas. The 2nd Platoon Marines are absolute lions. We protected each other.

After being briefed by LT Browne, the Marine Corps Hierarchy had no doubt about my character, integrity, and faithful service upholding The Fifth General Order. General Berger, SGT Major Jones, and the leadership at the 2nd Marine Division were verbally and declaratively disgusted on many stratified layers about Golf Company and the investigative campaign. The Department of the Navy thought they were going to abscond accountability and even tried to throw LT Browne, one of the best Platoon Commanders the Marine Corps has produced, under the bus with me. I wasn't going to let that happen. They simply don't understand the Fifth General Order or that it extends both on and off the battlefield and against enemies both foreign and domestic, like the oath we all swore to honor and uphold. General Berger had to appoint LT Browne, his personal adjutant, to send a declarative statement to the Pentagon and Bush Administration that if they pushed much further, after the battlefield decree, they'd passed to maintain political appearances and troop levels, there'd be a military branch mutiny on their hands.

I was the agreed-upon sacrifice that the Navy demanded for a truce and cease-fire. I was the prisoner swap. They were disgusted that Marines were medicated and information was compartmentalized further from their Platoon Commanders. They were also truly horrified that the same Company Commanders then sent those same vulnerable Marines into unrecorded battlefield interrogation chambers without even the courtesy of legal representation and acted oblivious. But when you have a monopoly across the Pacific Avenue and Park Place side of the board, those in power get to rig the game and choose

Chapter 15: Best Laid Plans

who passes go and who doesn't. Even the Battalion commander was forced to admit to my father that they "learned a lot from this" in a desperate attempt to maintain appearances.

The Defense Team was stonewalled from receiving the majority of NCIS enclosures, including all statements made by Navy and Marine Officers. They were listed as "exhibits," and any other mention or reference was completely redacted under national security, just like the pretrial confinement order indicated. The only reason they didn't just take me outside and execute me to cover up their growing scandal was because one lone officer never wavered in setting the disgusting record straight: LT Browne. It got so bad that he had to appoint LT Browne as his personal adjutant as a shot across the bow to the Pentagon.

Two months after leaving the hospital, I was allowed to go home on leave for the first time since before deploying. When I got there, I started having the most debilitating panic attacks because I had become institutionalized in solitary and hospital straight from the battlefield. My brain no longer knew how to do simple things like maintain hygiene. I felt the weight of the world on my shoulders, and no matter what the facts were, they were out for blood to deflect blame. My mom found me at the top of the stairwell at home, just rocking in panic. I was overcome with the fear of being sent back to solitary and the walls closing in. My adrenals were shot. I had nightmares every night that I was being dragged out of bed back to solitary confinement, waking up drenched in sweat and screaming.

LT Browne, always the tactful and honorable officer, only relayed pertinent information to compartmentalize the job of his subordinates. This, along with his honor, ranks high among his greatest assets and strengths. Around this time, he relayed a conversation while traveling with General Berger. He told me they had left their uniforms at home one night and went to grab a drink at a local venue to unwind. He sensed this conversation was coming but didn't want to overstep ever since he was conveniently appointed as adjutant. General Berger turned towards LT and said, "Cam, first and foremost, I need you to know that there are naturally things that I can't share with you and that certain decisions have been made well above my head. That being said…I need to know what the hell happened over there?"

LT Browne proceeded to take the convening authority systematically through everything that happened on that deployment and the overarching and verifiable Company Commander's incompetence from start to finish. He then pleaded with the General to meet with me, see and hear my first-person account, and witness the state of decline I was in at that time. I was deteriorating day by day due to the stress being placed on me by JAG persecution on top of solitary confinement straight from the battlefield after extraordinary combat operational tempo. He told him that if he sat down with me, there'd be no moral or ethical doubt about the cruel and unusual punishment of convicting me of any crime. He told him that if he was going to punish me, the Company Commander, Battalion Medical Officer, Battalion Commander, and Battalion Executive Commander should be sitting in the cells to my left and right.

When LT Browne finished taking the General through the intimate sequence of events, he said the General sat back and said, "Fuck, Cam…"

Around this time, my mom called 2/8 Battalion Aid Station (BAS) and contacted LT Douglas Pugliese with several medical in-

Chapter 15: Best Laid Plans

quiries after having been briefed by LT Browne on the events that took place on deployment. She requested all my medical and psych records. He very politely said he'd start the process. LT Pugliese was a classy, compassionate, and always extremely polite individual from the moment I met him before deployment, regardless of my non-concurrence or the level of medication he was prescribing, both officially and non-officially. That should be stated for the record. I would never defame them, though they told more lies about me than I can count—even if that meant guys like LT Pugliese kept quiet while others like Company Commander, Battalion Commander, and Battalion told the real lies. There'd be no honor in me stooping to their level. Many times, silence and omission are the biggest forms of cowardice and betrayal.

My mom got a call back about an hour later after Company Commander MB had gotten wind of the increasing inquiry by my mom and the civilian defense team, as well as LT Browne's intimate knowledge by this point of what the Navy and Marine Corps were trying to do to me. I got chills down my spine when my sick mom reiterated this story because I remember wanting to break out of the hospital and track down the commander. My mom received a call from Company Commander in what she described as one of the most "terse" and "threatening" conversations she'd ever experienced. The commander said, "If you have any questions, don't ever call the Battalion Medical Officer about a Golf Company Incident and go around me! You call me!" My father called the commander back the moment my mom had relayed the conversation, and the commander instantly reverted to his incompetent bashful self.

My father told him directly, "If you *ever* speak to my wife like that again, let alone after using and discarding my son like the feckless excuse of a man you are…you'll regret it…*Mark*." The Company Commander instantly went into submissive apology and said my mom "misunderstood." Guys like Captain Mark MB are only tough when they're talking to someone they deem vulnerable. That was a grave miscalculation to anyone who knows my mother.

Around this time, the prosecutor, negotiating with defense team, agreed to reduce the charges even more substantially than the General already had based on the salacious campaign of lies that were uncovered to allow the government the ability to save face during the debacle. Three weeks later, General Berger vetoed the deal. He would later admit to LT Browne that the decree was issued well above his head, indicating the Pentagon and the White House. I remember hearing news of that vetoed reduction of charges and, highly medicated from all the stress and torture, went to an even lower point. The Naval staff couldn't get me out of bed for a week. If not for my parents and LT Browne, I would've withered even more like a plant shielded from sunlight. I would've never made it through the hospital. My parents would fly down, and when they left, LT Browne would coordinate and come and spend time with me in the hospital. He demanded that the General let me go on weekend trips with him and his wife, even just to see a movie. I was so broken I didn't even feel comfortable leaving the hospital, which was why he knew I needed to. He knew the threat of institutionalization. They were the same threat that the Commanders had tried to employ to cover up their body bag full of command failures.

General Berger verbally admitted being overruled above his head. I hold him accountable for shuffling my file, allowing me to be de-

Chapter 15: Best Laid Plans

prived of mental health services, and allowing the Department of Defense to twist the facts and portray me as a criminal. If it weren't for my mother, I would've never survived. The fact that I'm even able to coherently tell this story is nothing short of a miraculous Testament to God. They discredited me in every way they could.

At Division, LT Browne also worked side by side under the tutelage of SGT Major Michael Jones, who reported directly to General David Berger, the future Marine Corps Commandant, who was responsible for looking out for the welfare of the enlisted contingent. SGT Major Jones and the young officer developed an unnatural friendship due to what the Pentagon and Bush Administration were trying to do to LT Browne and myself, as well as the tradition and reputation of the United States Marine Corps, all to cover up a bad war that we fought fiercely out of duty, not preference.

LT Browne, on numerous occasions, confided and reminded me that SGT Major Jons is "your biggest fan" after going over all the evidence and that I executed the orders I was given in remarkable fashion, even when wounded and left to fend for myself by ground command. All throughout this period, LT Browne would tactfully relay the intimate conversations between the two, as well as the 2nd Marine Division Gunner. The SGT Major and Division Gunner would hold off-the-books meetings with LT Browne and strategize and recommend what LT Browne could do to interfere with the Pentagon hamstringing General David Berger, the soon-to-be Marine Commandant. LT Browne relayed this to my family and me. The Senior Division personnel even put him in touch with a General with intimate ties to advise him.

CHAPTER 16:
ARTICLE 134

Many people within or outside the military don't understand the unconstitutionality of the Uniformed Code of Military Justice. It's a mechanism of duress that gives the Pentagon carte blanche power regardless of the facts.

Article 134 of the Uniform Code of Military Justice (UCMJ) is often referred to as the "General Article." It is a catch-all provision that addresses a wide range of offenses not specifically covered by other articles in the UCMJ. Article 134 covers three primary categories of offenses:

(1) Disorders and Neglects to the Prejudice of Good Order and Discipline. This includes any behavior or actions that undermine the good order and discipline expected within the armed forces. Examples might include conduct that disrupts unit cohesion or discipline.

(2) Conduct of a Nature to Bring Discredit Upon the Armed Forces. This involves actions that could harm the reputation for integrity of the military in the eyes of the public or other entities. Such conduct could include actions that are disgraceful or morally reprehensible.

(3) Crimes and Offenses Not Capital. This category includes a variety of civilian criminal offenses that are not capital crimes (i.e., crimes punishable by death). This can include offenses such as assault, theft, or fraud if they do not fall under other specific UCMJ articles.

Because of its broad scope, Article 134 is sometimes criticized for being overly vague, but it allows military authorities to prosecute conduct that is considered harmful or detrimental to the military, even if it's not explicitly covered under other articles. It can be used to address a wide array of behaviors, making it a powerful tool for maintaining discipline, order, and appearances within the military.

Even if you fight the main charges and win, the Department of Defense will still find an inferior and unrelated charge to convict you, like conduct unbecoming. These clauses are used to target enlisted, non-college-educated personnel, provide malicious shade for the D.O.D. and Officer Corps as a whole, and ensure what they refer to as continuity under the guise of good order and discipline. This is the article they deploy to force enlisted personnel into pretrial agreements, i.e., plea deals, and demoralize them against fighting the absurd and unjust charges. They know that most of the enlisted service members have been exploited and deployed to the fullest to combat and inhospitable postings and environments. They know that they will need healthcare and rehabilitation for the remainder of their lives because of those contractually demanded occupational hazards and for faithfully honoring the Fifth General Order.

If you don't sign, submit, and indemnify the Pentagon, you end up not only in a horrible military prison but statistically homeless and destitute, overcome with the ravages of military service. The most famous portrayal of Article 134 was depicted in the Navy and

Marine film *A Few Good Men,* where the Marines are acquitted, and the General is exposed for his commands. The two enlisted Marines are still awarded dishonorable discharges and disgraced. The civilian sector is under the impression that if a service member gets awarded a dishonorable discharge, it's because there are bad apples, and this factor is played up immensely in Hollywood depictions to drive the narrative.

This threat of duress is how the Pentagon bullies good service members into unwarranted plea agreements out of fear of their hometown friends and families hearing they were bad apples. The private sector won't even hire you with a less-than-honorable discharge, and that's another way the Pentagon intentionally reinforces this duress clause. These are all reasons why most were more terrified of the court martial than Al Qaeda itself on the battlefield and why Marines were terrified when agents like Steve Driess showed up at FOB Riviera to cover for Company Commanders and Battalion Leadership. People say anything to ensure they can go home and not be implicated.

Night Before Tribunal

The night before the court-martial, I was brought to the JAG office to go over everything with other witnesses. There was laughter down the hall, so we poked our head outside from the defense side and saw Major George Caldwelder (Marine Prosecutor), the Army National Guard witness, and his bodyguard laughing hysterically. This was a serious situation, as I had seven months of hell. However, the National Guard unit never took anything about perimeter security seriously. Around this time, the JAG defense attorney informed me that the prosecutor had met with LCPL Peterman numerous times and had tried to convince him to testify against me and validate the lie that

SGT Reagan had talked about the ambush where CPL Rapavi was killed. LCPL Peterman refused to collaborate, let alone validate a lie.

My defense attorney told me that Peterman had been disgusted by the prosecutor trying to drive that lie about my suppressive fire being anything but lifesaving when he and other Marines had been dragging the mortally wounded Marine. That's the extent to which the convening authority was going to pin this entire case on me. The prosecutor full well knew by this point that not only had it been a malicious lie, but that military intelligence had interrogated the sniper and knew how effective my suppression was. The sniper had been lining up another shot to kill Peterman and the other Marine who had come to rescue the fatally wounded Marine. No other turret gunner down below in the parking lot had a line of sight to suppress the exact area of the sniper. If I had allowed the Company Commander's fear-mongering to paralyze me, there'd be two more dead Marines on the Gold Company memorial. Still, the prosecutor only cared about winning, even at the cost of his soul, and bullied several Marines to falsely validate SGT Reagan's statement to investigators. This is how dirty these military leaders are and how far they'll go to get to manufacture evidence that serves their purpose. Sadistic arrogance personified.

CHAPTER 17:
PUBLIC ENEMY #1

The first part of the court martial centered around providence. The judge needs to determine and be convinced that a criminal act was indeed committed, and that the accused knew what they were doing now. He reviews all the investigative statements and documents before he methodically engages in a line of inquiry with the defendant. He breaks down what transpired to lead to criminal charges and engages in an intimate question-and-answer format without interference from legal representatives to get the accused's version of events and ensure the defendant is under neither duress nor coercion by the convening authority before proceeding to accept a guilty plea and litigation between defense and prosecution by calling witnesses.

The judge knew something was deeply off about these proceedings and made it clear it should've never reached his docket. He was visibly and verbally uncomfortable with the lack of providence from a mental health standpoint but also from the reports detailing the complexity of the night-time enemy engagement in question. He tried his best to review several witness statements as well as the intentional lack of substantiation by investigators for a coerced confession.

I was heavily medicated from combat and the stress the convening authority was putting on my shoulders, along with solitary confinement. I attempted to satisfy the legal threshold, or I stood to forfeit all military benefits and future access to physical and mental health care. As evidenced by the court transcripts, the judge repeatedly and assertively stopped the proceedings several times to address me and then my legal team outside my presence. Then, the judge ordered a recess to discuss issues of competency with litigators.

Each time, the judge and lawyers needed to reduce the firefight complexity to desperately satisfy the providence threshold, which is essentially what the civilian sector calls the burden of proof. The judge and lawyers kept eliminating all combat complexity to the degree that there was practically no firefight by the end of the line of inquiry, and they engaged in linear yay or nay lines of questioning. Providence suddenly became a cropped photograph stripped of all context and high-stakes reality. The prosecutor requested a recess to discuss sensitive matters surrounding providence, and the judge paused proceedings several times and met with the lawyers outside my presence.

>**Prosecutor:** Your honor, may we take a quick recess?
>
>**Military Judge:** We're in recess.
>
>Court Martial recessed at 1017 hours
>
>Court Martial reopened at 1046 hours
>
>**Military Judge:** The court will come to order. All parties present when the court recessed are again present.
>
>**Military Judge:** During the recess, an 802 conference was conducted between trial and defense counsel outside the presence of the accused, wherein counsel brought to my

Chapter 17: Public Enemy #1

attention a number of matters are going to—are anticipated to—would be coming up during the presentencing portion part of this trial that are likely to prompt a reopening of the providence inquiry.

The battlefield investigators were determined to drive the retribution narrative concerning the loss of fellow Marines. They were also determined to portray me as hateful towards the Iraqi Police when, in all reality, there's a difference between hate and universally held reservations about operational security being compromised. Operational Security and Tactics must be universal to be effective. Even as a Lance Corporal, I was taught that by Corporal Rapavi and LT Browne, who were brilliant tacticians.

Several admissions within battlefield statements were suppressed by minimizing and convoluting the actual complexity embedded in the larger text, which clearly gave the full bird colonel pause on top of combat tempo and stress by the time that complex engagement occurred a week before finishing deployment. Among these admissions that NCIS suppressed by embedding them in broader texts even came admissions from Iraqi Policemen themselves:

"When returning to the Iraqi Police Station, an IED exploded near the second vehicle. [Iraqi Policeman #1] drove in the direction of the IP Station. [Iraqi Police vehicle patrol] made an immediate right turn. He stopped, exited the vehicle, and began shooting [North] in the direction of the mosque. When the shooting stopped, all three vehicles drove in the direction of Iraqi Police Compound. I saw occupants of the first vehicle walking toward where the IED exploded to pick up AK-47 magazines when the shooting started again."

[Iraqi Policeman # 2] "When returning to the Iraqi Police Station, an IED exploded near the second vehicle in the patrol. His vehicle made an immediate right turn down a side street. Reported receiving fire from the direction of the mosque and somewhere east of the IP Station. Began firing in the direction of the mosque because that was the direction the other members of the patrol were firing. Once the shooting stopped, [Iraqi Policeman] instructed everyone to withdraw and get to the IP Station."

> **[Iraqi Policeman # 3]** "When the three vehicles were about 500 meters away, an IED went off, and the patrol began receiving Small Arms Fire from behind. After driving another 200 meters, the patrol stopped, got out of the vehicles, and returned fire behind them. [Iraqi Policeman] advised the shooting lasted 10-15 minutes. [Iraqi Policeman] reported the patrol was receiving fire from The IP Station rooftop at this time. [Iraqi Policeman] then radioed the Iraqi Police Station, telling them to stop shooting. Once the shooting stopped, all the policemen returned to their vehicles and began driving in the direction of the Iraqi Police station. [Iraqi Policeman] then looked in his rearview mirror and was able to see someone running and shooting at them. According to [Iraqi Policeman], they also began receiving fire from the roof of the Iraqi Police Station."

[Continued Discrepancies]
The Navy's own extensive RCM 706 Naval Forensic Board, after reviewing all testimony and evidence, noted:

> "It is of the opinion of the board, with medical reasonable certainty, that the accused was suffering from a severe mental disease or defect at the time of the alleged offense.

Chapter 17: Public Enemy #1

I come to this explanation upon review of his reports leading up to the incident, which led to charges against the patient, as well as my interview with LCPL Phillips. It was clear that he was suffering from Post Traumatic Stress Disorder and was beginning to withdraw, as well as experiencing significant depressive symptoms.

(continued)

Using the clinical data, the accused has the following clinical diagnosis: Post Traumatic Stress Disorder as evidenced by hypervigilance, irritability, avoidance, flashbacks, nightmares, and survivor's guilt present for the past five to six months. The patient was also diagnosed with Major Depressive Disorder, recurrent. At the time, the patient endorsed decreased sleep, irritability, hopelessness, low energy, problems with concentration, and poor appetite empirically present for the last month and a half."

"It should also be noted that [fellow Marine] mentioned the Iraqi Police contingent had been fired upon had actually turned around and come towards them, which could have been seen as an aggressive act at the time because they had been hit by an IED; however, at the time Lance Corporal Phillips was unaware that they had been hit by an IED and was unsure of their intentions."

The judge eventually got to the point about intent. By this time, the judge had already paused the proceedings several times and taken recesses to discuss the inappropriate nature of these proceedings.

Me: Sir, when we were engaged in the firefight, he was in the same direction we were being shot from, and he was there, and I lost any anger and control, and I fucked up.

Military Judge: In paragraph 18, you note that at the time you were suspicious of the trustworthiness and the loyalty of the Iraqi Police; is that correct?

Me: Yes, Sir.

Military Judge: So, do I understand then that at that time, you thought that members of the Iraqi Police, if not that persona personally, might be responsible for some of the things that were happening to you and your fellow Marines?

Me: Yes, Sir.

According to statements from several Iraqi Policemen, an insurgent with an AK ran up behind their vehicle and was engaging them on foot at close quarters, which was only one of the dynamic targets within the kill zone. He asked me what my response was regarding the firefight. I looked to my lawyer and randomly said the only thing that I could think of in all the absurdity: "I lost my cool, Sir." What was there to say to the absurdity by this point? Once the judge and legal counsel were able to fit the round peg in the square hole, the litigation commenced with opening arguments and witness testimony, both material and character.

While Marines were testifying to the extent that Lance Corporal Hale had been tortured, a Marine Captain sitting in the courtroom had to stand up and walk outside in tears to get fresh air. By the looks of it, he vomited once outside.

Chapter 17: Public Enemy #1

The defense was only able to call Marines from my squad that were still alive but wounded to testify. All other witnesses were either dead, in the Walter Reed burn center, out of the military, or in California for Combined Arms Training (CAX) preparing for their upcoming redeployment. The prosecution called the Battalion Medical Officer (M.O.), an Army National Guardsman. All from a prosecutor who didn't even believe in the charges or existence of providence as indicated by internal documents that my father prudently retained. Otherwise, there'd be no proof of the convening authority's collusion and undue command influence. My team leader, CPL Neal, though on base, did not attend the court-martial. He had better things to do, like trying to stay awake and not being the only Marine to fall out of combat patrols. For a guy like him, that's a full-time job.

The prosecutor, clear to anyone present, went above and beyond to discredit my character and military service, which completely lacked congruency for someone who'd endorsed a substantial reduction a month previously after General Berger had already substantially reduced the original charges. The message had been clear; the prosecutor had been overruled and told to destroy me. He even blamed me for the violence in the AO. He dug up anything he could from my childhood, no matter how illogical or impossible. It was a scorched earth campaign.

General Berger and the Marine Corps prosecutor had wanted to drop the charges and confinement entirely. He'd quickly learned of what the Golf Company Commander and Medical Officers were prescribing and their trail of negligence and deferential behavior resulting in the reversal of pretrial confinement national security directive on the 38th day after execution, along with the defamatory myth that I was deranged. SGT Reagan's statement was, by his own admission, invalidated, though it served as the bedrock for the entire case being referred by agents for prosecution. He reversed the part about me "being out of control" when responding to the sniper who killed CPL Rapavi and had been in the process of targeting LCPL Peterman and another Marine as they were dragging the wounded Marine to cover. Why SGT Reagan perpetuated that false narrative to investigators when he wasn't even on the rooftop is possibly the product of a controversial hypnotic and memory lapse side effects, further compounded by extensive sleep deprivation and aggressively biased investigators deploying duress against war-weary Marines.

The part about him being emasculated by me and willing to shoot me is compatible with that because I don't know many men, let alone warriors or Marine Squad leaders, who would write and sign such an admission, knowing others would one day see it. If it had been even five percent true, he or the officers would've transferred me out of the squad at the very least and back stateside at most. What the Company Commander and Medical Officer were doing with medication and exploitation and the deferential leadership by the Battalion was conduct unbecoming Marine and Naval Officers, plain and simple. SGT Reagan isn't one to be judged for the stress they put on us and for letting us be interrogated by malicious agents after seven months of hell. Back at Base Camp in Iraq after the interrogation, I walked past SGT Reagan on the dirt road near South Camp, and he walked right past me within ten yards. He didn't recognize or acknowledge me.

Later, when he told me that LT Pugliese had him on the drug as well, I made sense looking inwardly at my withdrawn behavior and the high-stakes nature of firefights, even on a good day with sleep—let alone medicated and thrown to jackals. SGT Reagan was a great squad leader, and like the rest of us, he was placed in an untenable,

Chapter 17: Public Enemy #1

no-win dynamic. He persevered just like the rest of us in his own subjective way, as did I. We all honored the Fifth General Order despite subjective wounds and deteriorating conditions. We all used the tools we were given, which were very few and extremely rusty. We relied on our training and cohesion to survive and complete the progressively abstract mission overseas. The blame rests solely with the Battalion Medical Officer, Golf Company Commander, and sadistic investigators, who intentionally deceived and withheld sensitive information from excellent Platoon Commanders out of emasculation, command greed, and exploitation.

The National Guardsman, who'd been previously laughing hysterically the night prior with a bodyguard, had been struck in the head with an RPG and spent months in a coma. He was called by the prosecutor to the witness stand. It was bizarre testimony from a soldier who was incapacitated and comatose from a head injury, making him a prime malleable witness for the prosecutor to exploit. These are the type of people who were villainizing me and claiming the moral high ground. Upon cross-examination by defense counsel, the soldier was questioned as to the trustworthiness of the Iraqi Police, and he said most of them were, by this time, automatically designated insurgents based on many events and suspicions. That was from a contingent who had barely been there for two months compared to our seven-month deployment, observations, and expertise.

> "Well, the RPG hit me square on the head—well on my helmet. I was dazed before I fell and got shot by a sniper in the side. I was in a coma for a while, and they had to pull out —they had to pull out my skull—they gave me a new one. I had a blood clot in my lung because I was sitting for too long. There were at least three Iraqi

The First General Order

Policemen who could not be trusted. We designated them the Three Stooges because they were too shady. They were always missing when the compound was attacked."

National Guard NCO

Upon examination, the National Guardsman admitted he could not identify me from 15 yards away in the courtroom, though we had been that same distance in the nighttime firefight, and admitted he could not remember me, indicative of his brain injury and the level of chaos in the rooftop nighttime firefight. I easily recognized him. He was also questioned on tips they received about AQI and ISIS moving into the area and the fact that we weren't fighting ordinary insurgents but highly trained sadistic terrorists overrunning the Syrian Border, setting the stage for what we later saw of ISIS overrunning the country within weeks.

Living with Iraqi Police you knew were playing for the other side brought the terror of being captured and tortured to a new level. It was bad enough being on missions and ambushed, but sleeping next to them made quality sleep non-viable and detrimental to operational security. It's important to put the blame on the military prosecutor, judge, and convening authority (General Berger) and not the National Guardsman. He was put in a horrible and isolated outpost overseas where 2/8 Battalion and Golf Company leadership refused to do their job to ensure unit and amalgamated cohesion. They forced him to fly across the country, torturing a semi-comatose wounded service member, disrupting his rehabilitation.

The Bush Administration never lets physical or mental incapacitation stand in its way. It's also worth noting after we left Iraq, the Army National Contingent was overrun at the Iraqi Police Station

Chapter 17: Public Enemy #1

when a suicide vehicle-borne IED (SVBIED) came at the compound from the very avenue of approach that I was suppressing and wiped out the entire compound. It was likely an inside job, combined with the fact that the Army National Guard contingent didn't take fire superiority or battlefield tactics seriously. They were wiped out.

The Prosecution called the Battalion Medical Officer (M.O.). He lied under oath, perpetuating the rumor overseas that I had lied, withheld, and fooled officers by understating my condition at every critical juncture. Detailed Battalion Aid Station (BAS) notes signed and dated by him show the extent of the lies and what they were doing. He also admitted to the JAG Defense Team how many times LT Browne had approached him and all other Company and Battalion Leadership and admitted the "extraordinary" nature of that informative campaign for months on deployment.

> is right". He had tended to minimize symptoms to his COC so as to not appear like he was giving up or otherwise not fully functioning. It was highly recommended that he not go outside the wire at that time. He was not found to be suicidal or homicidal or frankly psychotic or manic. Again it was marked combat operational stress heavy.

Battalion medical Officer LT Douglas Pugliese accusing Lance Corporal Jonathan Phillips of misleading Navy Officers and Marine Company and Battalion Commanders

Defense Counsel: You had LT Browne talk to you on several occasions, correct?

Medical Officer: He did.

Defense Counsel: Did any other Platoon Commander in the Battalion approach you about a Marine under their command?

The First General Order

Medical Officer: No, Sir.

Defense Counsel: So this would be fairly characterized as extraordinary that a Platoon Commander would come to you on at least three occasions to talk about a Marine he doesn't think should be in the field, correct?

Medical Officer: Yes, Sir.

> A   Yes, sir.
> Q   Did you ever go down and talk to the corpsman and say, tell me what you're seeing?
> A   Yes, sir.
> Q   You did?
> A   I spoke to Lieutenant ▓▓ like I said earlier, sir. I spoke to Staff Sergeant Bestman on the same day I spoke to Lieutenant ▓▓. Like I said, Dr. ▓▓ and I lived at OP Riviera. We were there our BAS was at OP Riviera. We took care of Marines who were injured from Golf Company. And in addition to that, sir, Dr. ▓▓ the RCT-5 psychiatrist, did a site visit in early November, where he did a morale and welfare visit, combat operational stress control visit, and he did a written report that he submitted to Lieutenant Colonel ▓▓ on the morale situation there, the fact that Golf Company had taken a lot of casualties. He submitted that report to Lieutenant Colonel ▓▓ so there were multiple opportunities for anybody who had concerns to bring them to us.
> Q   Well my question to you, though, was: You had a report from the corpsman who does have some medical training -- he may not be a doctor, but he does have medical training -- that he had concerns about Lance Corporal Phillips' mental status; correct?
> A   Yes, sir. The head line corpsman, HM3 Ogarra, we spoke to him on several occasions about Lance Corporal Phillips.
> Q   Did he tell you that Lance Corporal Phillips was withdrawn?
> A   Yes, sir.
> Q   And not eating?
> A   Withdrawn was the big one. That he wasn't acting himself, that he was withdrawn, et cetera, yes, sir.
> Q   Those are also indicative of post-traumatic stress disorder; correct?
> A   That is why I referred him to psychiatry, sir.
> Q   So you don't disagree with the diagnosis. You believe he does have PTSD; correct?
> A   Yes, sir.

Battalion Medical Officer LT Douglas Pugliese testifying about the rapidly attenuating state of morale on the ground at Forward Operating Base (FOB) Riviera and admits that both company and battalion commanders were both on board concerning the all hands on deck battlefield decree

Chapter 17: Public Enemy #1

LT Browne went head-to-head with the prosecutor, detailing every event overseas empirically validated. LT Browne detailed the prejudicial nature of the NCIS investigation at FOB Riviera, and those agents refused to allow witnesses to formulate their own statements and version of events or have video corroboration, which says all anyone needs to know. Naval investigators were vehement about structured and signed lines of inquiry, painting the picture completely asymmetrically based on pre-established motive.

LT Browne (USMC) said, "We were the only platoon in the entire Battalion taking casualties the way we did, and never once did anyone even go out to talk to the guy or encourage us or see how we were doing, not even once."

The Defense Counsel then cross-examined LT Browne about my state and demeanor immediately after the rooftop ambush at the time the Company Commander was jumping to biased conclusions and assigning blame within minutes that served as the foundation for the charges and court martial:

> **Defense Counsel:** Did you see LCPL Phillips shortly after?
>
> **LT Browne:** I saw him right after it happened. They brought him back to FOB Riviera. I walked him upstairs; we got some privacy.
>
> **Defense Counsel:** What did he look like? Describe his appearance for the judge.
>
> **LT Browne:** He was exhausted. He was distraught. He was breathing very heavy. He was confused. He was in a lot of pain. He was broken.

> **Defense Counsel:** You got a chance to talk to him?
>
> **LT Browne:** Yes, Sir.
>
> **Defense Counsel:** What did you talk about?
>
> **LT Browne:** I told him to stay relaxed. That we were a family, and we were going to stick together, and we weren't going to turn our backs on him. We didn't have all the facts about what happened and that he was going to be going back to Base Camp.

SGT Reagan, under oath, clarified the coerced assertion from the federal statement that I responded inappropriately during the ambush that CPL Rapavi was killed, confirming what both General Berger and the prosecutor knew all along and why they'd released me from pretrial confinement. There is no record of any Marine saying they felt anything but completely safe and protected around me. SGT Reagan asserted that he was somehow abstractly forbidden from transferring me to another squad, platoon, or billet and alleged that he was doing me a favor by keeping me in his squad as a fierce saw gunner. He alleged that it was all for my benefit and that if he allowed me to go to another squad, I would've felt abandoned. His testimony made clear that he'd never once suggested or asked if I was willing to move to another squad to escape the abuse. It was all hands-on deck. Orders directly from the Company Commander. The following dialogue relates to the day CPL Rapavi was gunned down:

> **Prosecutor:** You testified today that he behaved appropriately in suppressing fire at that point?
>
> **SGT Reagan:** Suppressing fire, yes, he did, Sir.

Prosecutor: Then, at some point, you thought he was too frantic, and he was out of control?

SGT Reagan: Out of control in the sense that I couldn't get an accurate situation report, yes.

Prosecutor: And that he was shooting way too many rounds?

SGT Reagan: I wasn't on top of the roof to see what exactly was going on. All I could see was my best friend lying in front of me with a bullet hole in his neck. Through a squad leader's perspective, I was pissed off because my friend is dead, and I can't get an accurate situation report, yes, Sir.

Next, the defense counsel cross-examined SGT Reagan.

Defense Counsel: Where was LCPL Phillips when CPL Rapavi was shot?

SGT Reagan: LCPL Phillips was standing post on the North Post of Iraqi Police Compound rooftop.

Defense Counsel: And would he have an observation of CPL Rapavi when he was shot?

SGT Reagan: For lack of a better explanation, he had a front-row seat.

Defense Counsel: When CPL Rapavi got hit, what did LCPL Phillips do?

SGT Reagan: He suppressed the most likely point of origin to the sniper.

Defense Counsel: Again, someone was able to retrieve CPL Rapavi and pull him back into shelter position?

SGT Reagan: Yes.

Defense Counsel: So again, LCPL Phillips reacted the way you hope he would react?

SGT Reagan: Yes.

Defense Counsel: And he provided suppressive fire to protect the life of other Marines?

SGT Reagan: Yes, he did.

The Defense Counsel then questioned SGT Reagan about the events surrounding the day we were ambushed in the alleyway and LCLP Mheule was shot by an enemy sniper.

> "LCPL Phillips laid down immediate and rapid suppressive fire with his SAW, enabling LCPL Parcels and myself to aid—and Doc Solbach to aid—LCPL Meuhle enough times so we could gain access into one of the residential courtyards and post security. The snipers, they were getting in a habit of taking two shots. Like LCPL March, they shot the squad leader first, then felt safe enough to reload and take another shot. Later in deployment, another Marine (HET SSGT) was shot twice by the same sniper. So, the sniper on this day only got off one shot because of Phillips' effective suppression."
>
> SGT Reagan (USMC)

Chapter 17: Public Enemy #1

The Department of Defense will perpetuate lies, convolute the narrative, bury inconvenient facts in larger body of texts, and call you a cold-blooded murderer and homicidal maniac one day, only to release you 38 days later when your parents hire an experienced litigator and start asking for records. Then they'll walk back charges and allegations but say someone has to answer up for the events. The military prosecutors and convening authorities are in bed together. Prosecutors will investigate, quickly realize the charges are salacious, and endorse the reduction of charges, only to blame you for everyone's injuries, even leaving the battlefield at the behest of the convening authority who vetoed the reduction and dismissal of charges.

These people will use comatose, wounded veterans to testify against you, so they can't even remember material parts. They manipulate facts, omit material exculpatory evidence, and sling allegations of murder, then retract. They engage in email collusion. They make you look even crazier by dragging you through the mental mud. These are who these people are. These are the people who think the Fifth General Order is simply a piece of paper that can be used when they need to use the restroom and can't find another source of material for comfort.

Next, the prosecutor cross-examined and attempted to badger my mother while dishonoring my military distinction. The prosecutor did his best to tear her to shreds and put her in tears. I turned to Major Woodard on my left and said, "If you don't do something, I will." But he was transfixed. Without even turning to me to quell the rage, he just leaned forward and said audibly, like he was really talking to himself, "I can't believe he's doing this. I can't believe he's going this far." The message was clear: they had orders from the Pentagon to wage a scorched earth campaign. This case was being used to set a landmark precedent, and it was now a matter of policy and liability. They were never going to admit fault for what the Bush Administration had decreed, so they had to crush the threat, which was me. I felt it, too. Like the weight of the world was pushing down, and nothing anyone said or did could mitigate it.

Question and Answer by Marine Prosecutor badgering my mother:

> **Military Prosecutor:** I want to ask you a few questions about your son's medical history prior to joining the Marine Corps. In his 707 examination, it said that he was treated for ADHD. Is that correct?
>
> **Mother:** When he was very young. In fourth grade. He had it for only a short time.
>
> **Marine Prosecutor:** Was he treated with medication?
>
> **Mother:** Yes, but he didn't stay on it.
>
> **Marine prosecutor:** Ritalin?
>
> **Mother:** For only a week.

The prosecutor went first with closing arguments:

> "All the what-ifs, all the perhaps if he'd been diagnosed earlier, maybe if the command had made a different decision, this wouldn't have happened, it doesn't change the act that with the intent to kill, LCPL Phillips stole his life."

Now we know that LCPL Phillips didn't deliberately target him.

Chapter 17: Public Enemy #1

I was silently contemplating all the what ifs he was conveniently omitting. What if the Iraqi Police had never left the compound that night and only returned two minutes later, with typical shady behavior, endangering all of us? What if the Iraqi Police patrol had followed orders and not dismounted, ran in multiple directions, and drove through the ambush? What if the Army National Guard hadn't breached established protocol and blocked the entrance control point with their vehicle out of a sense of false dominance? What if the Company Commander hadn't rushed to judgment out of fear of his trail of deployment-long negligence being exposed? What if we weren't medicated with controversial hypnotics to maintain troop levels? What if we weren't inundated with caffeine to the same effect? But unlike those petulant officers, I wasn't in the industry of What-ifs.

My profession was to execute shots with complete violence of action while under constant duress of making the wrong decision and being judged and dissected. My profession was making sure Marines and sailors were safeguarded, and everyone outside of that was collateral damage if necessary. That's the promise and covenant Marines make to fellow Marines and sailors. The Company Commander, NCIS Agents, and Battalion Leadership violated the Fifth General Order that night, and they were fast-tracked for promotion to bury the national security event at the expense of a lance corporal with insidiously systemic ramifications. I'm not the one who negatively affected "the reputation of the Navy and Marine Corps and Nation as a whole." Am I sorry? I'm sorry for every single person who died in Iraq. I'm especially sorry that Lance Corporal John Hale was burned alive for over 45 minutes. I'm sorry those three Army soldiers were castrated alive by a demonic adversary. I'm sorry that Washington, D.C. was playing politics with the midterm elections at the expense of American lives. But besides that, I'm not discriminately apologetic for any specific foreign individual with inappropriately contrived guilt. Every day was nothing but downside over there.

The Marine Prosecutor said, "The military hierarchy ensured Golf Company Commander and Battalion leadership were absent from the court proceedings, though irrefutably implicated in a trail of premeditated carnage throughout seven-month deployment so that they couldn't be called as witnesses and cross-examined by the defense with no way of justifying their guilt, which brought significant discredit upon the Navy and Marine Corps and the Nation as a whole."

The prosecutor then dropped a bombshell about how corrupt the Iraqi Police Force was based on his examination and interviews:

> "Now we know that LCPL Phillips didn't deliberately target him and that one of the many tragedies that permeate this case is that of all the Iraqi Police that had to be killed, it was the one that everyone admired and looked up to, and who was admired by the U.S. Military who served with him. But it wouldn't have happened had LCPL Phillips not killed him. Had he not pointed his machine gun at that Iraqi Police convoy and pulled the trigger. Although he did not deliberately target this individual, his actions killed him and stole his life."
>
> Marine Prosecutor

That right there was the admission as to why he didn't want to prosecute the case and enforced dropping the charges to General Berger. He had done his homework and combed through all the witness statements and events on deployment. He was well-versed

Chapter 17: Public Enemy #1

that the Iraqi Police Force were not the heroes the Navy and Marine Corps were portraying them as. The IPs wouldn't even leave the compound to rescue a wounded Marine. After a month of deployment, no Marines were willing to die or trust that corrupt force. Not one Iraqi Policeman was killed or injured before this event because they refused to fight. Spare me the patriotic spiel about Iraqi Police courage. To make matters worse, Golf Company Commander sat back at Base Camp, taking showers, eating warm meals, and deferring responsibility.

The Marine Defense Counsel went next with closing arguments:

> "We're sitting here for one reason: because the Department of Defense wanted more dime for their buck. They placed a premium on manpower. And they got every cent out of LCPL Phillips."

When the sentence was spoken, the Battalion Surgeon, testifying for the prosecution, walked past me and took a knee next to my mom. Putting his hand on her shoulder, he said, "Mrs. Phillips, not a day goes by that I don't regret what we did to your son." In his mind, he was morally indemnifying himself in a pathetic fashion after just testifying against me, lying under oath, and accusing me of misleading officers. These are the types of people we're talking about. Epitome of snakes. They stab you in the back, then smile apologetically when coming around to your front side to morally indemnify themselves. Complete arrogance.

The prosecutor walked over to SGT Reagan and said how disappointed he was in him as if the prosecutor had a moral high ground. There was more finger-pointing by this point, from combat all the way to the tribunal, which lasted a lifetime. Somehow, a single LCPL was public enemy number one and was ardently accused of negatively affecting the reputation of the United States of America in one of the most controversial wars in American history, which speaks to the absurdity of the Iraq War in totality. SGT Reagan was used by the Company Commander and wounded just like me and many others. We all did the best we could with what we had. We survived a command that no Marine should have to. Company Commander may have missed the court-martial, but everyone involved knows what a feckless coward he is, and that's his legacy. The one thing that allowed us to survive that deployment and horrid command was the legendary leadership of LT Cameron Browne. He led from the front and stuck by his guys to the end of the line. He single-handedly scrapped with the Pentagon and challenged them to an old-fashioned duel, and they blinked. He will always be the Captain and Commandant of Fear Factor Zero.

Three Days after Tribunal

Three days after the tribunal, the front-page *Marines Times* article hit the newsstand, proclaiming on the front page in big, bold letters: "Sent for eval four times then snapped and killed a friendly." Large letters horizontally across the top read, "I lost my cool, Sir." They then cropped the narrative, misleading the target audience about the complexity established in court martial and deploying a picture of me that had been taken while I was medicated in the morning, walking into trial after solitary confinement, after three months medicated in the hospital and six months of JAG persecution. It was a microcosm of defamation at best and a case study of treason at worst.

The article was also included in *Leatherneck Magazine* for all to see. The only quote they took from me was the forced providence

Chapter 17: Public Enemy #1

quote: "I lost my cool, Sir," as we were forced by General Berger to do whatever was necessary to satisfy providence to regain my medical benefits. They didn't mention a single word about the judge not wanting to accept the forced plea deal due to lack of providence, as also evidenced by internal emails between the prosecutor and future commandant. Instead, they said I heard an explosion, ran up to the roof, and executed a friendly.

Front Page Cover of Marine Times Article — Post Tribunal (Page 1)

casualty

4 of his friends died. He was referred for mental care 4 times. Then, he snapped

By Trista Talton
talton@militarytimes.com

CAMP LEJEUNE, N.C. — Lance Cpl. Jonathan A. Phillips' fellow Marines all knew one thing: He should not be in combat.

His reaction to the deaths of four friends in the span of two weeks gave Phillips' commanders enough concern to send him to a mental health expert. Then again. Then two more times.

But whatever the battle-hardened Marine was dealing with inside, his outward demeanor was of a man ready for duty. At least that's the impression he gave the doctors. And to the chagrin of his fellow Marines — including his platoon commander, who personally contacted a psychiatrist at Camp Fallujah — he was sent back in.

"He didn't need to be out there," said Stephen Reagan, former 2nd Platoon squad leader with 2nd Battalion, 8th Marines. "I knew that. His buddies knew that."

After Phillips killed an innocent Iraqi man, everyone else knew it.

Now, after pleading guilty to a crime that his friends and family believe could have been prevented, Phillips' story stands as a cautionary tale for anyone who's ever lied to get back into the fight, buried his feelings too deep or overlooked the pain of a co-worker in obvious need of help. Phillips pleaded guilty to voluntary manslaughter and solicitation in a small Camp Lejeune, N.C., courtroom Sept. 21. He was sentenced to two years in prison.

After the guilty plea, his friends and fellow Marines took turns at the stand, telling a military judge how the man standing trial that day was not the same jovial leatherneck who deployed to Iraq in the summer of 2006.

Lance Cpl. Jonathan A. Phillips, left, of 2[...] courtroom at Camp Lejeune for the start

"This kid could not sit down to save his life, and just look at him now," said a teary-eyed Sgt. Patrick Lajuect. "He was just as pure as life could be. He had so much potential."

Phillips wanted to become a squad leader, intent on learning from other Marines in that position. The goal was something Reagan believed Phillips had the potential to achieve.

All that changed Oct. 6. Second

Marine Times Article Continued (Page 2)

Chapter 17: Public Enemy #1

RANDY DAVEY

d Battalion, 8th Marines, walks to the
f his court-martial Sept. 21.

Platoon had suffered its first casualty just days before, when a friend of Phillips' was killed by a sniper Sept. 24.

Just 12 days later and shortly after the memorial service of the Marine killed by the sniper, Phillips' squad was hit by a u-shaped ambush. A vehicle carrying four Marines and an interpreter was blasted by a roadside bomb.

The explosion instantly killed three Marines and the interpreter. A fourth Marine was inside burning alive. Phillips, said to be in a state of panic, and another lance corporal ran to the fiery vehicle to try to rescue the only surviving Marine.

After they pulled the Marine out, Phillips rode in the vehicle with the dead and wounded.

"As far as I'm concerned, he was just as much a casualty as the men in that truck were," Reagan said.

The once-outgoing Marine became withdrawn. He wouldn't eat. He talked to his weapon. He talked in his sleep. He wasn't calling home like he used to. He hung a poncho from the rack above his to obstruct the view from his bed, a room of empty racks where his friends, now dead, once slumbered.

The changes concerned those around him.

Shortly after the Oct. 6 attack, Phillips was sent to Camp Fallujah for a psychiatric evaluation. Reagan said he was surprised when Phillips returned to his platoon, which was set up in a police station in Saqlawiyah.

Phillips was sent for psychiatric evaluations three more times before Jan. 20. He was evaluated in early December, shortly after witnessing another friend, his first squad leader, take a sniper's bullet to the throat from the rooftop of the Iraqi police station. Each time, he was proclaimed fit for duty and returned to his unit.

Navy Lt. Douglas Pugliese was not one of the psychiatrists who assessed Phillips, but said he saw

See next page

Marine Times Article Continued (Page 3)

> "No one expressed any interest, which really upset me," he said. "We know from Day One, Oct. 6, that this Marine was a great Marine, but he was a casualty. We're here because he was not taken care of at their level. We're here because they dropped the ball."
>
> Then came Jan. 20. Phillips, after hearing small-arms fire, spotted an Iraqi policeman in a marked car and shot him in his chest. After the shooting, he asked a fellow Marine not to report him.
>
> "I lost my cool, sir," Phillips told the military judge.

Marine Times Article Continued (Page 4)

Marine Times Article Continued (Page 5]

The optics made the Pentagon's job even easier. Instead of quoting SGT Reagan for contradicting his original statement, the Pentagon chose a much more compelling quote: "It was a bad case of I told you so." What he really meant was he couldn't understand how I survived everything he threw at me for five months after the bridge ambush, taking out his hatred on one Marine asymmetrically. What he failed to account for is how my grandfather trained me: to be dropped

Chapter 17: Public Enemy #1

into bad situations, surrounded, and fight my way out. He deeply resented that he could never break me. That's what he really meant when he was quoted at trial. He had tried to provoke a confrontation for five months in the most vitriolic manner and failed. Even when discovered by other Marines. That's why he told investigators that he carried his sidearm around me when I was unarmed. He indeed felt he had ample reason to be intimidated, knowing what he was doing in the shadows. But I always kept in mind that the Fifth General Order was bigger than any one person.

LCPL Kelly, a wounded Marine from the Wounded Warrior Battalion, had sat through the entire kangaroo court-martial from start to finish. The morning the article hit the newsstand; he was grabbing coffee with the other wounded Marines at the base convenience store. Another Marine in the store picked up the front-page article and said to his friend, "Hey, this is the kid I heard waxed three Marines." LCPL Kelly got livid and told them to shut the fuck up and that the article was a complete hit piece meant to drive the shame factor so that I didn't go public with the real narrative, as they knew several news outlets had reached out to me wanting an interview. I wasn't going to subject my sick mother to that, and the convening authority knew it. Just imagine how many other Marines and sailors picked up that article across all domestic and international Navy and Marine Corps installations without being set straight by someone like LCPL Kelly.

> "When Jonathan returned stateside, he was thrown into solitary confinement. Our family wasn't given the respect of being notified. It wasn't until our parents found out inadvertently that our mother called the 2/8 Battalion Aid Station, demanding Jonathan's medical and mili-

tary records after speaking to his Platoon Commander, who was the only one who notified her. Jonathan's squad leader didn't notify us. Minutes after speaking with the Battalion Medical Officer, our mom was called back by Golf Company Commander. He accosted her and warned her never to circumvent his authority again. My mom said she'd never had a more disturbing interaction and immediately knew something dark was in the works. Our father, outraged, called the commander back from work and told him if he ever spoke to his wife like that again, he'd regret it.' The commander quickly apologized and claimed there had been a misunderstanding.

Shortly after, the General released Jonathan from solitary confinement and offered him a full honorable discharge for battlefield distinction—if he stayed quiet. But by then, the 2/8 command had sparked a firestorm at the Pentagon, which was in full panic mode, looking for a scapegoat.

Because of the physical and psychological damage from battlefield exploitation, compounded by complete solitary confinement, deprived of sunlight, fresh air, or human interaction, and degraded by daily strip searches. Jonathan was sent to the naval hospital for over three months inpatient before he could even speak and semi-process.

Jonathan was then granted leave to fly home because the military realized how severely they had damaged him on top of his battlefield distinction and perseverance. They changed the narrative overnight from national security

Chapter 17: Public Enemy #1

unhinged flight risk to 'Hey, we need him to go home and see his family so we can look honorable,' when really, they just wanted to pawn off his severely compounded injuries while ascertaining a scapegoat for all the 2/8 Company and Battalion Command negligence. He came home, but he couldn't process much. I remember him sitting on the stairwell, rocking back and forth, having panic attacks. My mom and I had to stay close, trying to calm him down.

At his court-martial, the Marine prosecutor viciously attacked our mother on cross-examination, though she was merely a character witness, making her cry as they tried to destroy Jonathan's character. They even dredged up an absurd childhood fight where Jonathan was defending a sibling. After the trial, my mom and I both concurred [that] she had been used as bait by the prosecutor who was clearly trying to provoke a reaction from Jonathan, one that almost came but, thankfully, didn't due to his restraint. He has an uncanny level of control. But people take that for granted until the moment guys like him strike back. Then they realize the quiet guys are the ones who don't want to fight because they know their true power and what it can do. Afterwards, the Battalion Medical Officer took a knee by our mother, put a hand on her shoulder as she cried, and, after having testified against Jonathan and lying under oath about him misleading him in medical evaluations, profusely apologized to our mother for what the military was doing to him as the fall guy.

"A few days later, I was at a restaurant with my firefighter coworkers when a former Marine friend brought in the front-page newspaper. It claimed Jonathan had walked onto a rooftop and executed a friendly after misleading the officers and Navy Doctors. We were all in disbelief—that wasn't even remotely true.

The Department of Defense smeared Jonathan to keep his confidence down and to prevent him from speaking to the media when reporters were asking for interviews."

Danielle Phillips (Sister)

"Was he a good Marine? Depends on whose version you choose to believe. The defamatory reports you'll find in newspapers? Or the opinions of the Marines and Sailors who fought alongside him in combat? More than being just a good Marine, he is a good man and a loyal friend. Plenty of people would give you the shirt off their back—but John? He'd give you his socks, shoes, car keys, expecting nothing in return.

Some Marines were 'afraid' to engage the enemy for fear of punishment from command under threat of court-martial, only to see those same Marines throw others under the bus for doing exactly that. It was diabolical fear-mongering and cost many Americans their lives and injuries unnecessarily.

I wasn't there for every moment recounted, and I don't need to have been. I know everything I need to know from John's character, the failures of our chain of command, and the way people who once called him 'friend' acted during NCIS and JAG proceedings. No one felt anything but supremely safe around Phillips and his mission commitment, which was the safety and preservation of fellow Marines and Sailors. God forbid Civil War ever breaks out again. I want him at my side without question. He's a guarantee, and that's a rare thing in this day and age. It's about the guy next to you. He's a true enemy to the enemy. Political qualms and abdications have no place in the equation."

Lance Corporal Kyle Mercado

Days later, Gunny Rowe called me apologizing and saying he didn't even need to open the article to know it was all lies and that the command had thrown me to the jackals. He was extremely apologetic. I told him not to worry about it, that it wasn't his fault, though I was legitimately terrified about being relegated back to solitary confinement. But I didn't see any upside in deferring responsibility onto to someone like what was done to me.

Base Barber Shop

LT Browne was in the barber chair being swiveled around as he received his weekly haircut. Suddenly, 2/8 Battalion Executive Officer Mark Reardon came charging through the door like Ferdinand the bull, gripping the *Marine Times* article and ambushing my Platoon Commander for exhibiting the uncommon 2/8 command virtues: honor and integrity. This was not an unplanned ambush, as evidenced by the fact that the Executive Officer had searched for LT

Browne and made sure to have the front-page article with him at that moment. Deduction, not speculation.

Major Riordan began accosting LT Browne, saying, "You threw me under the bus, LT Browne??!!" while holding up the newspaper as if anyone for one moment believed he was literate. LT Browne nearly jumped out of the barber chair at the sad excuse for a Marine officer and said, "You have some balls running in here acting tough while you're responsible for betraying a 19-year-old gunfighter, leaving him to rot in solitary confinement." The more disturbing part may be the fact that Major Reardon had the article with him when he saw LT Browne in the barbershop window in the first place. Major Reardon may not have seen combat, but he was clearly well-versed in hunter-killer ambush tactics. It's safe to say he left the barbershop that day without a fresh line-up for his comb-over—though his spine got a trim, and his testosterone got a high and tight to accentuate his crisp, starched uniform. The hunter became the hunted on the dangerous battlefield of Camp Lejeune, N.C., where distinguishing friend from foe was more volatile than in the Middle East. On base, tribal alliances shifted daily, with promotion being the overriding campaign medal.

I was forced to wait in a purgatory state for the future commandant to make his determination as to whether he'd suspend the remaining confinement portion of the sentence like all logical Marines assumed he was going to do based on his behavior. All the officers at the Wounded Warrior Battalion went to bat for me and even personally met with General Berger on my behalf since she wouldn't meet with me because, as some said, he wouldn't be able to send me back to the brig if he met me and saw the condition that I was in and what the JAG persecution was doing to me after distinction in battlefield.

Every sign from the General indicated that he was going to suspend the sentence and let me start my rehabilitation.

Months After Court Martial

General Berger had specified that twelve months after court-martial, if I had remained infraction-free (which I'd always been), he would suspend all punitive discharge, giving the illusion that there would be no logic in subjecting me to 19 more months of the Brig and making me go downhill just so I could eventually go uphill with medical retirement. In the writing, he stated that he had four months following the court martial to act on and execute the confinement portion of the sentence. He waited until the very last day of that period to act and relegate me to the Brig.

I sat in panic mode, reliving all the what ifs after having the Pentagon tear apart every decision I'd ever made overseas. I continued to vomit. I was reunited with LCPL Mule at Wounded Warrior Battalion East. Battalion Commander LT Colonel Thomas Siebenthal thankfully made the incisive call to assign us to rooms beside each other for cross-coverage. I couldn't fathom being sent back to the Brig—partly because of the claustrophobia and partly because of the humiliation of being portrayed as a cold-blooded murderer, no matter what the facts were or how I proved them. It was like in Rome when they'd captured the opposing leader after an arduous Gaul campaign and marched him through the streets so everyone could see their victory and his subjugation. I would spend all day in my barracks room, refusing to come downstairs with the other Marines. Because of the article and unflattering picture, I was ashamed to be seen anywhere. So, I would only venture out late at night—pre-dawn hours. Once again, my friend was the cover of darkness.

The First General Order

I was a wreck. I still didn't trust people, and the acting Company Commander at Wounded Warrior Battalion (WWB), who had all sat through court-martial, said that it made no sense that General Berger would send me back to the Brig in light of how asinine he knows the charges and conviction to be in light of all the officer and enlisted testimony. The fact that he made my Platoon Commander his personal Aide De Camp seemed like the message was loud and clear. They said it was clear he was letting the grace period lapse, and then a day after that grace period, my sentence would be suspended by default, and I could begin my med board evaluation to medically retire and finally start the arduous rehabilitative and transitioning period.

Around this period, one night, a group of senior men from Golf Company's 3rd Squad took me out to Texas Roadhouse to get me out of my room because I was losing my mind and was in jeopardy of having a mental meltdown. Brent Mule had called them, and they said they'd come to get me to make sure I remembered who my kin were and that they were behind me. I was losing myself day by day.

The 2nd Platoon and Golf Company are some of the best men I know, and I'm supremely blessed to have been fated to 2nd Platoon. Neither they nor I deserved what Company Commander did along with the investigations. The prosecutor and future commandant were intimately aware of that and felt horrible behind the scenes, yet vehemently upheld their subjective version of the Fifth General Order to perpetuate the smoke show. On top of that, they knew continued incarceration was a statistical death sentence for combat operators having to be confined with no way to exorcise the demons from the battlefield that were an occupational hazard. They were briefed extensively by LT Browne. The Golf Company Commander, current Commandant, and prosecutor have no right or basis in playing the

Chapter 17: Public Enemy #1

moral high ground. Unfortunately for them, I've always had a high standard deviation and haven't been relieved from my post. The Fifth General Order remains in full effect.

This had zero to do with good order and discipline and everything to do with polarizing what they were doing with manpower overseas, which was a top-down decree.

LT Browne confided in me that the General was placed in a horrible position by the Pentagon. I told him that I sympathized, professionally speaking, but the General's decision after being intimately briefed by a well-acquainted officer was a moral abdication. LT concurred and admitted that politics aside, he found the abdication an act of moral and ethical cowardice. LT Browne also found General Berger's refusal to meet with me the ultimate admission that the General knew what he was signing off on was morally and ethically wrong. The General didn't even ensure I got decent therapy in the Brig. He just signed off and abdicated himself. True character is revealed when one is up against it.

CHAPTER 18:
MUZZLED

Before being escorted back to the Brig for the remainder of my two-year sentence by 1st SGT Russel Hill from Wounded Warrior Battalion, I had to go to medical and receive pre-incarceration medical evaluation. The wounded LCPL that escorted me said, "Take off, dude. I'm not gonna be the guy who turns a good Marine over to the wolves. I'll delay as long as possible." I said I really appreciate it, brother, but the enemy always hopes you'll turn and run and make their job easier. When you stand your ground, it scares them.

Marine Corps Prison was the pinnacle of physical and mental survival. Guards oftentimes attempted to strip inmates of all dignity, service, and distinction. They felt inferior that a good majority of inmates were seasoned combat veterans by this time in the war. Every waking day was status quo mental cat and mouse games. I had no iPod to shift my reality and provide a nominal reprieve. In the general population, you had 15 minutes to inhale and devour your chow. Guards would strip-search you and laugh. All you really had to look forward to was recreation calls at night in the courtyard, but oftentimes, they would use the notion of inclement weather to deprive prisoners of that at will. As if the Marine Corps were genuinely concerned with the welfare of the subjugated inmates under their lock and key with the daily goal of breaking down pride and dignity.

The First General Order

Exercising indoors was cruelly prohibited. I was sent to solitary at times for opposing this while performing push-ups and lifting the medal tables up in military shoulder press fashion. Window slats were seldom opened to allow fresh air intake. No matter how frigid the temperature got, you received only one olive-drab wool blanket. There were no pillows. We slept on a two-inch-thick rubber mattress on top of steel metal slabs. There were no commissary privileges, cigarettes, headphones, or CD players, which takes the survival aspect of the Brig to heightened levels. I had been recommended for S.E.A.R. school at the end of deployment, and the mentality of preparing to attend that and the Marine Recon Indoctrination Program proved vital to surviving Marine prison.

There was nothing to separate time or space. Minimal light. Sometimes, an inmate would cruise by with a book cart and throw me something to galvanize my mind, only to be stripped away by a sword team in riot gear the moment a petty staff NCO realized I had a book. He knew it was my mental and psychological lifeline to distance myself from the hell of solitary, which afforded no ventilation, AC, heat, or fans. During the summer months, I'd have to strip myself naked to keep my body and brain from overheating in a 5 by 8 heat box. Solitary confinement was directly atop the boiler room, which burned hands and feet when trying to engage in exercise without insulation between the floors. During the winter, you got one thin, world-war olive-drab wool blanket.

At times, the migraines would get unbearable. I'd take my T-shirt, wrap it around my head, and just lie down, imagining life outside the present environment, away from the stench of sewage next to my head. The migraines from deployment only intensified with the stress of legal persecution followed by prison.

Chapter 18: Muzzled

At times, my motivation became so nonexistent that my hair and beard would become long in solitary, and the Brig Master Gunnery SGT would threaten to deploy a sword team of guards in riot gear to forcibly remove my body hair. I told him the threat gave me a hard-on and that the blood would be on his hands, and it wouldn't be my blood. I vividly recall the Brig Master Gunnery SGT coming to my cell on D-Row in solitary confinement because he was indignant that I refused to shave like a Marine while getting dressed and paid as a prisoner. He called me a murderer, and I said, "Stand by your words, open this cage, and let's see who the real Marine is." I then attacked the bars, lunging at him. I don't think I've ever seen someone run away that fast. It was sad. But I wasn't going to let one more individual who hadn't been in combat tell me what happened. Cowards judge from thousands of miles away and only when there's a cage separating them. Oil and water don't mix. It's a testament to the detrimental and corrosive effects poor leaders can have on an institution. That's what happens when the world's foremost premier fighting institution allows politics and political correctness to permeate its rank and insidiously spread throughout like a small but potent virus.

Wild as it sounds, the mice were welcome friends of civility and socialization and would come frequently to my cell at night. I'd name them. The cockroaches were vicious. They swarmed at night from the vents. If you dropped a shirt on the floor at night, you'd see a bunch of them scurry in all directions, like in the movie *The Mummy*. The Brig was so old that it was being decommissioned during my last two months in solitary, and inmates were being transferred to the Chesapeake Bay Naval Brig. My drinking water was from a base that became legendary for its contaminated water source.

In solitary, I would inscribe "Free Phillips" in Sharpie on the back of my shirt. Certain guards took it one way, but it was a Declaration of Independence against the matrix of forced subjugation and a covenant of never being their prisoner for even a single day. If anything, they were mine, and I'd make their lives living hell in the instances they would denigrate my relegation to the Brig. Pretty soon, the senior guards would be hazing the junior guards who had fucked with me because of the chaos it would engender in me and how it would reverberate to the other inmates.

I never let myself entertain the notion of being a prisoner, nor did I ever act accordingly. A prison is simply a matrix and cage of thought, and I was never one to engage in that type of paradigm. You're only a prisoner when you allow subjugation to vanquish your mind.

I would mentally and visually cling to distant worlds and alternate realities. I'd visualize the woman of my dreams from the *Maxim* magazines we'd all pass around on deployment. I'd think about luxuries I'd have one day, like the ability to exercise without having to do handstands in my cell, which was the only way to make the small 5 by 8 layout work. I would ruminate on books I'd read in the past and recreate salient scenes, except the scenes wouldn't end in an epilogue but keep going.

Before I knew it, I was the protagonist, and I was taking the novel in directions of my own volition. I'd previously gotten hooked on the authors of Vince Flynn and Brad Thor. I'd wake up on certain days and convince myself I was the leading character, which would inundate me with the strength and fortitude to resist the unpleasant ecosystem. Anything to live outside the walls of that sewage-ridden cement cell. The poet Emerson eloquently said, "The mind once

Chapter 18: Muzzled

stretched by a new idea can never return to its original form," and in a way, I don't think I ever left solitary confinement the same person I'd once been. I struggle with it to this day. I'm not sure if that's a good or bad thing, but I inherently gravitate towards optimism. If you have any chance to survive that type of claustrophobic habitat, you better force your brain to create new neural pathways and find some level of meaning in the pain, or the suffering will overtake you. I'd lay on my back looking up and imagine I had a Bright yellow tennis ball that I was bouncing off the ceiling. I'd count each time it came back down. Anything to take my mind off the sweltering humidity and lack of A/C and fresh air.

At one point, a Brig gunnery sergeant made a comment about how he didn't like my positive attitude and how I focused on micro goals like a simple PB&J sandwich. He said I was lucky that we weren't in the days of corporeal punishment consisting of bread and water. I had recently lost another of my four clemency appeals and was ready for a fight. With a look of superiority in my eyes, I told him he'd just made the most foolish miscalculation possible. Right there and then, I commenced a three-week hunger strike. I went into delirium at some point. The Staff NCOs told me the command leadership was contemplating involuntary intravenous infusion to restore me. I just remember that was the only way at that point that I could turn the tables and take back control of my life. I remember I was willing to starve myself to death to let every guard and the General know they were my prisoner, not the other way around. They would remember my name with their last breath should I die. That was one of my lowest points in isolation. The Staff NCOs suddenly began begging me to eat as if I wasn't a prisoner.

Either one of two Gunnery SGTs, whom I highly respected or, more likely, the Brig executive officer whom I hold the utmost reverence for, delivered beautiful rosary beads from my parents and made a length exception as the great Catholic and leader he is. He has another spot on my guardian angel list. From that point forward, I would pray and recite the Rosary on my knees every single night in solitary, visualizing the Stations of the Cross while in recitation. That incantation took my mind to another realm and pushed me forward in the lion's den. That Rosary submission every night, like Psalm 91 bandanna from Mrs. Lynn Johnson, enabled me the fortitude to mentally dominate and persevere through anything the enemy threw at me.

Prisoners get three or four clemency petitions throughout their sentence. The Department of the Navy denied each one, no matter who testified on my behalf in Washington, D.C., or wrote letters validating the absurdity of the prosecution. They got every ounce of blood from the altar of deferred blame. All they effectively achieved was enabling and perpetuating incompetent and drunk officers caught in the act and shuffling them around throughout the military to defer the situation. The Naval Board denied my third clemency appeal and cited that I had been caught with peanut butter contraband. I was emaciated and had stashed some peanut butter packets to maintain calories so I wouldn't die off after a hunger strike.

> "I still recall with absolute clarity my first encounter with Jonathan Phillips. It's a rare occurrence when you stand before young men who believe in something bigger than themselves. It's an even rarer occurrence when you are afforded the privilege of leading and serving alongside such men in battle.

Chapter 18: Muzzled

From the very beginning, I knew Jonathan possessed the character traits to be successful on and off the battlefield…because he had an uncompromising commitment to the mission and, most especially, to the men at his left and right.

The Fallujah suburbs were like a grizzly bear; you never knew what was going to happen. You can train for that environment for your entire life, but until you experience it at ground level, out in the street where the metal meets flesh, you can never understand how it impacts your total state of being, nor can you comprehend how it challenges your inner constitution."

LT Browne (USMC)

"The day after Thanksgiving 2006, Jon had a front-row seat to the murder of his former squad leader. Jon was on post on the roof of the Iraqi Police station, overlooking the vehicle parking lot. As the other squad was loading their vehicles for patrol, the squad leader was shot in the throat by a sniper. He fell directly below Jon's post. Jon, who had proven in prior engagements to show discipline and composure, began firing his light machine gun into the traffic circle at what was later described by Marines in the parking lot as the most likely threat. I tried to contact him by radio to get a situation report and only got an erratic response of 'He's shot, he's shot, I'm shooting.'

Again, we sent Jon back to Camp Fallujah to be seen by the Navy doctors. They sent him back again, fit for duty."

SGT Reagan

SGT Reagan was a good squad leader and merits full credit for writing a clemency petition and setting the NCIS record straight during cross-examination by disgusting military prosecutor. The only people who can understand the totality of our emotions and psyche are those who were present on that bridge evacuating casualties from the crash site while holding off the enemy as they tried to capture us alive.. The Company Commander used all of us and discarded us like human trash. SGT Reagan did his best to try and rectify the horrific position he was placed in by the Company Commander, Medical Officer, aggressive investigators, and the deployment we were all was subjected to. That stands in stark contrast to how Golf Company Commander threw me, SGT Reagan, and the rest of the war-weary and sleep-deprived fellow squad mates to the wolves immediately after the rooftop ambush. After framing me by prejudicing the investigative narrative and walking away that day in solitary confinement, the Company Commander never once spoke to me or drafted a single word for clemency petition. He simply continued to climb the hierarchical ladder after using Marines and medicating them on the battlefield, then washing his hands of us.

For the entire 20 months, I could barely call my sick mom because of how much the military charges prisoners to use the phone system because of the technology as they record every call. It's one more way they subjugate and punish the inmates. They cut them off from the rest of the world. My parents spent their life savings on civilian defense to prevent the Pentagon from being able to lock

Chapter 18: Muzzled

me up and throw away the key on top of terminal cancer treatment and their other four children. The only one who would see me every few months was my extraordinary case manager, Linn Wiedow, from the Wounded Warrior Battalion, when she could find time from her overloaded patient workload—and the private attorney my parents had retained to sit and talk with me for ten minutes or so every couple of months. The attorney went beyond providing legal assistance but also offered companionship and mentorship. The Brig XO Joseph Moschetto would come to sit at my cell and mentor me whenever he could find time away from his busy duties and treat me like a human and fellow Marine. All the above are my guardian angels.

> "I had heard the rumors about the inmate in segregation raising hell, but this was the first time I laid eyes on him. Anytime an inmate from Seg was moved, the rest of us were put on lockdown, unable to move. I was sweeping one of the downstairs hallways when I finally saw Phillips for the first time. Stories about what he was charged with flooded the brig, and everyone knew he was being pushed past the brink – yet, somehow, he was slated for a full honorable discharge.
>
> The latest word was that he was on a hunger strike, protesting the brutal mistreratment he was enduring. He'd supposedly quit shaving, and there were rumors he'd gone naked in his cell. As the guards marched Phillips through the hallway, shackled hand and foot, he waddled like a duck. His hair and beard were wild – way out of regs. He looked he'd just walked out of the Peshmerga Valley after years of fighting. But there was no hesitation in his

stride, no fear in his eyes. He didn't speak, just kept his shoulders squared and his head held high. The consummate professional.

As he passed by, he glanced at me, giving a quick subtle nod and quick grin. It was discreet, but it said it all: he wasn't going to be broken by concrete, steel bars, or forced isolation. He wasn't going to conform, no matter how much they tried to break him. That kind of unshakable defiance earned him the respect of both inmates and guards alike. They knew, like we all did, that he wasn't just another marine inmate; he was an innocent man, standing firm against a corrupt system.

Having served at the very tip of the spear for ten years, working alongside the most professional, intelligent, and surgical soldiers on the planet, Phillips and I hit it off immediately."

SGT First Class November Romeo
(Pseudonym) - Unit Redacted

"When Phillips wasn't in solitary, we were often assigned to Squad Bay 4, which was considered the wild west of squad bays. For a guy as dangerous as Phillips, it was torture because he was provoked daily by junior guards who were envious of the respect and admiration he commanded. Everyone knew he didn't belong in the Brig, yet he never once so much as acted like he was better than anyone. The junior guards taunted him inveterately, but I never saw him raise a hand, even in the face of some of

Chapter 18: Muzzled

the worst provocation I've ever seen. One time, an inmate threw a tantrum at Phillips, practically screaming in his face and inadvertently spewing spit. Phillips didn't want to leave the group we had, so he stood there straight-faced. Because the guards didn't like him, they ended up taking both inmates to solitary. Phillips quickly learned that it didn't matter what you did or didn't do—it was just another no-win battlefield. Months later, he returned from solitary, emaciated with long hair and a beard, smiling like he'd never left. That guy's a warrior. It's inspiring. He'd show back up and ask what good nights he'd missed, wanting an instant recap so he could live vicariously through the films."

Lance Corporal Joey Morales

In solitary confinement, I'd be awarded max status due to my deteriorating mental and physical health and non-compliance with guards like Brig Master Gunnery SGT calling me a murderer. Every time they wanted to move me or bring me downstairs for anything, they would lock down the entire facility and stop all movement. I would be marched like a penguin to the destination, and the other prisoners would be locked down in the hallway. I'd waddle through with a long beard and hair, lethargic and out of it. I'd try my best in those moments to bury all the pain and make a show and say something hilarious to inspire the other prisoners who knew me and the bullshit of the conviction. It was challenging. But inspiration is imperative and goes both ways. Seeing their faces and hearing their words of encouragement amplified my fortitude. When you're at your lowest, it's like in wrestling days; I had to mentally embrace the upside of going against the monsters, knowing that others were drawing inspiration from the victory and I them. Not staying down while shackled or accepting subjugation for even a second was a valiant statement. It was bigger than any one person. I had to maintain that aerial terrain map perspective. Victory was contagious.

After 19 months, I was nearing the end of my sentence. The Brig Company Executive Officer had, by this point, on numerous occasions told me unequivocally that my being incarcerated was a travesty to the Marine Corps, and I did exactly what any Marine in their right mind would've done and not to second-guess it for even a second. I hold that man in reverence to this day and consider him as another one of the guardian angels God introduced in my path to sustain me in the roughest of seas. Without his leadership, my mental kayak would've fully capsized, bullet-ridden, and taken on water with carnivorous sharks circling.

Chapter 18: Muzzled

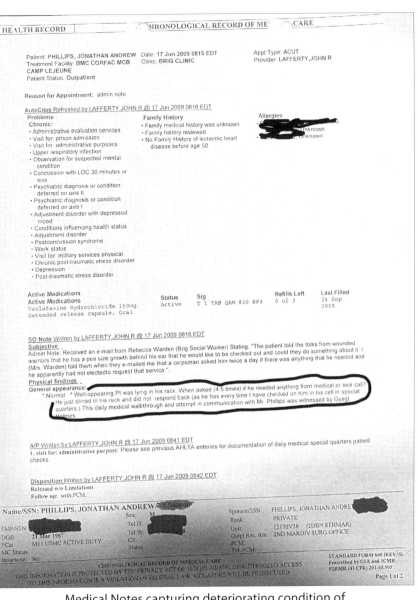

Medical Notes capturing deteriorating condition of LCPL Jonathan Phillips in solitary confinement.

The First General Order

Phillips, Michael

From: jonathan phillips [jonph0311@yahoo.com]
Sent: Friday, April 01, 2011 3:02 PM
To: Phillips, Michael
Subject: Last one,Thx!

Marine Claiming PTSD Denied Clemency

July 01, 2009
Associated Press

JACKSONVILLE, North Carolina - The Marine Corps has denied clemency to a Marine who pleaded guilty in the death of an Iraqi policeman but is suffering from post-traumatic stress disorder.

The decision came despite pleas from his Navy doctor to release him because confinement is aggravating his mental condition.

Pvt. Jonathan A. Phillips pleaded guilty to voluntary manslaughter in the shooting death of the policeman in Saqlawiyah, Iraq, in 2007. Before the shooting, Phillips was sent for psychiatric evaluations three times. Each time, he was proclaimed fit for duty and returned to his unit.

"I have no concerns that Pvt. Phillips is a threat to anyone or himself, but I am concerned about the emotional impact of continued incarceration. I suspect that prolonged incarceration will also lead to a more protracted, complicated recovery," wrote his Navy doctor, Lt. S.J. Stephens, in his clemency petition.

Stephens treated Phillips, a 22-year-old infantry rifleman from Middlesex, Massachusetts, until April when he was deployed to Guantanamo Bay.

Phillips' unit was a week away from finishing its deployment when the Jan. 20, 2007, incident occurred.

The tour in western Iraq had been bloody and several members of the unit were killed. One of his roommates was burned alive, according to court testimony. Stephens said Phillips told him he didn't want to leave his unit short-handed, so he kept coming back despite his mental problems.

According to testimony in his Sept. 2007 hearing, Phillips had gone onto the roof of an Iraqi police station after his unit heard an explosion.

Two marked police vehicles pulled up in front of the station and the victim - identified only by his first name, Monthir, to protect his family - got out of one of the cars. Phillips shot Monthir in the chest, according to testimony.

Phillips is scheduled to get out of prison in September. McNeil said he will likely return to the Wounded Warrior Battalion at Camp Lejeune so he can get a medical discharge.

Associated Press Article including Naval Officer Sam Stevens as whistle blower against injustice campaign being waged against LCPL Jonathan Phillips and his deteriorating physical and mental condition in solitary confinement

At this time, a great Naval Psychologist, LT Commander Sam Stevens, had reached his tolerance threshold of seeing the military pissing on the Hippocratic oath while witnessing first-hand the mental

Chapter 18: Muzzled

and physical decline for no reason other than allowing certain officers to climb the Marine hierarchy. He went to the Associated Press as a whistleblower, and his comments were subsequently published in the Associated Press exposé. He was the second whistleblower who stood up about the black eye the Navy and Marine Corps were engineering.

Brig Executive Officer Chief Warrant Officer Joseph Moschetto confided in me after the Associated Press Article hit the newsstand that the General from the division ran over there indignantly and questioned his take on me. He told the General, "What the fuck do you expect? I'd be behaving the exact same way or worse if you did me the way you've done him! You think this kid is stupid? This isn't what Marines do to good Marines." The Brig XO is the type of Marine Officer, like LT Browne, who makes the Marine Corps the premier fighting force it is. What General Berger failed to understand is that real Marines stick together. They fiercely defend the perimeter and repel all attacks against it. An attack on one is an attack on all. Testudo. On the last day of my 20-month sentence, the Brig XO came to my cell. I didn't want to leave. I'd grown accustomed to the conditions.

Adapting and overcoming is the easy part. Reintegrating is the terrifying prospect that makes war and military prison unthinkable. One part that I feel guilty about and that I told the Brig XO on that last day was my impact on the Brig. They had a job to do, even if they didn't believe someone should be there. They trusted the Generals to never confine someone who didn't belong there, and for good reason. It violates good order and discipline. I never once accepted that I was a prisoner, so it instantly sent shockwaves of belligerence throughout with respect to all the other inmates and guards alike. Unlike the other inmates, the captors had no leverage on me as far as threatening solitary confinement. The resistance was infectious. I didn't take orders from anyone except the XO, Gunny Wright, Gunny Mercer, SSGT Sullivan, and SSGT McMillan. As a result, the good order and discipline in the Brig was compromised. It was war by that point, and the level of polarization was extreme. But to this day, I conversely see no way around it. I was deprived of mental health care. Resisting is what kept me alive there.

CHAPTER 19:
EMANCIPATION

I left the Brig emaciated and broken. I was never a prisoner. Not for one day. Nor did I conform to that forced ideology while confined. When I got released from the Brig, I was physically and mentally emaciated. LT Browne, along with my parents, knew that I was in a precarious state and didn't know how they were going to navigate this point of reintegration. LT Browne flew to Boston to be with my parents under the logical corollary that their leave request for me to come home and be with those most comfortable would be automatically accepted. It was denied. Once again, it made no sense. Why would the Marine Corps want me walking around Garrison in that type of state without anyone to turn to?

My sister, Danielle Phillips, said, "After two years of confinement in a Marine prison, Jonathan came home emaciated. Our terminally ill mother had to hold his hand, guiding him from one PTSD program to another, though he didn't want to go because of the damage the military's smears campaign had done to him and to our family. Our mom let Jonathan get a five-week-old pit bull to galvanize his mind even though he was in no shape to care for his K-9 best friend, so our parents raised her during that first year while Jonathan was in and out of VA inpatient and outpatient rehabilitation programs.

Without that dog and my parent's ability to raise her at Jonathan's most vulnerable, I don't think Jonathan would have survived post-military prison reintegration. What they did to him is 20 times as bad as the book attempts to capture. Our family banded together. Like the Marines, we don't leave a member behind. That's a lesson our patriarch grandfather instilled in us from a formative age."

If it weren't for my mother, father, Aunt Sheila, Uncle Paul, and Charles, I would've never survived the aftermath of military prison. I was highly subsidized. By the time I was released from confinement, I was admittedly a vase shattered into a thousand fragmented pieces. If my mom, family, and four-legged best friend Sam hadn't been there to protect and talk me through all the hospitalization programs, I wouldn't be writing this story. My mom said, "We're going to get through this. And remember, don't ever let a few bad actors make you bitter. That's what people like that want. That's how they transfer their guilt. Starve them of that oxygen."

Before being able to medically retire me with full military honors, the Marine Corps was forced to dispatch me to several inpatient hospitalization programs to restore me to a status where I could speak coherently and actively participate in the Physical Evaluation Board (PEB). Once I was able to be medically retired, I was left in rough shape. My mom and dad raised Sam while I was in and out of inpatient hospitalizations and flying back and forth to base. . She gave me the capacity to persevere through those programs.

I spent the first four months in the VA psych ward, further isolated from all who I served with. The military, once again, told the VA less than half the true story, which portrayed me as psychotic, especially following twenty months in Marine prison and solitary confinement. The only thing that got me through week by week was

Chapter 19: Emancipation

my mom bringing Sam to see me on the weekends when she wasn't too sick from chemotherapy. I would lie in my rack and just picture the prospect of seeing them in a few weeks, and that would sustain me. My anger at what the Department of Defense put my parents through still haunts me. But she told me she needed me not to let them get the best of me. They'll get their due. Not one of those offenders has escaped retribution for their falsehoods, lies of omission, and deceitful career advancement.

"I was a patient in Ward 7 psychiatric unit Northampton VA. I had arrived around two hours before Jonathan Phillips arrived. I recall it being later at night. I recall the nurses talking to each other at the front desk. I was sitting close to my desk alone. They started talking about a patient who would be arriving shortly and that he killed two Iraq police officers without provocation and had been in military prison for the last two years. Phillips arrived and was shaken down, strip-searched, showered, and given a hospital uniform. It was late at night, and I recall Phillips entering the opening main area because they locked our rooms until bedtime. He was asking me questions in a military manner. Always addressing me as 'Sir.; I never at the time mentioned that I knew what his situation was or that the nurses were publicly talking about it in front of other patients. I was 49 years old at the time. I was sure I heard the nurses say he was 22 years old. Within minutes I felt safe around this kid and knew that whatever the military said was complete bullshit because why else would he be out of military prison after two years if even 1 percent was legitimate.

The First General Order

From that moment on, we stuck together and watched each other's backs. Even straight from military prison and solitary confinement and thrown into an inhospitable VA ward where the nurses were already biased and on guard, I never once saw Phillips get physical or raise his voice. He was liked by everyone. We would crack jokes incessantly and keep each other as upbeat as possible. I was going through one of the lowest periods of my life at the time, and that kid would cheer me up no matter what he was going through. He would just do push-ups to keep sane since we were locked in ward. One of the only things besides our camaraderie that kept his mind going was his sick mom, who would bring his six-week-old Pitbull puppy up to see him on the weekends between chemotherapy when she could muster the strength. That woman was extraordinary. She would ask me, 'How's he doing… I'm worried he won't come back from this,' and I would tell her, 'Mrs. Phillips…nothing keeps a guy like that down…no matter how much is thrown at him. He's more worried about you.' When his mom and puppy Samantha would come up on a Saturday here and there, he would light up. Everyone would run over and play with Sam."

Mike Cibelli (United States Air Force)

My mom would have to tuck me in at night while on leave between hospitals because of how much I was used to sleeping in a 5 by 8 solitary cell and not going outside for months on end. She would tuck my three-month-old Pitbull and best friend Sam, who she raised while I was incapacitated and hospitalized, in with me, and I would just pet

Chapter 19: Emancipation

her. Between her and the elevated levels of medication, I would drift off. At the time, the military had been prescribing me maximum doses of Seroquel, which would induce seizures. My mom would find me lying on the kitchen tiles unconscious, having collapsed. My brain would work one minute, and the next, I remember collapsing vertically.

My main champion, my mother, passed away from terminal ovarian cancer nine days after I medically retired. We lost the final years of her life together. Up to that point, I could handle everything, knowing she was there leading the charge. I still haven't grieved to this day. I miss her so much. She was the warrior.

Retirement Citation for LCPL Joanthan A. Phillips

The First General Order

I bounced from VA hospital to VA hospital inpatient program, cycling through several programs, trying to make sense, rationalize everything, and reestablish the chronology of who I once was. I was angry. Bitter. Resentful. I was placed into an involuntary VA psych ward for six months at one point. After getting out of solitary, I had to teach myself how to cook and put myself to sleep at night without being forced to do so. I wouldn't want to go outside because I was institutionalized. SSGT Rivers would text me daily to give me instructions on how to walk to the end of the block and not think about anything else while at my lowest point.

I ended up needing to spend another six months inpatient in the VA Psych Ward, where we barely got to go outside for fresh air under the excuse of being short-staffed. But being in those war, prison, and psych ward environments showed me what many people are dealing with, just how much the American youth have sacrificed, and how they were treated. I was mentored by some of the most amazing Vietnam veterans who were treated like subpar citizens after their heroic distinction and instantly formed a camaraderie with those great men. The nurses at the Bedford VA Michelle, Rosanne, Steve, and Eric—especially Michelle—provided me with the human connection, laughter, and smiles that made it possible to rebound from that terrifying phase and write these very words

Veteran Jack Johnson was, from all places, Arlington, MA, and he took a liking to me at the Bedford VA and pushed me to a new veteran nonprofit organization called Home Base as he could see how broken, disoriented, and directionless I was in that absolute low point in time. Home Base and Serenity Mental Health exemplify how the Fifth General Order applies to the civilian sector.

Chapter 19: Emancipation

Home Base laid the foundation for further assistance and inspiration through the Semper Fi Foundation—a nonprofit organization that provides financial assistance and support to wounded, ill, and injured members of the U.S. Armed Forces and their families. They offer a range of services, including financial relief, family support, and resources for recovery and rehabilitation. The organization is highly respected for its dedication to helping service members transition to civilian life and achieve long-term success.

Semper Fi & America's Fund, originally known as the Injured Marine Semper Fi Fund, was founded in 2004 by a group of military spouses led by Karen Guenther, a registered nurse and wife of a retired Marine. The idea for the fund arose from the need to provide immediate financial assistance to injured Marines and their families, who were facing significant challenges during their recovery from injuries sustained in combat, particularly in Iraq and Afghanistan.

Karen Guenther and the founding members were driven by the desire to ensure that no service member or family went unsupported during their time of need. The organization quickly expanded its scope beyond Marines to include all branches of the U.S. Armed Forces, and in 2012, it launched America's Fund to extend its services to other military personnel and their families.

The organization is known for its hands-on, case-by-case approach, offering direct financial support, assistance with housing, transportation, and adaptive equipment, as well as long-term recovery services. Semper Fi & America's Fund has since grown into one of the most respected military charities in the United States, providing critical support to thousands of service members and their families.

These organizations are a true testament to the private sector and how it picks up the slack when the government messes everything up with impulsive and poor planning when executing its military agenda. One of the things that continues to impress me to this day about Semper Fi Foundation is the personalized care. I get texts from my case manager. It may sound silly, but I look forward to adding the annual customized Christmas ornament to my growing collection and hanging it on the Christmas tree as it weighs the branch down. It serves to remind me of just how much military veterans have had to bear the weight of the world and how far we can come when I see all the annual year inscriptions on the ornaments. It reminds me of the Fifth General Order and how much the private sector embodies it.

EPILOGUE

The Department of Defense, through UCMJ, has done things like this to countless fiercely loyal and selfless warfighters who gave everything they had and then some throughout the 20-year Global War on Terror until the moment they became politically expendable. The rain ceased, and the umbrella canopy of freedom retracted, so services were no longer required.

There are entities in Washington operating under the guise of patriotism and servitude while subsidizing this democratic nation, leveraging the blood and sweat of warriors. Like all risky investments, the balance eventually comes due, and there's a margin call. The Pentagon "lost" trillions of dollars during the Iraq war on top of the stipulated price tag. As you can deduce, those funds went everywhere but to the troops fighting. And they certainly didn't go towards taking care of those fortunate enough to make it home and exchanging one battlefield for another. Both with survival as the precarious objective. The Department of Defense further found ways to increase the available funds to siphon off to unknown destinations and causes by stripping many combat veterans of their healthcare and military entitlements with bogus criminal offenses in combat and stateside before their contracts were up. Being in the Brig gave me a first-row seat into the toll of the war. Where did all the taxpayer dollars go? As a combat veteran, military retiree, and accounting major, I'm intrigued yet apprehensive to know the answer.

I knew I had to find purpose quickly and recapture who I was and not the inmate the military assiduously tried their best to portray me as. I decided that the motto No Man Left Behind applied just as much off the battlefield as it did while deployed in combat. I refused to leave myself behind. Consequently, I enrolled in university and began studying business.

God led me to a treatment facility by the name of Serenity Mental Health. They took me in like a broken orphan and helped set me on a positive path forward. I went into mission mode, attending treatment every single day, Monday through Friday, for 20 months on top of university academics. Twenty months was the same amount of time I'd spent incarcerated in the Brig. I Serenity Mental Health and my treatment tech, Maddie, for enabling me to process all the compound trauma and psychological abuse and enabling me to work assiduously with my talk therapist every week. With treatment, I was able to lower my resistance and become capable of waging a campaign against the areas of my memories I was previously unable to confront and the matrix of thought that was maintaining control over my sovereignty and self-confidence.

Serenity Mental Health focuses on gratitude while engaging in alternative therapeutic modalities. Serenity Mental Health took a complete approach to my wellness. He takes the time to get to know you and make an accurate assessment. I'm not just a file with a social security number. I don't just walk in there for two minutes and leave with a bottle of pills or Ambien like the Department of Defense or Department of Veterans Affairs. At Serenity, I matter as an individual. I'm no longer treated like an inconvenient statistic. Besides grati-

Epilogue

tude and patient care, the part about Serenity that truly transformed me was the revolutionary construct centered around set and setting. Their organization isn't in a hospital where there's a ubiquitous sickness, death, and shame factor in the mental health department. Their clinics are located in other corporate offices and locations with the rest of society. That made me suddenly WANT to work hard at getting better and moving forward. It reminded me of what the point was every single morning when I'd show up for treatment.

I'm now a graduate of Suffolk University's Sawyer School of Business with a Bachelor of Science in Accounting. I was inducted into the Honorary Accounting and Finance Organization, Beta Alpha Psi, for exceptional accounting and finance candidates. I served on the Student Government Association and co-founded the Suffolk Student Veteran Association as Treasurer.

What gets me through the day and enables me to stay in the fight is the same mentality that I always deployed: Gratitude. Focusing on what I have versus what I lack. Micro-motivation. After seven months of combat, two years of military prison, and a year of inpatient psychiatric programs, I have luxurious amenities at my disposal that are easy to take for granted if you don't count them as blessings: a bath when I want to relax, a mattress and pillow, restored mental faculties, and the ability to sleep throughout the night. God has yet to relieve me of my Post and the mission at hand. The Fifth General Order remains in full effect. Unlike the military, I'm not leaving anyone behind, and that involves not leaving myself behind. I'm supremely grateful.

My hope is that this book will serve as a reminder to both military veterans and nonmilitary veterans of the mental health revolution that is currently commencing and harnessing the active hope of such a long-awaited advent. No more. Not one more left behind. If you've made it this far, just hang in there and keep the faith a little while longer. Day by day. Not only will you get better, but you'll be leaders of tomorrow in a world desperately thirsting for the strength and resilience that is a mere prerequisite for warriors. We're the torchbearers. The living legacy of those who can no longer speak. This is bigger than us.

I'm also writing this book for each veteran sitting unjustly and ignominiously languishing in military prison because they were bullied and lacked the financial resources, advocacy, or mental wherewithal to participate in a viable defense. The night before I was released, one of the other inmates said, "Phillips, don't forget about us." I haven't. Nor will I.

When I enlisted, I stood and took an oath to defend this nation against all enemies, both foreign and domestic. I took an oath to uphold the Fifth General Order. This memoir is commensurate with both covenants. The perimeter is being breached. There are polarizing enemies within the lines posing as patriots on the military and governmental fronts. In my mind, one of the biggest destructive factors dishonoring the United States Marine Corps and its legacy is the jurisdictional carte blanche autonomy given to the Naval Criminal Investigative Service (NCIS). Their reputation and legacy of detached scrutiny and deceit speaks for itself and is completely antithetical to the core values of the Marine Corps: Honor, Courage, and Commitment. The Marine Corps, through the Navy and NCIS Gestapo, has allowed more great Marines to be destroyed, shamed, and humiliated than I can count. I stand in solidarity with that Marine Subset. I no longer seek vindication or validation. I've

Epilogue

found my brotherhood. One that I'll continue to fight for with every breath.

> *"Careerism and political expediency are corrosive to the principles of truth-telling. In either case, the individual's hope for personal gain outweighs his or her personal integrity and or patriotism."*
>
> General Anthony Zinny - USMC (ret.)

IN CLOSING

True leaders and gunfighters don't abdicate their responsibilities; they focus on their lane and scope paradigm. All those other individuals have nothing to do with my scope and line of sight. I stand by my shot. How I survived that deployment is the real question. The Lord had his top angels at work, considering that command leadership. Otherwise, I wouldn't be here as a literary torchbearer. Here I stand establishing fire superiority and suppressing with literary precision, hoping it leaves no man behind on or off the battlefield. Alive and kicking. The Fifth General Order in full effect.

It's hard to convey, but it is imperative to know how many miracles needed to happen health-wise to get me to this very moment of writing.

Until Serenity Mental Health Organization, I'd wake up at night screaming, fighting with the recurring notion that agents had come to my bed inexplicably dragging me away again back to solitary confinement. That's the absurdity. To my mind, it still doesn't make sense. There's no congruence. It can't be rationalized.

I learned throughout my experience that, like the battlefield, facing down the demons and fire superiority are the only ways to persevere. Stand your ground and look your enemy in the face. Usually, if you don't stand your ground and confront them, they only amplify in strength. There's no easy or linear way through crucibles. But there's no pathway of circumvention or circumnavigation. Even while writing this book, which took a decade of rehabilitation, there were several chapters I was naturally inclined to run from. Events I'd rather not relive. The motivation is that, like in wrestling or on the battlefield, the upside stems from standing your ground and envisioning yourself on the other side of the fear and pain. The only time you learn who you are is when you're up against the ropes and confronted with the option of quitting and staying down. Put a smile on your face, knowing that there's only potential upside in pushing forward through the kill zone and repelling the ambush. If someone labels you crazy for refusing to stay down, it's a reflection on them. Not you.

This book is intended to illuminate the population subset that was unjustly persecuted by the Uniformed Code of Military Justice (UCMJ), many recipients of whom are guilty of but one legitimate charge: faithfully honoring and upholding the Fifth General Order. I urge the Executive Branch and Congress to launch a longitudinal probe and audit all combat-related convictions and incarcerations and fully restore medical and compensatory benefits. Many recipients have been stripped of their military, medical, and educational benefits, left homeless, destitute, and indigent. It's time to defend the perimeter. I hereby urge the United States Congress and Senate to pass unanimous and sweeping legislation that exorbitantly expands the VA Choice Program, initially expanded under President Donald J. Trump, and allows combat veterans to choose who and where they seek private medical and mental health care. You have no right to send young men and women to war and then force them into a single, subpar healthcare system.

We're not asking. It's not a request. It's time you passed sweeping congressional and senatorial reform and earned your salary and

In Closing

healthcare that you're afforded under the protection of those whom you deployed to the frontline to keep what you alleged were the wolves at bay.

Like growing up along the Historical Paul Revere Trail, I'm sounding the alarm to a polarizing enemy at the gates. I'm just not sure what side of the gate is more dangerous. If freedom has any hope of resistance, it'll be the veterans of the 20-year Global War on Terror who will be the last line of defense to walk forward, establishing fire superiority.

MY FELLOW VETERANS

We must stop wasting energy and mental bandwidth with the perpetually inveterate what-ifs of the mission we were tasked with overseas and start asking ourselves this: Do George W. Bush or Dick Cheney have an ounce of sorrow or regret for the mess they threw us into, only to be thrown to a bureaucratic single healthcare system and told that we should consider ourselves lucky to be getting 20 bottles of pills? We all know the answer. It's time we start reminding ourselves of it.

We were put in a situation of complete madness and then told that we couldn't defend ourselves or our fellow comrades. I take everything that happened as a badge of honor. The Pentagon is so incompetent it can't even prevent the safest building on earth, surrounded by restricted airspace, from being rammed by a commercial 747. That's all we need to know about how competent they are at the top. In fact, I have a message for them: <u>You, gentleman, should've taken the shot!</u>

Anyone who's having a rough time right now: try changing the paradigm to that of how tough you had to be to survive all that you did foreign and domestically to be reading these very words. Hold your head sky-high. No wonder why many civilians tend to be intimidated. If we can make it through all that, we can dominate industry or endeavor. We need to stop questioning and blaming ourselves for decisions that were made well above our heads and decisions we were forced to make in split-second volatile dynamics. Whatever you're blaming yourself for or having a tough time moving past, you made the right decision in a situation that was lose-lose. No more guilt. It's time we start wearing our existence as an extraordinary badge of honor.

Years ago, SGT Jefferson told me a story recounting a conversation when his close friend CPL Santiago was cheering him up about not going down the victimization route. The story helped me while on the precipice at a critical juncture. He said, "Jefferson, don't do that. Don't devalue your experience and trauma contrasting to other people's injuries. I may've lost my legs, but every one of us left a part of us over there." Words of wisdom.

The below letter from the VA Choice Program under President Joe Biden delineates how much his administration has detracted from the executive orders invoked under President Donald J. Trump, to whom I owe my life and mental health. This disparity between what politicians say and do is unacceptable. Combat veterans aren't even given lifeline continued talk therapy as a thanks for their service. That's how expendable veterans have been made to be. However, those same politicians and elite who send the troops to foreign battlefields are often enriching themselves and their cronies in the process and afforded the best healthcare and decency in perpetuity. Washington is sending 80 million dollars a week to terrorist organizations in Afghanistan after all the trillions of taxpayer funds allocated throughout the war, while veterans who valiantly upheld the Fifth General Order in those wars are being pushed off the chessboard at an exorbitant rate. Unacceptable. There is a threat at the gates, all right. But it seems like, as during the Iraq War, the designation between friend and foe is heavily polarized.

And if history is any key performance indicator, I don't plan on dying off until those veterans who have contractually earned and fought for decency of care are given Carte Blanche access. Anything less is another stain on democracy and every person who paid the ultimate sacrifice and never made it home. Washington, one way or another, will start honoring those they called into service to uphold the Fifth General Order.

The VA doesn't inspire much confidence as an organization. There are some phenomenal nurses and social workers, but the system is defective. They don't talk about the private sector treatments that are changing lives. But they are. The reality is systems fear change and disrupters. It's no different than when Uber and Lyft disrupted the taxi industry through innovation and efficiency. The government is reluctant to adopt revolutionary treatments, which can be demoralizing when walking the halls of the VA, thinking that's all life has to offer. Private sector organizations like Home Base and Serenity Mental Health Clinic are successfully spreading across the country. If I hadn't been led by an older veteran to these organizations, I don't know where I'd be, and I prefer not to surmise. I urge President Donald J Trump to continue what he started in 2016 and bring it to completion. Hold the line just a little longer. Hope is on the horizon. The Fifth General Order is still in effect, and we haven't been relieved of our post.

Made in the USA
Monee, IL
12 April 2025

a646be91-4fc6-4eb2-80e7-3af05f8e3f8eR01